Student's Rorschach Manual

Student's
Rorschach Manual

*An Introduction to Administering,
Scoring, and Interpreting Rorschach's
Psychodiagnostic Inkblot Test*

Revised Edition

ROBERT M. ALLEN, Ph.D.

INTERNATIONAL UNIVERSITIES PRESS, INC.
New York   *New York*

Library of Congress Cataloging in Publication Data

Allen, Robert M   , 1909-
    Student's Rorschach manual.

    Bibliography: p.
    Includes indexes.
    1. Rorschach test. I. Title.
BF698.8.R5A53 1978   155.2'842   77-14710
ISBN 0-8236-6201-2

Cop. 1

Manufactured in the United States of America

To all the people I have met in my forty years as a student, a teacher, a researcher, and a practitioner of Clinical Psychology.

To all the teachers, professors, and colleagues with whom and from whom I learned to be a useful person.

To the students and clients who taught me about human behavior.

To my family, nuclear and extended, who tolerated me — THANKS.

R.M.A.

CONTENTS

FOREWORD

Over the years the *Rorschach Psychodiagnostic Inkblot Test* has grown in stature and in frequency of usage as a clinical evaluative procedure. Many research articles and papers have been published and/or presented at meetings of learned societies purporting to enhance, extend, modify, and some even to obfuscate, Rorschach Test theory, administration, interpretation, and application. Some of these ideas and techniques have been assimilated into the Rorschach Test procedure, while as many more have proven to be passing fancies.

The organization of this revised edition conforms to my method of teaching the Rorschach Test technique to graduate clinical psychology students. The focus is on the *basics* of the theory, administration, interpretation, and application of this test. Once these have been assimilated, then the students should be able to explore and/or evaluate the extensions, modifications, and experimental esoterica that are certain to be published.

The format of this volume is based on the student's need for intensive training in the complexities of the administration, scoring, and interpretation of the test protocol. This may be achieved by approaching the three major subdivisions of the testing technique in a systematic, albeit molecular, manner. Whereas the Rorschach Test is best handled as an attempt to see the whole person responding to stimulation both from within and outside of himself, ideas can be presented only

singly and in sequence. If there is sufficient integration of percepts and inferences to yield a total picture of the testee, it is
because the tester is the locus and the source for the integration — not the book from which the technique is being learned.
Therefore, the student will be exposed to each of the three
major aspects of Rorschach testing — administration techniques, methods of inquiry leading to scoring, and finally, to
the elements of interpreting the Location, Determinants, and
Content elements of the test protocol.

I do not believe that the advanced level of interpretation of
the Rorschach Test can be learned solely from a book. The
insights that emerge from experience with this and other tests,
from clinical interviews, and from the suitable use of case-
history data, are a function of time, supervision, and the
tester's astuteness as an observer of the human scene. It is for
this reason that only the elementary interpretive aspects will be
presented in this volume.

Those phases of the Rorschach Test which have an integrative function are presented in the latter portion of the book,
followed by suggestions for writing reports and illustrated by
actual case material.

The reader of this volume will probably wonder why the important attributes of validity and reliability are not discussed.
In general, the author is of the opinion that the user of this
book will be concerned mainly with the techniques of administration, scoring, and interpretation of the Rorschach Test protocol. Issues involving the validity and reliability of the inkblot
test should have, or will have, been considered by the course
instructor, the supervising clinical psychologist, or by the student's reference reading. This should be construed as part of
the approach to projective psychology and the projective
method.

The validation studies of the Rorschach Test vary from the
validity of a single variable to the validation of the total protocol with no reference to a particular element or combination of

elements. Methods employed for ascertaining this attribute include matching, use of identified groups of subjects (usually patients), follow-up studies, factor analysis, and qualitative estimates of the test in describing the testee.

Reasonably satisfactory validity has been found for this test in studies revolving around a variety of methodological approaches by Cox and Sarason (1954); Allen, Stiff, and Rosenzweig (1953); Allen Richer, and Plotnick (1964), and others. Rosvold, Ross, and Dorken (1954) have also reviewed the validity of the Rorschach Test, and offer the opinion that there is sufficient evidence to warrant its continued use experimentally and clinically. Zubin (1954), on the other hand, points out the impossibility of testing the basic hypotheses of the congruence between perception in the "artificial Rorschach space" and perception in the "real space." He does state that global evaluations do "work," that content analysis is satisfactory, but that the atomistic approach is not a valid method of relating to personality attributes (see Cronbach, 1948). Zubin sees the Rorschach Test situation as an interview and, as such, contents can be revealing. The reader is urged to consult Chapter 10, Projective Techniques, in Vernon (1964) for a broad survey and review of the validity status of several prominent projective tests, especially the Rorschach Test. Also see Harris (1960), and Allen (1966).

As for the second attribute, reliability, definition would play an important role in arriving at a conclusion about this facet of the Rorschach Test. The matter of single-variable reliability would not be too difficult to ascertain if such complicating factors as effects of previous experience with the test, memory, recall, surface and deep-seated personality changes, and tester-testee relationships could be controlled satisfactorily. There is a wide variability in the so-called reliability of the different Rorschach Test elements. I have suggested (Allen, 1957b) the use of the term "consistency of responses" until it can be decided whether reliability, as applied to the Rorschach

Test, is a matter of test-retest response similarity, or agreement of response scoring among different testers, or congruence of interpretation (or testee identification) among judges (see Chapter 1). The consensus of serious students of the projective method is that the projective techniques are reliable in accordance with their own definitions of reliability, which seem remarkably alike in that they reject the orthodox operation in favor of a global "it works" approach. Excellent discussions are contained in Holzberg's paper (1960) and in Jensen's monograph (1959).

A comparison of the early and current practices and thinking with and about the Rorschach Test theory, administration, interpretation, and application confirms the adage: *Plus ça change, plus c'est la même chose.*

I wish to thank the many persons quoted and referred to in this volume, and to express appreciation to their publishers for permission to use their material.

Robert M. Allen, Ph.D.
Professor of Psychology and
    Pediatrics, Emeritus
Director, Psychology Services,
    Grant Center

South Miami, Florida
May, 1977

Part I

THEORETICAL ISSUES

Chapter 1

PERCEPTION, PERSONALITY, AND APPRAISAL

The past four decades have witnessed thoroughgoing modifications of the concept of personality testing, description, and interpretation of the dynamics of behavior. In contrast to the currently held views of personality theory and personality assessment, there is the long-held posture, a traditional position best characterized as molecular. The understanding of the person was segmental, and upon this atomistic formulation the modes of appraisal were predicated. The individual was described in terms which were reducible to cognitive, conative, and affective components — each separately defined and measured. The specific instruments of personality evaluation were derived from this theoretical position. This further nurtured the conception of the human organism as discretely knowing, willing, and emoting. The psychometric-quantitative findings drew a picture of a fractionated person reacting in a molecular fashion in a series of seemingly unrelated situations. Observation of actual behavior over a period of time was usually sufficient reason for doubting the validity of this disjointed discrete approach to personality description.

This traditional concept of Man resulted in theoretical hypotheses and experimental designs conceived within this framework. Difficulty ensued when the experimenter (or psychologist) was required to put the parts together to form a picture of a real, live, everyday functioning individual. To read

3

the report of testee's appraisal grounded in *pars pro toto* discrete entities could be a stultifying experience. At times the reader could easily extract separate sentences or paragraphs from the report without obviously affecting the rest of the protocol. It was a mental feat of no small proportion for the reader to realize that these paragraphs referred to the same person. In a way it is reminiscent of the educational methods of high school days when the student was exposed to Caesar of Shakespeare, the Julius Caesar of *Omnia Gallia*, and the Julius Caesar of ancient history. It was quite sometime before one realized that the teachers in English Lit., third year Latin, and Ancient and Medieval History were all talking about the same person. The element of integration was lacking.

Most of the tests derived from this view of man were anchored in the clinical experience of the test constructors who favored an empirical or an "it works," problem-centered framework as the basic rationale for the construction of their personality tests. Another model for the empirical basis for test construction was the factorial view of personality. This even further fractionated man by the very nature of factor analysis and what Cureton (1949) has characterized as the compulsion of the factor analysts to combine wishful thinking with higher mathematics to prove their original notions.

The difference between "it works" and the factorial rationales lies in the method of arriving at the allegedly independent problems or factors that form the bases for the individual questionnaire-type test items.

A new outlook in the psychology of personality, in perceptual psychology, and in projective psychology, referring specifically to the role of perception in perceptanalysis, has its origin in many sources. Freud's psychoanalytic psychology, the revolt of the Gestalt school against the mechanistic atomism of the behaviorists, the research of Lewin (1935) in group dynamics, and the holistic tenets of the psychobiologists—all were directed to the study of the person as an organized functioning unit in a social surround. In short, the human being was to be viewed holistically rather than actuarily.

The operationism of Bridgman (1927) the philosopher-physicist, and the time-space relationships of Einstein, (Clark, 1971) and quantum physics contributed to the field-theory interpretation of man. This posture looks at the whole individual in his field or the life space in which he is behaving. This life space includes the physical, social, and biological forces at work. Thus, personality, while still a semantic abstraction, is seen as determined behavior by an organism in response to the external and internal forces impinging upon him. Most appropriate to this position is Frank's (1948) definition of personality as consisting of those ". . . processes or behavior by which the individual establishes, maintains and defends his private idiosyncratic world" (p. 15). This, coupled with Mursell's (1947) definition of a test, set the stage for perceptanalysis as an evaluative procedure.

Within the framework of this theoretical position there is no need to postulate personality types or to consider personality as an additive picture of discrete hierarchical traits. It is sufficient to describe what is immediately observable — behavior — and to interpret this in terms of the current situation and its place in the larger life space. This includes not only the interacting social, physical, and biological forces, but also the time dimension resident in the individual: his past experience, n-t, the present situation, n, and the future, n + t, as he perceives, organizes, and reacts to these variables both below and above the level of awareness.

Somewhat antedating the field-theory concepts in personality in American psychological literature is the work of Hermann Rorschach (1942). Physically near the analytically oriented psychiatric center of Europe, he could not help but come under the influence of the psychology of the Freudian circle. Rorschach was not the first one to utilize the vague unstructured inkblot as a vehicle for eliciting responses, but he was the first one to use it more completely in the sense of Mursell's definition of a test. Actually, Rorschach was preceded by Shakespeare and Galton. In the United States Sharp (1899) was the first to write a doctoral dissertation based on inkblot perceptions. Others (Binet, 1903; Brittain, 1907) attempted to use the inkblot technique as a test of intelligence of the basis of the individual's creativity.

Rorschach made the earliest organized attempts to evaluate personality from the content of the person's responses. He applied his knowledge of personality dynamics, coping mechanisms, and their behavioral manifestations to adapt this medium to personality appraisal. The necessary task, as he saw it, was to relate the spoken responses—i.e., oral-perceptual—verbal behavior—via inferred coping mechanisms to the underlying dynamics. In this inferential process of reverse-cycle reasoning as to "What Makes Sammy Run" lies the core of the usefulness, or concurrent predictive, or construct validity of the projective procedure.

The projective techniques purport to appraise the structure of the personality, to yield insights into the thought content and the ideational processes of the individual. Their particular value is the feasibility of teasing out the psychological dynamics and coping methods reflected in the testee's behavior or responses. The theoretical context of the projective methodology leans strongly on the determined nature of behavior in the complete sense of Mursell's definition of a test; that, in his responses, the individual reveals certain psychological personality characteristics.

For the individual, the causes of his behavior lie in the internal and external fields (using the skin as the convenient boundary between the fields) as these have meaning for him. This notion helps clarify much that has remained esoteric and mystical because consideration was formerly given only to what could be observed. Similar to the confusion between IQ—an obtained score—and intelligence—an abstraction—there is a tendency to confound percentile ratings and T-scores on personality inventories with personality dynamics and with personality structure. With the insights made available by the projective method, in which overt behavior is noted and covert thought content is elicited, man's more deeply rooted motivations are exposed for detailed study, description, interpretation, and utilization.

At this juncture, attention should be shifted to the perceiver in the testing situation. The perceiver, the known principles of perception, and motivation, are important to personality theory and to projective psychology. Klein and Schlesinger (1951) called attention to this issue by pointing out that to study perception is actually to study the perceiver, the "see-er, the hearer." To ignore this phase of perception is to approach personality theory building and personality evaluation without the person who does the behaving. The manner in which the person responds to stimuli in his field and the organization of response systems, Klein and Schlesinger suggest, *is* the individual's personality.

The philosophical roots of perception may be traced, at least one direction, to Leibniz (1949) who wrote, " We perceive the universe of objects but we do not perceive the units of which the universe is composed." This recognizes the unity of a situation. The synthesis takes place within the person. A suitable starting point, with regard to the experimental literature of perception and the concept of experimential continuity in perception, is the study by Braly (1933). The purpose was to ascertain the influence of past experience on the perception of forms. The method employed was to expose tachistoscopically a given type of geometric form as an *impression-series* and then have the subjects look at a *test-series* of forms composed of new figures, among which were interspersed the impression-series forms. Braly concluded that present situational stimuli are not interpreted solely on the basis of past experience, but depend in great measure on the context within which these stimuli are embedded — thus supporting the important roles of the time-dimension and the experimental context in perception.

Duncker (1939) performed an interesting series of experiments in which he exposed subjects to various stimuli and noted their responses. In the first of three phases Duncker showed part of a male figure which was usually identified as the head of a dog or a whale with a white eye. Then he exposed the total figure and noted two reactions; (1) that the manner in which the part-figure was perceived influenced the configurational features of the whole figure; and (2) if the new configurational situation was of such a nature as to *dominate* the past stimuli embedded in it, the past stimuli underwent configurational changes in keeping with the *new* frame of reference. Duncker concluded that changes in total figural perception could not be attributed directly to mere addition of separate parts of the total figure.

In the second phase of the investigation of the relation between past experience and current perception, Duncker exposed his subjects to an artifical green leaf and a donkey made of exactly the same material as the leaf. Both were presented in a red-lighted chamber. Previous experiences with leaves and donkeys yielded definite impressions of green leaves and gray donkeys. In this study of *"memory color,"* each subject matched a color wheel in a normally lighted chamber with the color of the critical object — first the donkey and then the leaf. Of eleven subjects, six selected a deeper green and two chose a slightly greener shade for the leaf than for the donkey. The remaining three subjects could see no difference between the green of the donkey and the green of the leaf. At no time did the donkey look greener that the leaf. The "more-green" perception of the leaf, as compared with the donkey, could come only from the subjects' past experience with green leaves and grey donkeys. Thus, in contrast to the first phase of the study, the present situation did not so dominate the sitmuli as to lose them entirely. Rather, the old stimuli — past experience or color memory — so dominated the present stimuli as to transcend the present stimuli and produce leaf and donkey percepts in keeping with the color memory of these previously exposed objects.

It may be seen, thus far, that the influence of past experience is not uniform under all circumstances. The degree and kind of influence are dependent upon the nature of the past experience, the content of the present situation, and the person's perception of the interaction of past and present. That perceptual properties are a function of the perceiver who brings with him his past experience into the "to-be-perceived situation" was confirmed by Duncker in the third phase of his study. This centered around a new type of white chocolate, which, despite its coloring, tasted like most chocolate candies known to the subjects in the experiment. Duncker sought to ascertain the effect of the visual appearance of white chocolate on reported taste. The results were in the hypothesized direction, i.e., four of the six subjects who tasted the white chocolate with their eyes open reported a milkier taste than when they compared the taste of real chocolate blindfolded. Under the latter condition there was no difference between the two chocolates reported by the four subjects.

Bruner and Postman (1949) carried on some relevant investigations. In one of them they emphasized motivation as an important factor in perception in terms of the individual's needs, attitudes, and habit systems and their affect on subsequent behavior. The reader should be acquainted with the details of their *associative reaction time* and *speed of recognition* study. In the analysis of their data, Bruner and Postman identified two phenomena at work: the defense and sensitization processes. The first they defined as defense against anxiety-laden stimuli engendered by the recognition of a stimulus-word and its manifestations as either an *avoidance of recognition* or *delayed reaction time*. The sensitization process accounted for the comparatively rapid recognition times for certain words.

An earlier study by Bruner, Postman, and McGinnies (1947) involving personal values and related words validated the role of personal values in perception. The reaseach that followed the lead of Bruner, Postman, and McGinnies is best summed up in Gardner Murphy's (1947) comment that the organism's perceived world pattern mirrors the "organized need pattern within." Contemporaneous with and supportive of Bruner, Postman, and McGinnies findings are the investigations by Atkinson and McClelland (1948, McClelland, Atkinson, and Clark, 1949) in motivation. By manipulating the condition of the subjects, hunger in one instance, they demonstrated the influence of need on response to unstructured stimuli, such as vague pictures, smudges on slides, and TAT plates. Along the same lines, Murray (1943) placed young girls in a manipulated social situation to yield definite evidence of the effects of pleasant and fear-invoking conditions on the characterization of photographs of persons. From the phenomenological viewpoint, the emotional state engendered by the manipulated experimental-social conditions altered self-concepts to the extent that these tensions required some avenue of discharge. The need to reduce these tensions and the anticipation of a change in the state of the organism were reflected in the subjects' lowered threshold of sensitivity to particular stimuli, and facilitated perceptual distortion of neutral stimuli.

Thus far the theory of perceptual phenomena indicated herein is neither classical nor systematic. Rather, it rests on an "it works" frame of reference. There are excellent books that present and interpret theories in detail. Zubin, Eron, and Schumer (1965) have introduced a directive-state theory which has emerged as a result of the new look in personality theory. (Yet this is not an entirely new idea, since in the newlook posture the perceiver also counts, to paraphrase these authors—who, incidentally, are not sympathetic partisans of the Rorschach test method.) Essentially the directive-state view that holds perception and its consequences are directed by the organism in terms of his needs, drives, etc., or his state, has seven major tenets:

1. Bodily needs influence what is perceived.

2. Past learning (including rewards and punishments) associated with stimulus-perception determines subsequent perception of that stimulus.

3. Values play a role in stimulus-recognition and utilization.

4. Perceptual defense and sensitization or vigilance are present in the individual's response to the forces in his field. This implies the presence of the time dimension at the moment of observation, including the testee's past, present, and future.

5. The locus of personality and perception is the perceiver, and the responses are related to his personality characteristics.

6. The mediating mechanism between the central motivational state of the individual and his perceptual response has been given many labels — all are constructs since little is really known about how the "state" performs its "directive" function. This is a major failure of the directive-state theory of perception. And, finally,

7. Evidence has been suggested by Lazarus and McCleary (1951) for discrimination without awareness, or subception. In other words, it is possible for a stimulus to be recognized before its conscious identification is made, as in sensitization; and it is possible for recognition to be absent after identification has been made, as in perceptual defense.

How can this be brought within the purview of a test such as the Rorschach Inkblots? As Bruner (1948) indicated, there is a need for integrating the Rorschach Test approach with perceptual theory. The task is not an easy one. Perceptual purists decry the contention that the inkblots are unstructured stimuli, insisting that, for an inkblot, an inkblot has as much structure as a picture has structure for a picture. But inkblots are merely pictures of low fidelity, and, therefore, the subject may not be reporting his direct perceptions. How readily this criticism may be used to validate the basic rational of the Rorschach Test: that it is not the purpose to report direct photographic perceptions, but to elicit "engrams." At the other extreme are such authorities as Brown (1953) and other orthodox analytically oriented Rorschach Test users, who see in every response adequate reasons for taking off into flights of fancy that extrapolate much beyond what the data could justify. It seems that some of the problems related to projective perceptual theory need to take into consideration not only the perceiver but also the nature of the stimuli. The presence of popular responses, sex populars (Shaw, 1949), the cardpull of Ranzoni, Grant, and Ives (1950), and the card-meanings research call attention to this issue. Is this part of personality or does personality determine the responses? Which came first, personality or perception? Such a question as "Does personality influence perception?" is superfluous. Perception adduces overt manifestations of the larger process called personality. Perhaps Graham's (1963) model offers an approach to the answer when he indicates that:

$$R = f(S, T, O, E \ldots \ldots X_1, X_2, \ldots . X_n)$$

in which R is the response which is a f (function) of S (properties of the presented stimulus), T (time of exposure), O (state of the organism, including set, motivation, tonicity, degree of fatigue, etc.), E (past experience), and $X_1, X_2, \ldots . X_n$ (personality characteristics of the individual).

In this model, the focus is on the response, but the background contains the person in whom all the variables reside, within whom the transactions among the variables take place, and who responds or behaves. The $X_1, X_2 - X_n$ are the modes of coping (learned and reflexive) available to the organism. Any one or combination enters into the transactional process to culminate as a unified segment of behavior or structure which, in essence, involves the total organism regardless of the extent of the observed verbal and/or motor behavior.

More specifically, this may be reworded to characterize Rorschach theory: the manner in which a person interpets the inkblot mirrors the way in which the individual perceives, organizes, and behaves. All of the elements of Graham's model can be found in the Rorschach Test situation. In the final analysis, one must agree with Hermann Rorschach that the testee's responses are not the products of his imagination *qua* fantasy, but actually indicate how he perceives his world visually and responds to the pattern of forces within it, including himself.

It seems that it would be useful to think of Rorschach Test theory as belonging to a personality theory that will explain all typical and atypical events occurring in nature. Since perception is one modality contributing to human behavior, this process should be a definite part of the over-all, unified behavioral theory of personality.

Chapter 2

FOUNDATIONS OF INTERPRETATION: THEORETICAL CONSIDERATIONS

The basic hypothesis that sustains the interpretive evaluations of the Rorschach (1942) Inkblot Test protocol has been succinctly stated by Frank: "What is of major significance for understanding the individual personality is that the individual organizes experience as he warps, twists, distorts and otherwise fits every situation, event, and person into the framework of his private world, giving them the affective significance which they must have for him in his private world" (1948, p. 15). Thus, a protocol is a momentary picture of the fluid, dynamic process. This process depicts the manner of experiencing situation, how they are handled, and the mechanisms employed (should they be necessary) for the maintenance of dynamic homeostasis.

Any theory of personality that applies the inferential use of projective test responses must center about the understanding of the processes inherent in the term "perception." In recent years a New Look group of investigators has become essentially interested in the dynamics of everyday perception. A variety of experimental designs has sought to ferret out the molecular composition of the total perceptual phenomenon as reflected in the behavior of the organism in its (biosocial and biophysical) phenomenological field. An overview of these studies suggests the selectivity of perception, and subsequent behavior, in keeping with the organism's presents needs and press, the influence of past experiences, and aspirations for the future. In addition, the structure of the testing situation, e.g., inkblot, picture, attitude induced by instructions, and even the tester, serves as an additional variant that must enter into the interpretation (Bruner, 1948). These become increasingly important when dealing with protocols obtained with TAT pictures and Rorschach inkblots. The interpreter should approach the problem of protocol evaluation from the point of view of what the stimulus means *to the subject* and not what it might mean to the examiner. The focus shifts from the device and the tester to the testee. How the subject molds the test material or the stimuli is expressive of his needs, goals, interpretations, of social pressures, organic stresses, fears, anxieties, aspirations, and other personality dimensions which may be observed and described. It is on the basis of these behavioral descriptions — inkblot responses, picture stories, sentences completed, figures drawn, etc. — that evaluative inferences may be made by the clinician.

Before the beginner attempts to interpret test responses he should be grounded in personality theory, perception, learning, and behavior dynamics. Rorschach (1942), writing about the theoretical formulations for the test that bears his name, has this to say: " The theoretical foundation of the experiment is, for the most part, still quite incomplete." White (1946), on the other hand, represents the *Zeitgeist* of opinion with regard to Rorschach Test theory in this statement: "The principle that every performance of a person is an expression of his whole personality." To this, Bruner (1948) adds two words: "perception included." Such a theory must hearken back to Frank's definition of personality in which this abstraction stands revealed as *a process* by which the individual "established, maintains, and defends his private idiosyncratic world." Thus, a theory of perception grounded in perceptual postulates should make a place for those activities in which the subject functions in a structured milieu with the structure deriving from society (external to the subject) and from the individual's needs (internal to the subject). The person is constantly striving to bring harmony into the biosociophysical field within which he is operating. The defense of the private world he has built, his interpretation of the phenomenological field, and his conception of his own place in it will determine his perceptions and reactions. Normal perception is a function of the minimal anxiety threat in the field stimuli *as the person sees them*. Misperception, or apperceptive distortion, generally describes those reactions to stimuli which are fraught with actual and/or potential danger for the personality integration of the perceiver. Stern's dictum still holds true: "*Keine Gestalt, ohne Gestalter.*" Lord (1950) has presented evidence of the differences in perception resulting from conditions imposed on the testee by the examiner, again lending support to the thesis that the subject's responsiveness is a function not only of the self-percept, but also of the atmosphere in which the technique is being applied. Schachtel (1945, p. 421), in a canvass of the subjective definition of the Rorschach situation, declares: "By a person's definition of the Rorschach situation I do not mean merely . . . the conscious ideas of this person about what is going on in his taking the Rorschach Test. Rather, I want to designate . . . the person's total experience of the test situation . . . *the togetherness of two people*, the tester and the subject, in the relationship of the test situation. The fact that a *task* is given to the subject by the tester. . . ." The importance of the interpersonal relationship between the tester and the testee was investigated by Allen and Dorsey (1954). They find that the suggestion "to see a person or persons doing something" made to the subjects by the tester who was also their instructor in a psychology course results in a significant increase in retest M productivity. It is concluded, in part, that the prestige value of the tester-instructor for the subjects in the Rorschach testing situation is reflected in the subjects' system of values. This influences their perceptions of the inkblot stimuli.[1] McCue, Rothenberg, Allen, and Jennings (1963) investigated the relationship between the publicly admitted values (on the Allport-Vernon-Lindzey *Study of Values* Test) of the *T*(heoretical)-*A*(esthetic) man and the *P*(olitical) man, on the one hand, and several Rorschach Test variables, on the other. They reported that the *T-A* man and the *P* man were sufficiently different with regard to these personality variables on the inkblot test to clearly reflect somewhat dichotomous value systems. The dynamics involved in the nature of the Rorschach Test percepts were found to relate appropriately to the two A-V-L value types. If there is no causal relationship, at least two A-V-L value types have a common mode of coping with life's problems that yields co-related inkblot percepts and selected self-rating questionnaire items.

Vernon (1964) points out several characteristics of the projective method of personality assessment that merit consideration and repetition. He feels that the unstructuredness of the inkblots, for example, encourages diversity and spontaneity of responsiveness by the testee. Emphasis is given to the fact that the testee is less aware of how his percepts are to be interpreted. This adduces a less guarded response set which is not present in taking a paper-and-pencil self-report test. The less than complete structure of the inkblot stimuli tends to divert attention away from the possibility of deliberately prejudicing responsivity in one direction or another. Vernon goes on to indicate that the absence of predetermined directional answers gives the testee every opportunity to permit his conceptual and personality dispositions to disclose major (as well as minor) personality trends. This is manifested in the repeated themes in

---

[1] This conclusion does not jeopardize the basic rationale of the Rorschach Inkblot Test: that it taps basic and relatively permanent personality dimensions. On the contrary, it supports this fundamental tenet in that it is sensitive to the changes in apperceptive and perceptive flux.

the picture-story test or the accumulation of signs in the ink-blot test.

In sum, the client in a testing situation gives of himself, with and/or without reservations that may be on a level of awareness or below it. He projects in varying degrees the role that his self-percept impels him to assume. This projected role contains the basic personality structure *plus* the superimposed reactivity to the current situation. It is these modes of experiencing and behaving that the Rorschach interpreter uses as his raw data.

Another consideration is the answer to Hanfmann's question: "What makes a given technique a projective one?" It is important that this query be given serious reflection in view of the possible abuses of this extremely helpful and easily perverted method. One would have to address this question inwardly since the answer "lies neither in the test material nor in what *the subject* is induced to do with it. . ." (1952, p. 3). It is an axiom of scientific progress that refinement and accuracy of measurement and evaluation lie in three factors: (1) the definition of the phenomenon to be measured; (2) the accuracy of the measuring instrument; and (3) *the carefulness of the person doing the measuring*. The issue seems to inhere in the third factor — the "projectiveness" of a test derives from the manner in which the tester deals with the responses. In keeping with this central concept, voiced by Hanfmann, *any* pattern of stimuli may be used as a projective test depending on the method of reading and interpreting the raw (behavioral) data, the signs. In any test situation the signs are present, it is a matter of reading them. Thus, a Bernreuter Personality Inventory could conceivably be evaluated projectively as well as psychometrically. The assumption is that the tester is skilled in reading and interpreting the signs. Central to this method of signs is the previously stated additive assumption of both White (1946) and Bruner (1948): ". . . every performance of a person is an expression of his whole personality, perception included."

A final consideration to which the Rorschach protocol interpreter must be sensitive is the problem of the interrelationship
that exists among the discrete Rorschach Test determinants.
Ulett (1950) has devised a helpful chart to show the interde-
pendencies among the various factors.

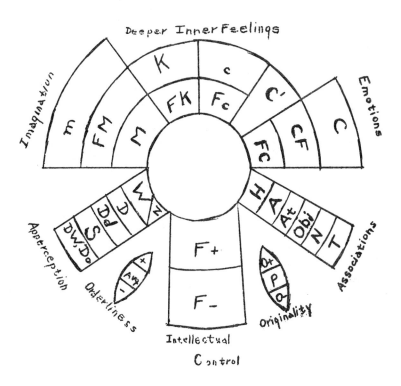

Modification of Ulett's Interpretive Diagram. From: Ulett, G. A. *Rorschach
Introductory Manual.* St. Louis, Mo.: Educational Publishers, 1950, Figure
1. (Reproduced and modified with the permission of the author and
publisher.)

One of the important features of this chart is the clarity with
which the basic meaning of each determinant is indicated *plus*
the modification of this essential interpretation in different

contexts. The reader is cautioned not to use this chart as re-produced above literally since many of the salient interpretive elements have been omitted by the present author.[2]

Summary Remarks

The current literature is replete with statements regarding the status of theory in the Rorschach Test. The most succinct and direct one comes from a paper by Hertz (1952, p. 109): "It is true that the Rorschach method is still without a theoretical basis." Schofield (1952, p. 20) uses strong language in de-scribing the popular usage of projective techniques: "Some clinical psychologists prefer to be more artistic that scientific in their practice; projective devices, at their present state of de-velopment, invariably encourage creativity in the examiner even though they fail to titillate the examinee!" The writer be-lieves that this is an excellent caution against going off into flights of fancy, but beyond this the case against projective tests is a poor one. No test is better that the person who uses it — no matter what type of instrument is involved. The answer lies, it seems, in better training in theory of behavior dy-namics, experimental techniques, and theory of test construc-tion, as well as practice in testing skills. Too much concern and criticism has been directed toward the test rather than the tester who makes running motions before he is able to crawl (see Allen, 1965).

[2] Profitable experience may be gained by the serious Roschach student by consulting the original Interpretive Diagram and the directions for its use which are contained in Ulett's *Manual*.

Chapter 3

THE PLACE OF THE PROJECTIVE TECHNIQUES AND PROCEDURE IN THE UNIVERSITY CURRICULUM

The title of this chapter is open-ended, since it presents broad vistas for exploration. One must wonder, though, whether the real issue is training in the university versus training in the practicum situation for the clinical psychologist. Why does this question arise with reference to the projective techniques only? Why not with regard to projective theory, or personality theory, or intelligence testing, or even psychopathological labeling? May there not be justification for insisting that since clinical psychologists deal with troubled persons then clinical psychology trainees should learn all applied aspects of their profession in the best place for it — in the clinical facility, the haven for troubled people. It is not compelling to view the issue as one of either-or. Learning in the university classroom and in the practicum setting need not be discrete events, but continuing and interwoven experiences. Why not consider university courses in projective techniques and the application of these procedures in the practicum under didactic supervision as two sides of a single coin?

A review of the recommendations by various sub- and *ad hoc* committees of the American Psychological Association

This chapter originally appeared in the *Journal of Genetic Psychology*, 1960, 96:321-325.

which have studied the problems of training in clinical psychology at the graduate and internship levels furnishes a wealth of expert and near-expert opinions. In 1945 Shakow (1945a,b) noted four approaches in clinical psychology which might be helpful for thinking through the values in conjoint academic and practicum training. Two of these belong primarily in the university curriculum — the dynamic and experimental approaches. In the dynamic, the interest is focused on understanding the development of human motivation and personality organization. Courses in the psychodynamics of behavior, motivation, psychopathology, and perception form the core for introducing the student to these essential concepts. The experimental approach is imparted directly in graduate courses and seminars centering around specific and general topics in personality theory, developmental psychology, and assessment procedures, in addition to those mentioned above. In each of the courses and seminars, the attitudes engendered and encouraged are a function, in part, of the instructor's own approach to the subject matter. The university climate usually fosters the experimental-research view. Projective skills taught in the university department within the framework of the dynamic-experimental approach could accomplish three ends: First, to discuss with the student the theoretical assumptions underlying the procedure; second, to train the student in the techniques of administration, scoring, and interpretation of the evaluative tests; and third, to expose the student to the experimental literature for his continuing consideration of the areas of agreement, controversy, strength, and weakness of the test methods, theory, findings, and applications.

The advocates of assigning projective test training primarily to the internship facility will find solace in Shakow's diagnostic-therapeutic approaches because of their service character. This aspect of the training program is self-explanatory. The student is presented with practical learning opportunities — learning that is best based on previously acquired information and skills. Moreover, the intern in most instances is a graduate predoctoral student responsible for carrying on dissertational research. He must look beyond the service function as he works with people and tests to the reseach referents that abound in the clinic. Much of this opportunity for growth in research interest and competency may be lost to the trainee who is absorbed in learning elementary testing techniques. With these skills already part of his apperceptive mass, he is freer to take advantage of the internship as something more than a time of learning new technical proficiencies. It becomes an added opportunity for thinking about tests, data, people, and research ideas as possible sources for supporting or modifying concepts.

In another report, a committee under the chairmanship of Shakow (1945b) recommended as part of the second-year graduate training program in clinical psychology a course or courses in the theory and practice of projective devices. The formal work should consist of lectures and some type of clinical practice. These would be followed by supervision in the administration, interpretatin, and reporting of test results. The committee also felt that part of this introductory work could be accomplished in a clerkship setting. This recommendation lent itself to a variety of interpretations and many modes of implementation. One view would establish a course in which the student concerns himself with the rationale of the projective procedure, the issues involved, and the experimental literature. The Rorschach Test could serve as the prototype method with emphasis on administration and scoring in the context of the location, determinant, and content elements. To present these concepts, the teaching would involve a discussion of personality theory, motivation, perception, and introductory psychopathology. Classroom lectures, laboratory demonstrations, and supervised practice should include individual and class critiques. This procedure permits exposing a larger number of students to a greater variety of situations in much less time than if each intern were to be given individual instruction by a single supervisor. It is important for the trainee to become acquainted with diverse problems of administration, scoring, and interpretation rather quickly. It is doubtful whether an individual clinic supervisor could present for an intern's consideration during any one supervisory hour nearly as many issues as a classroom instructor could introduce in the same period to a number of students. From a practical point of view, time is on the side of university preparation for the practicum.

In a discussion of the graduate professional program, the APA Committee on Training in Clinical Psychology (1947) suggests a broad curriculum with no attempt to turn out a specialist. Of the six recommended major areas of study, two, psychodynamics of behavior and diagnostic methods, are deemed vital to a clinical psychology training program. Furthermore, "The program should concern itself mainly with basic courses and principles rather than multiply courses in techniques" (p. 543). The interpretations of "multiply" and "techniques" are not given. Instead, these terms are wisely left to each department for definition as it plans its own program. The variety of training proposals is testimony to the differences in interpretation extant today.

In a further analysis of expert opinion, the report of the 1950 Boulder Conference states: "The university department has the responsibility of teaching the administration, scoring, and elementary levels of interpretation of some tests for clinical use and of certifying to the clinical practicum agency the student's readiness for clinical practicum use of such tests" (APA, 1950).

Finally, the 1950 report of the APA Committee on Training in Clinical Psychology (1950) recognizes that there may be a lack of integration between academic and theoretical training on the one hand, and the practical experience received in the field agency on the other. The report elaborates on the issue (p. 598):

Because it is only in the practicum that the student can develop proficiency in the use of psychological techniques, the question is sometimes raised as to the desirability of giving the initial laboratory level of instruction in techniques in the practicum agency. It is sometimes contended that early contact with patients and clincial problems gives greater motivation to learning techniques, that they may be learned better in practice with patients in the practicum under the instruction of psychologists who themselves are engaged in professional service work, rather than in the academic setting.

This problem really resolves itself to the question of how, when, and where instruction in testing techniques can best given without inroads upon the best theoretical and practical training which may be given by the graduate department and the practicum centers in collaboration. The Boulder Conference was in general agreement that "the university department has the responsibility of teaching the administration, scoring, and elementary levels of interpretation of some tests for clinical use, and of certifying to the practicum agency the student's readiness for clinical practicum use of such tests." The committee continues to see no reason for changing this recommendation concerning the teaching of testing techniques at the university level. Because of individual unique circumstances, the committee suggested that the university, perhaps after consultation with its practicum supervisors, should decide for itself when, and under whom, and where clinical techniques may best be learned.

These somewhat open-ended recommendations, stemming from the broader view of clinical training, imply that there cannot be only one road to clinical training to the total exclusion of any other approach. The committee has wisely foreseen, or perhaps it was divided within itself, that valid differences of opinion in training programs will continue to exist.

The members, therefore, have determined to ensure the student of the best training available in the variety of circumstances.

Once more the question arises—the place of the projective techniques in the university cirriculum. The Kass Committee on Training of the Society for Projective Techniques (1958) points out that "All major projective techniques are taught in all the [APA approved university—author] programs." This refers to the 30 departments of the 45 contacted which responded to the committee's questionnaire. The committee reports that more than half of the responding departments taught the Rorschach Test in connection with "courses on projective techniques in general or in some other context. Courses exclusively on the thematic techniques are offered in 30 per cent of the programs" (p. 121). Offering formal university courses and seminars in projective techniques enables the student to spend classroom, laboratory, and library time learning the rationale of the projective method, reading the pertinent research with regard to the problems and issues involved in the validity and reliability of the procedures, and integrating test theory and application. The usual interchange between student and instructor during lecture and laboratory sessions is feasible. Formal semester reports and frequent papers on current research provide essential referents. Much that can be exchanged in the atmosphere of the classroom, with stimulation to both student and teacher, may be lost in the busy clinic where service-demands can effectively reduce the time spent in teaching by the supervisor. The imparting of projective skills is a dual responsibility which neither the lecture hall nor the clinical faculty can do alone efficiently.

The aim of the internship is to furnish experiences with people so that the student may apply knowledge gained in the classroom. But the intern must come to the practicum with basic information and skill. Elementary competence with projective devices, a theoretical point of view, an understanding of behavioral dynamics and how these are rooted in perceptual psychology enhance the value of the practicum. It removes from the agency the responsibility of conducting clinical training "from the ground up." The reply that "We want to train the intern our way" implies that "our way" is *the* right way and that other modes are somehow wanting. If clinical psychologists were dealing with a subject matter other than human behavior, this argument might be tenable. But this discipline is not ready, as yet, to admit of only one way to assess human behavior for the purpose of yielding inferences and for making predictions therefrom. It would be unwise to send an intern to the practicum agency without prior contact with the tests to be used. It is less frightening to the trainee and gives the training supervisor some assurance of the "student's readiness for clinical practicum use of such tests." Projective testing courses in the university do not usurp the role of the practicum supervisor. The latter completes the work of the former, which do belong there.

In 1977 the discussion still rages, but with more biased participants — the proponents of the academic traditional Ph.D. curriculum, on the one hand, and the applied less broadly trained Psy.D. adherents on the other hand. But the usage of the Rorschach Test continues unabated and it still yields a harvest of research papers, doctoral dissertations, and ever-widening areas of application (see, for example, Erlemeier, Monike, and Wirtz, 1974; Klopfer, 1974; and Willemaers, 1973).

Part II

GENERAL ADMINISTRATION PROCEDURE

Chapter 4

THE RORSCHACH INKBLOT TEST

THE CARDS

This test is known briefly as "The Rorschach" after its designer, Hermann Rorschach, who was the first to fully utilize inkblots as a deliberately designed and organized personality probing technique. There are ten cards or plates in the standard set. The ground in each card is white, with a design centered thereon. Some of the designs are symmetrical, while others, upon close examination, are not bilaterally identical.[1] Five cards are printed in varying shades of black and gray — the achromatic or noncolored cards, I, IV, V, VI, and VII. Two plates, II and III, are printed in black and red. The remaining three, VIII, IX, and X, are all colored in different hues. The shapes have been deliberately designed and the placement of the colors, black, gray, and white, are the result of Rorschach's experimentation and belief in this method of personality analysis. The order of the presentation of the cards also plays a role in this percept-analytic process.[2]

[1] The observation of the presence and absence of symmetry in the designs may be used in personality evaluation.

[2] We are indebted to Piotrowski (1942a) for this term. Rabin and Sanderson (1947) indicate that: "1. Rorschach's empiricism in presenting the cards in customary order is justified, since the order (I-X) tends to produce more responses, more accurate responses and richer records in terms of Rorschach factors involved" (p. 224).

The details of giving this test vary with the preferences of the many psychologists and psychiatrists who use it. For the beginner the following is suggested until individual modifications come as the result of experience with the test. The adminsitration involves: facility in handling the testee and the cards, note-taking, timekeeping, and the constant interchange of words.

A. Physical Arrangement

It is essential that the subject and tester be seated so as to enable the latter to observe every detail of the subject's behavior—psychomotor activity, changes in facial expression, breathing rate, eye movements, to name a few. This may be accomplished best with the tester seated to the right or left and slightly behind the subject. The diagram illustrates this:

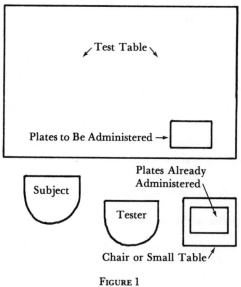

FIGURE 1
Physical Seating Plan

The subject is requested to sit on a chair while the tester moves his chair to a position which will enable him to see the subject's face easily. The cards are placed face down on the Test Table with plate I on top and X on the bottom. Next to the tester is a small desk, table, or chair on which are placed, face down, the cards that are returned to the tester as the subject is finished with them. For use in writing the tester should have a clip board which can hold a sheet of paper 8½ by 11 inches. The paper for recording the subject's responses may be ruled like this:

Name:		Date:	Ex. by:	
Card & R No.	Pos'n & Time	MAIN STAGE	INQUIRY	SCORING

8½ in.

11 in.

FIGURE 2

Suggested Form for Record Sheet

The average Rorschach protocol will require eight to twelve sheets. A sufficient number of sheets should be attached on the clip board to obviate the necessity for stopping to hunt for more sheets during the testing period.

A stop-watch calibrated for seconds in precise enough for timing in this test. A large watch with a second sweep hand will do if the Rorschacher is careful to note the starting and stopping times in relation to the large minute hand of the watch. A tester should not rely on counting to himself—there is too much to do during the test to be able to attend to the important element of time by this method.

B. Rapport

Many testees come to the psychologist's office with preconceived ideas about the need for testing and the nature of the tests to be taken.[3] Rapport is an integral part of the entire test situation. There are no general rules applicable to all subjects, but some suggestions may be in order—to be modified, ignored, or elaborated as each new test session will require:

1. Greet each subject cordially and warmly.

2. Give the testee a pretest indication of the reason(s) for referral to the psychologist. This will range from a frank statement to a disguised explanation of the need for an "appraisal of personality." In each instance, however, the client must be impressed with the fact that he is not there for experimental purpose (unless it is an actual experimental situation) and that all of the testing is designed to help the subject.

3. The nature of the test (in this instance the Rorschach) should be briefly indicated. This is especially necessary since some subjects will not cooperate if the face validity of the inkblots is not immediately apparent. Do not hesitate to tell the subject that he is to be given a personality evaluation test, and indicate the approximate length of time for the testing.

4. Tell the subject your plan with reference to the test findings: *The test results will be sent to Dr. Smith, who*

[3] The author recalls one subject who entered the test room, sat down gingerly and resignedly, and said, "You can turn on the raw shock now, I can take it." The importance of the subject's set is patently shown in a study by Hutt, M., et al. (1950) in which they found significant shift in Rorschach variables from test to retest in their control and experimental groups. The import of this study for testing and follow-up cannot be overemphasized. The serious reader is urged to consult this report.

referred you for examination. I am quite certain that he will discuss the matter with you further. Or, I will go over the results and make proper recommendations most helpful to you. No matter what is told to the client, he must appreciate that his time is not being wasted and that he is participating in a process that is centered about him and his problem.

C. Directions[4]

The variety of verbal directions to the testee is limited only by the number of testers. Some favor giving the subject plate I immediately upon being seated and saying, *What do you see there?* or, *Tell me what this means to you.* This is the simplest set of instructions. Others are far more elaborate and detailed. The following is suggested for beginners, since it contains all the elements that will facilitate obtaining an adequate protocol. After the subject has been seated, say: *I have ten cards here* (indicating the pile on the Test Table, face down) *which I will show you one at a time. These cards have inkblot designs on them made by squirting some ink on a piece of paper and folding it in half* (while saying this illustrate by pantomiming ink being splashed from a pen onto paper, then folding and opening the simulated piece of paper). *You probably played this game when you were a youngster* (if client is an adult) — *it's called blotto. When I give you a card, please hold it in both hands like this* (illustrate by holding a plate, back side to the subject, in both hands 12 to 14 inches in front of and below the eyes). *I want you to tell me what you see there, what it means to you. There are no right or wrong answers. It is simply a matter of what it means to you or what you see there. Tell me what you see as soon as you see it so that I may write it down. Some people see many things, others see a few. It is entirely up to you. When you cannot see anything more on*

---

[4] The suggested verbal instructions are subject to modification in keeping with the testee's ability to comprehend such directions. This is a *sine qua non* in projective testing.

a card, turn it over and place it face down on the table in front of you. I will give you the next one. Remember, hold the card in both hands, tell me what you see or what it means to you as soon as possible, and turn the card face down on the table when you can see nothing else. Are there any questions? Answer the subject's questions. Do not tell the subject that he may turn the cards. If that question does come up either before or during the test, the examiner may indicate, *That's up to you, you may do as you please.*

If the subject gives only one response to the first card, it is good test technique to urge the subject to hold the card a while longer to try to see more than one concept. This may be accomplished by a statement such as, *Most people see more than one thing on these cards, won't you try to tell me more about this card?* As soon as the subject has indicated that he is through with the card by facing it down on the table, the tester should remove it immediately and give the testee the next plate.

It may occur that the subject will recognize the inkblot after he has been given the first plate. Or it may be that upon his introduction to the test situation he may indicate that he had taken this test before. In either instance the examiner *should not* inquire into the circumstances surrounding the previous testing situation, but should take steps to insure the adequacy and progress of the present test. A statement such as the following will usually suffice to enlist the continued co-operation of the subject: *I'm glad you told me that you took this test before. We'll talk about it later. For the present, let's go on with this since it doesn't make much difference in the results. However, don't try especially to remember your previous responses nor should you avoid giving them. Just go on as if this were the first time you're taking the test and tell me what you see or what it means to you. Any further questions?* Emphasize that there is no need to recall previous concepts, and assure the testee that the present test is not spoiled by an earlier exposure to the cards. After testing the limits, the examiner should attempt to ascertain the facts regarding the previous Rorschach administration and to whom he may write for a copy of the report. Allen (1951a, b; 1954a) and his co-workers (1952; 1953) have found a fairly high degree of consistency in test-retest productivity. The author recalls the case of a psychiatrist undergoing analytical training who presented himself for Rorschach evaluation. The doctor protested the futility of re-testing since he had studied the Rorschach technique with one of the recognized authorities after his first experience as a Rorschach subject a year or so earlier. He averred that he knew the "acceptable" responses and would be able to recall quite vividly his previous concepts. The examiner verbalized the above directions and urged the testee to co-operate, even if only for scientific interest. The resultant protocol was very interesting and revealing. After giving the obvious popular responses, along with some excellent ones, in a plate, the testee followed with something like this: "I know I should not say I see this, but — ," And he proceeded to give concepts that contributed materially to insights into his personality and adjustment mechanisms.

D. Recording Responses—Main Stage

Before giving the subject the first card, the tester makes the following entries on the record sheet as shown in Figure 3. This indicates that the testee has plate I in his hands and has not yet made his first response, nor has he turned the card. The cards are *always* presented with the top up.[5] Therefore the first entry in the position column should always be ∧ . Any turning is

---

[5] In order to make certain of card presentation in the correct "top up" position, it is suggested that the beginner make a large arrow on the back of the plates with the apex always toward the top. The Roman numerals I, II, etc. printed in the upper left hand corner of the back of the card indicate the top. The imprint of the publisher is in the lower left hand corner, a guide to the bottom of the cards.

Name: J. Smith		Date: 8-15-65		Ex. by: R. M. Allen
Card & R No.	Pos'n & Time	MAIN STAGE	INQUIRY	SCORING
I* 1**	∧ ***			

　　* Plate No.
　** Response No.
*** Position in which card is given to subject.

FIGURE 3

Preliminary Recording Data

shown by $>V<$, depending on the direction of the *top* of the card. Excessive turning may be recorded thus: ⊘.

　　Immediately upon placing the plate in the subject's hands start the stop-watch. To aid in the recording the tester should reach for the plate with his preferred hand (right hand for the right-handed) keeping the pencil in the hand at the same time. In the nonpreferred hand will be the stop-watch. It might help a bit, in the early stages of Rorschach administration, to tie a loop of string around the index finger of the nonpreferred hand and through the top ring of the watch. This will prevent the watch from slipping and keep it ready for starting and stopping. As soon as the subject utters the first intelligible response the tester should glance at the watch and write down in the proper column the elapsed time as well as the position of the top of the card. This first time recorded is the "reaction time," giving the time that has elapsed between the presentation of the card to the subject and the first intelligible response. The watch is kept going until the testee turns the plate

face down on the Test Table. As this occurs, the tester stops
the watch and records the full time indicated on the dial. This
is the "response time," showing the fully elapsed time between
card presentation and placing the plate face down on the
table.

Every verbalized response must be recorded verbatim.
Sometimes a subject will turn the plate one or more times prior
to giving a response. These turns must be recorded in the position column. The following is an illustration of the record of
responses to the first two plates in the Main Stage:

Name: J. Smith		Date: 8-15-65	Ex. by: R. M. Allen	
Card & R No.	Pos'n & Time	MAIN STAGE	INQUIRY	SCORING
I 1	∧ ∨ ∧ 10″	this is a bat		
2	∧ ∨ 73″	1.1. an officer cap insignia		
II 1	∧ > ∨ 3″	a btfly up here		
2	∨ < ∧ 38″	2 clowns play'g pat-a-cake		

FIGURE 4

Record Sheet for Plates I and II
Main Stage

E. Main Stage [or Free Association]

If the subject speaks too rapidly for proper recording, the
tester may request the testee to slow down or repeat parts of a

particular response at the time it is given. This should be kept to a minimum since it may interfere with the desired degree of spontaneity and freedom of association. Experience with this test has led to the impression that in most instances limits may be set to the time and/or number of responses that will be recorded for a card. Unless unusual circumstances dictate otherwise, a five-minute time limit for each card is reasonably sufficient for sampling the behavior of the subject in this test situation; a second limit that is acceptable is to restrict the subject to a maximum of ten responses to each card. If a testee is so productive as to give ten or more responses to a card, there is no need to wait for him to give up the card voluntarily, for these additional responses will not alter the test results or interpretation. Needless to say, the card should be taken from the testee with tact so as not to offend him or to inhibit further responses.

A time-saving aid in recording inheres in a personal shorthand scheme. The following list of suggestions will give the beginner a start in setting up a personal system:

> look(s) like — l.l.;
> some sort of, some kind of — s.s., s.k.;
> something, anything — s'g, a'g;
> "ing" ending to a word — 'g, i.e., going — go'g;
> butterfly — btfly;
> could be — cld b, (shld, wld);
> cannot — cn; don't know — dnk; have or has — h;
> some — s; any — a; thing — t'g; body — bdy;
> man or male — M; boy — b; people — pple;
> woman or wife — W; girl — g; female — f.

Thus, to record the response, "Looks like some sort of an animal" — "l.l. s.s. A." The adept Rorschacher is continually finding new ways of writing responses quickly so as to keep up with the verbose subject. If a record is to be read by another psychologist or by other members of the clinical team it is

urged that the administrator immediately rewrite the protocol in full words so that there can be no misunderstanding of
responses.

F. Suggestions for Audio Recording the Rorschach Test

Essentially, audio recording is desirable in order to capture
and hold the meaningful nuances that may be entirely lost in
the usual method of hand note-taking by the tester. After considerable experimentation with various types of recording devices, the disc type has been found most satisfactory. The disc
can be filed in the testee's case folder without appreciably increasing the cost of testing. Furthermore, it assures a permanent verbatim record for scoring, interpreting, follow-up
study, and research, and is excellent staff-conference material.
It also serves as a facile teaching medium in an introductory
course in the Rorschach technique. It frees the examiner from
note-taking and affords increased opportunities for observing
behavior in the testing situation. It is thus possible to see many
behaviors not otherwise attended to in the multiplicity of tasks
necessary for obtaining an adequate protocol.

This procedure is used in counseling research and with the
TAT. However, the Rorschach Test does not lend itself to
complete machine recording because of the Inquiry. This
phase of the test calls for verbatim repetition of the testee's free
associations prior to inquiry into the location and determi-
nant(s) for each percept. It appears that two machines are
needed, one to play back the free association response and the
other to record the subsequent Inquiry data. The other alternative would be a continued jockeying back and forth on the
recording tape or disc between the free association percept and
the place on the tape or disc where the Inquiry is to be recorded. The first of these methods is too expensive in that it
ties up two machines and two tapes or two discs. The second
alternative results in a messy record and in frequent tape
breakage.

A third method emerged from repeated trials with the disc type of audio recording machine. This procedure produced a clear protocol with the least amount of difficulty and disturbance in the testing atmosphere.[6] The optimal procedure is as follows: After the usual rapport talk, the testee's permission for recording his responses is requested. A brief explanation may be necessary in some instances, but the testor will experience little difficulty in securing the desired consent. The subject is given the Rorschach Test directions, and the tester writes the free associations. Upon completion of the free associations to all ten plates, the testee is then introduced to the Inquiry phase. He is also informed that the machine recording starts at this point and will continue to the end of the testing period. The subsequent verbal give and take between the testee and the tester is machine recorded.[7] The tester then reads from his written notes the subject's first response to plate I, but prefaces this repetition with the statement, "On card I your first response was . . ." As the testee indicates the location of the per-

[6] It was noticed that some subjects, especially anxious neurotics, were visibly disturbed, along with the examiner, when the recording procedure was interrupted by breakages and entanglements.

[7] A conference type microphone with a very sensitive pickup and a hand operated snap switch to start and stop the machine is best in this situation. The tester has two choices of how he will record. He can snap the switch on and let it run until the end of the complete test, or he can operate the snap switch so as to record only when actual conservation is going on. In the former instance the play-back will be the same as the original recording time, with large gaps of silence. This may require more than one one-hour disc. In the latter case, starting and stopping the machine, playback time is shorter and an entire Rorschach test may be completed on one side of a one-hour disc or at most both sides may be required. The major difficulty here is to anticipate when the testee will begin to speak and complete verbalizing his ideas. This may be a bit more disturbing to the neurotic patient. With experience, however, a modification of these two extremes may be possible. Turning the disc or changing discs takes very little time and may be accomplished smoothly by engaging the subject in trivial conversation while making the change. For playback a foot-type switch is most convenient since most are equipped with a device for starting and stopping the machine and also a gadget for positioning the disc to play at any desired point.

cept, it is recorded directly on the Location Chart in the usual manner. It is important that the tester preface his inquiry into each percept with identifying numbers: the plate number is spoken when each plate is placed in front of the subject and the response number for each percept in the particular plate is verbalized. Thus, the tester says: "On card IV your first response was . . ." The next response to the same plate is prefaced with, "The second response was . . . ." Another requisite is to mark off the location for each response in each card and to identify each with the same response number as spoken into the microphone. In this way the tester will recognize the Inquiry (location, determinants, and content) data for each response when playing back the disc with the Location Chart in front of him. For those additional new responses given in the Inquiry, the tester makes the usual inquiry and identifies the percept on the recorder and on the Location Chart with "1a." A second additional response is labeled "2a."

Testing the Limits is similarly recorded. After arranging the plates as required by this phase of the test, the tester asks the questions to be answered by the testee's choice of percepts. The tester speaks into the microphone the plate number and the location of the percept. This should be supplemented by noting the location on the Location Chart.

Further uses of this technique include recording clinical impressions and test-behavior observations. The final interpretation may then be added to the record to await convenient transcription. This method does not eliminate note-taking, but confines it to the free-association stage only. It does enable the examiner to pay more attention to the other more important facets of the interpersonal and social situation labeled "test administration."

Part III

LOCATION — WHERE?
DISCUSSION OF LOCATION

Chapter 5

THE SCORING SYMBOLS

INTRODUCTION

The testee isolates a portion of the plate or uses the entire design in which to organize a percept. The location, or Where, of the percepts is an integral part of the process in which the interaction of Where, How, and What educe a meaningful engram or memory picture. An inspection of the cards reveals several designs which are easily organized into percepts using the entire blot area. Other designs resist being organized as a unit into a meaningful gestalt.

Within each plate certain portions of the blot and space-areas are more easily organized into concepts than others. These less-than-the-whole blot-areas are called details. Within the category of details there are variations in size, natural lines of articulation, and frequency of selection by the testee. These variables determine the scoring symbols assigned to the location of the concept on the card. The ease and difficulty of detail-organization may also be measured on a continuum with some more and others less feasible with reference to scoring.

The third portion of the plate that may enter into the formulation of a response is the space-area surrounding each blot or enclosed within the design (such as the four white spaces within the blot on card I). The space-areas may be used as primary or secondary (additional) components in a concept.

WHOLE

The W response is easiest to locate and score. The testee readily ascribes his concept to the entire blot. Whole responses are normally seen very readily in plates V, VI, I, and II; less easily in IV, VII, and III; while the greatest amount of difficulty in forming W's is encountered in plates VIII, IX, and X (Ranzoni, Grant, and Ives, 1950, p. 128). The organization that is required to give some meaning to the whole blot may be scaled on a continuum ranging from the least to most effortful.[1]

Klopfer and Kelly (1942) introduced the cut-off Whole for scoring the area of the concept which included all but a minor portion of the blot. If the beginner in Rorschach decides to use the cut-off Whole, W^{χ} , in scoring, the symbol must be tabulated in the W row and computed in the W total and percentage. No matter what the decision, the careful interpreter must keep in mind the type of whole response, how well organized, its originality, banality, or impoverishment of conception — in addition to quantitative considerations.

An atypical whole response that is given by the mentally deficient and the psychotic is the confabulated whole, DW. This location symbol is used to characterize the response in which a small portion of the blot gives meaning to the entire blot. For example, the subject may see the two small clawlike pincers at the top center of plate I and on the basis of only these two de-

---

[1] The amount of effort that is necessary to form the total blot into a meaningful gestalt has been called "the organization activity: Z" by Beck (1950, pp. 58-82) who defines "associationstrieb" as: "The number of W is, before all, index to the energy at one's disposal for the organization drive" (p. 58). Organization can take place at location levels other than W. This is seen in the numerical "Z" values assigned to detail concepts in all cards. The "Z" scheme of weighted values is quite complex. Wilson and Blake (1950) found that there is no particular gain in applying Beck's weighted "Z" scores to each response. The tester may do as well by estimating the organizational level (through all of the factors entering into the response) of each concept and emerge with a final conclusion as to the subject's organizing ability.

tails call the total design a "crab." The main principle differentiating the confabulated from the normal whose response is that the entire takes meaning from a part and that in the Inquiry the testee is unable to account for the response except in terms of the radiation of this small part to the whole.

Some of the more usual whole responses given to the individual cards are:

Card I: a bat, butterfly, or two-winged bird or insect; face of a cat or fox (with white spaces as eyes, mouth), (Halloween) mask; crab; map; two witches hanging onto or pulling apart something in the center (usually a woman); officer's insignia V.[2]

Card II: Two clowns, men, women, old ladies, may be playing a game with or without colored costumes; butterfly; map; cave or tunnel with entrance; two animals with fancy hats.

Card III: two vaudeville actors on a stage with a red decorated curtain (most concepts in this card omit the red details and are scored as cut-off whole in the Klopfer system, and large detail by others).

Card IV: a monster, gorilla, or human (college boy wearing a 'coon skin coat) — the testee must include and account for the middle bottom detail; an animal skin or rug; bat.

Card V: a bat, moth, butterfly ∧V ; a dancer in costume.

Card VI: an animal hide or rug; animal form; smoke, cloud; atomic explosion V ; airplane; map; fan V ; two masks on a theater program V .

Card VII: two human forms (usually female) ∧V ; map; two animals on a base; cave; wig V ; archway or architecture V ; featureless face and hair (wig) or Washington type V .

Card VIII: heraldic design; response integrating side

[2] V < > indicates the direction of the top of the card when the response is given by the subject. Absence of arrow implies that the top of the card is held in the normal position. If an item is followed by ∧ V the indicated response is produced with the top of the card in both directions.

animals with the rest of the card (climbing up a tree); anatomy; Xmas tree and decorations; microscopic slide.

Card IX: (a whole response to this card is usually either O + or O −)[3] an old-fashioned gown ∨ ; explosion, with smoke and fire ∧∨; ; anatomy; map; plant or flower.

Card X: underwater scene, marine life; scene on a microscopic slide; design or emblem. (See Card IX regarding the quality of W responses.)

This list by no means exhausts the variety of whole responses a Rorschacher is bound to obtain during the course of experience with the test.

DETAILS

No complete agreement exists among Rorschachers on scoring detail locations. There are two guiding principles:

1. frequency of selection of an area in a large number of protocols, and

2. the "naturalness" of the separation of the detail from the rest of the design making it a completely articulated unit. The details meeting both of these criteria (with emphasis on the frequency) are scored D — large detail.[4]

[3] A beginner should consult a standard reference for original concepts. See footnote 4 for recommendations. "O" signifies an original response, + and − indicate the quality of the concept as well or poorly conceived. An original concept depends on the rarity of its appearance in a number of protocols, traditionally set at one time in 100. Obviously, only experience with a minimum of 100 records can begin to give the neophyte an appreciation of an original response.

[4] Prepared detail location charts for scoring may be found in: Beck, S. (1950, pp. 13-57). A detailed list differing in some scoring details from Beck is: Hertz (1970). Many students prefer L. Small's *Rorschach Location and Scoring Manual.* See also, Alcock (1963).

The author has marked up an old set of Rorschach plates in accordance with Beck's scoring system for location. This has proved to be a timesaver, since direct comparisons may be made with the testee's circled responses on the achromatic reproductions of the ten designs usually found in commercially available record forms. These reproductions may be purchased from

The normal or usual details contain most of the popular responses.[5] These large details — D — form the core of the protocol in most instances. Any concept embracing less than the entire card is a detail. Examples of some of the more common details are presented in Figure 5. The contents of these percepts are given below:

Card I: a claw; hand or mitten; female figure; bell with clapper; donkey or elephant; profile $\vee$; crab; bug or insect.

Card II: bird; turban; castle; phallus; pliers; bear (whole bear or upper half); butterfly; blood; fire and smoke; dog(s) $\wedge \vee <$.

Card III: two human figures; elfin, monkey, or rooster; chicken or ostrich head; fish; leg of horse or cow; Negroid head $\vee$; chest area (X ray or skeleton); anatomy; bowtie; butterfly.

Card IV: flower; vagina; snake; arms; oriental face or mask; dog $>$; shoe(s) or boot(s); head of cow; tree stump.

Card V: rabbit; horns; penis; human legs; leg (human or animal); face of Peter Pan; animals rushing together; person with fancy hair-do or hat.

Card VI: totem design; phallus; animal hide; butterfly, newel or bed post; figurine; snake; vagina; submarine on surface of the water $<$; face with beard $\vee$; road or river; projectile shooting; feathers.

Card VII: Indian with feather in head; faces (female);

Grune & Stratton who publish a one-page location form; Harcourt, Brace and Jovanovich publishes the Klopfer and Davidson Individual Record Blank with a Location Chart for the ten designs, place for scoring the individual responses and tabulating the symbols; a psychograph for plotting the distribution of determinants, and the formulae for statistical computations which aid in the interpretation. Other forms are printed in booklets and single pages. The Psychological Service Center has developed a 16-page Standard Rorschach Psychodiagnostic Record Booklet which permits recording of all responses, inquiry, scoring, computations, locations on design-chart, and duplicating the interpretation.

[5] Popular or P responses are those which have appeared most frequently by actual count in accumulated protocols.

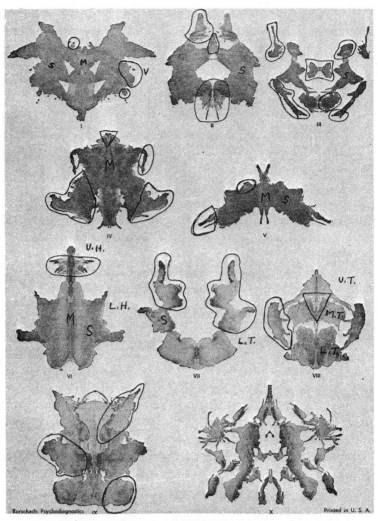

FIGURE 5
Sample Large Detail Location Chart
By courtesy of Hans Huber, Publishers, Berne, from Rorschach,
Psychodiagnostics.
S—entire side of the ink blot; M—entire middle of the ink blot; V —card
held up-side down; L.H. —lower half of the blot; U.H. —upper half of the
blot; U.T. —upper third of blot; M.T. —middle third of blot; L.T. —lower
third of ink blot; (plate X)—almost every part of the blot is a large detail.

female figure ∧∨ ; butterfly; North and South America; wig ∨ ; dog's head; clouds; elephant head and trunk; wire-haired terrier or scottie <.

Card VIII: animal; tree; ribs; pillow(s); flag(s); rocks; ice cream; animal head ∨ ; butterfly ∨ .

Card IX: witch or human form; face; animal; spinal cord; vagina; deer or camel face; head of Mark Twain > ; cherry tree ∨ ; grass; anatomical parts; boulders.

Card X: crab; octopus; lobster; sheep; phallus; rabbit's head; worms or caterpillars; collie dog; poodle; blue birds; elf; sea horse ∨ ; anatomy; parachuter ∨ .

The list and illustrations do not approach the variety of ver-balizations and locations of large detail, D, responses. It should be noted that the plates do not lend themselves equally well to detail organization. Plate X usually evokes the greatest number of D concepts, followed by VIII and IX. Least pro-ductive of D responses are cards VI, IV, I, and V in descending order (Ranzoni, Grant, and Ives, 1950, p. 128).[6] The con-sideration of these details leaves areas of the plates still un-touched. These nonindicated areas form the body of the re-maining types of detail responses—the small or infrequently given locations. Location-areas not scored W or D, and not in-volving white space, are scored in one of the following cate-gories:

1. Dd: these are portions of the plate which are smaller in size than D and are less frequently perceived. This is so because their size, isolation, and position are less impressive than D and so draw attention less often. In many instances Dd responses

[6] It is interesting to speculate that the Rorschach protocol is like a closed energy system—there is a normal or usual distribution of location and deter-minant factors. Deviations from this normally expected distribution must come from the internal composition of these factors in the personality structure. This finds expression in the statement that what is not whole is de-tail or space, i.e., deviations that apear in the location-distribution must come from within the system. Therefore, overpredominance of W is at the expense of detail and/or space, and vice versa. This is one of the ingenious aspects of the Rorschach Test.

are difficult to differentiate from D. Listed below and illustrated in Figure 6 are some small detail percepts:[7]

Card I: breasts; hooded heads; belt buckle; egg; profile of
man with turned-up nose; tree; head of Abe Lincoln; eagle or
dog head ∨.

Card II: apelike face (prominent chin and hooked nose);
profile of old man; icicles; vaginal opening; horn of unicorn;
tongue of flame; broken bridge.

Card III: head of bull ∨; rope; alimentary or eustachian
tube; penis; breast; lung.

Card IV: profile <; beak of bird; castle; pair of feet; horn;
nun or senorita with mantilla ∨.

Card V: head with derby hat; profile of person; person in
long or flowing robe; tail; chicken leg or bone.

Card VI: bird's beak; claw; cat's whiskers; statue or sculp-
tured bust ∨; testicles ∨; two vague heads, maybe ghosts.

Card VII: walnut kernel; canal; snout; Turkish minaret;
bubbles.

Card VIII: feet ∨; spine; vagina; head of sheep ∨; ghost;
statue.

Card IX: fingers; antlers; pointing finger; rays of sun; gun
or revolver; figure or person; mask; bridge.

Card X: tooth; fried egg; hazel nut; profile of child or
cherub.

2. *Dr:* This scoring symbol is assigned to those areas which
are very infrequently used alone to form a concept and is
known as a rare detail. Rare details may be very small or large
in size, so that extent of area is not the main consideration.
Usually, rare details cut across natural lines of articulation and
include in one concept portions of the plate which require
either unusual creativity and originality on the one hand, or

[7] An examination of two widely used references for scoring (Beck, 1950
and Hertz, 1970) indicates wide divergences in the scoring of some details.
Also consider Klopfer's and Davidson's (1962) D, d, dd.

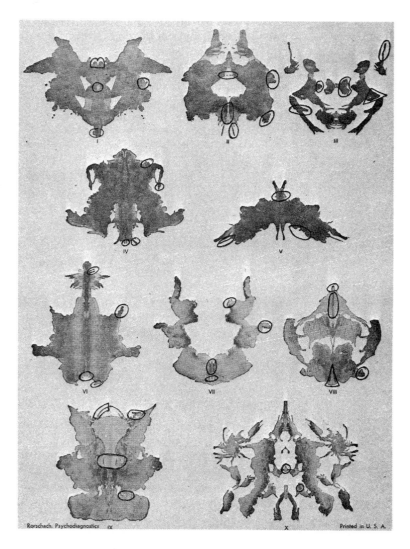

FIGURE 6

Sample Small Detail Location Chart

By courtesy of Hans Huber, Publishers, Berne, from Rorschach,
Psychodiagnostics.

distanciation from reality on the other. The recognition of Dr responses depends upon experience with a large number of protocols and with various psychiatric and psychological categories of subjects. Some illustrations may be of value (see Figure 7):

Card I: 1—butterfly; 2—three prehistoric animals; 3—profile of a man; bowling pin, a large one.

Card III: 1—two front teeth; 2—a bomb; 3—face of a Hottentot with a sharply pointed nose.

Card VI: 1—snake or worm; 2—head of a collie dog.

Card IX: 1—woman jumping or falling off a cliff; 2—a razorback eating an animal.

3. De: This is an edge detail and is scored when the testee gives a concept which utilizes only the outer edge or contour of the blot, or any portion of it. This type of location is illustrated in Figure 7:

Card II: 1—profile of a man with a firm protruding chin V; 2—shoreline at Lake Sebago.

Card V: 1—the profile of Peter Pan, just the side view of the horns, forehead, nose, mouth, and chin—looks exactly like him. The De is a bit difficult to determine but this test is applied: a concept which adheres only to the periphery of the blot or portion thereof and does not go *into* the blot is an edge detail. The rationale for this type of response precludes going beyond the edge.

4. Di: A concept which is predicated on an area located entirely inside the blot is an inside detail. It is an area which is entirely surrounded by chromatic or achromatic portions of the blot.[8] In this the subject literally ". . . pierces a blot area which seems to be an unbroken area to a preponderant majority of all subjects . . . . using the most minute shading differences for their delineation" (Klopfer and Kelley, 1942, p. 103). Di responses are illustrated in Figure 7:

[8] An exception to this is the response in Card IX, camel or deer head, which is scored D.

FIGURE 7

Sample Dr, De, Di, Do Detail Location Chart

By Courtesy of Hans Huber, Publishers, Berne, from Rorschach,
Psychodiagnostics.

Card IV: 1—face of a woman inside here, see her hair, nose, eyes, mouth, and chin, an excellent side view.

Card VII: 1—an eye; 2—a scottie dog < .

5. *Do:* In the oligophrenic detail (dx of Klopfer) the testee reports a part of an animal or human concept (Adx or Hdx) where normal expectation is to perceive the entire animal or human (A or H). In Figure 7, Card III: in place of the popularly perceived human figure in the entire side detail the deviant response will give only the upper portion of the human figure from the head to the hips or waistline, thereby cutting off the lower portion of the body concept.

6. *DdD:* This characterizes a confabulated concept in which an infrequent detail gives meaning to a larger detail. This is seen in the response, "This whole orange is a buffalo; here is the head and so the rest must be the body," to orange area of Card VIII, response 1∨ in Figure 7.

Space

The remaining portion of the plate as yet not differentiated and discussed is the white space that surrounds all of the designs and also occurs inside the designs on plates I, II, VIII, IX, and X. The testee may at times utilize only the space and the whole or part of the surrounding or adjacent blot area. The first of these—pure space— is scored S. Where blot and space share a concept the scoring may be WS, DS, DdS, DrS, etc. S—in these the blot area is primary and the space is secondary or additional. The converse—SW, SD, SDd, SDr, S, etc.—holds if the use of space in a response reflects a modification of the figure-ground (or blot-space) relationship inherent in a design of the Rorschach type.

1. *Pure space—S* (see Figure 8)

Card I: 1—ghost walking; cartoonist's drawing of a man's head.

Card II: 1—a sting ray; ballet dancer; top.

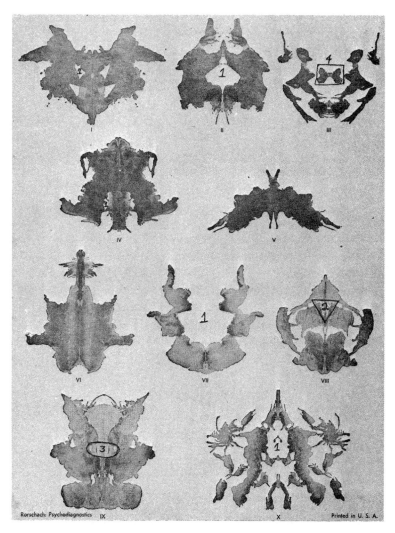

FIGURE 8

Sample Space and Positional Location Chart

By courtesy of Hans Huber, Publishers, Berne, from Rorschach,
Psychodiagnostics.
The numbers refer to types of responses indicated in the text.

Card IV: a man in an academic cap and gown, he fell asleep over his book.

Card VII: 1—a bust of George Washington ∨ ; a vase or urn.

Card X: 1—a catcher's chest protector ∨ .

2. Space primary and blot additional—SW, SD, etc.

Card VII: a bay with its outlet into the ocean surrounded by a coral reef—SW.

Card VIII: 2—the bleached skeleton of a longhorn's head —SD.

3. Figure and space—WS, DS, etc.

Card I: a mask with holes for the eyes and mouth—WS.

Card II: a tunnel, looking in through the entrance—DS.

Card IX: 3—a bridge over the water here—DdS.

ADDENDUM

Two types of responses that are not primarily problems in location should be mentioned—the contaminated or spoiled response and the positional or Po percept. The contaminated concept may evolve from a W, D, or Dd area. The basic formulation in a contamination process is the fusion of two concepts to the same area of the plate. The testee is unable to inhibit or delay one of the associations in favor of the other and gives two separate responses. The result is a "double talk" type of response which contains elements of the two and becomes an original concept, to say the least. Rorschach's classic illustration is the spoiled concept to all of Card IV: "seen as a degenerated liver, and then as a happy man sitting on a stool; the two responses are contaminated into the (one) response, liver of a solidly living politician" (Klopfer and Kelley, 1942, pp. 353-354). The location is scored W.

The positional response is usually a detail which derives its content primarily from its placement on the card in relation to surrounding or adjacent portions of the blot. Other factors may enter into the response. For example, in Figure 8, Card III: 4—the hearts of two men. Inquiry into this response elicited that this was two hearts because the blot is "exactly in the center and that is where the heart is." Many genital responses have a bit of the positional element in them, especially the lower middle areas of plates II, VII, VIII, and IX. However, in most instances the shape and shading play the primary roles so that these responses are not usually scored Po.

A third somewhat common problem is the borderline D or W location. In any of the plates a testee sees a concept on one half of the blot and asserts that it is repeated on the other side. For example: in the entire side of Card II a subject sees "an old maid sitting at a table, the same in the other half of the card." Scored: D-WM + . The "detail-leading-to-a-whole" (D-W) response is not a well-organized W response and is tabulated with the D location in the final totals. This same question arises with so-called symmetry responses.

Chapter 6

THE INQUIRY

An integral part of the Rorschach administration is to question the testee in order to ascertain those factors which entered into the association of the blot stimulus to the given verbal report.

The freedom of the Main Stage in which spontaneous association is encouraged does not appear in this phase of the test. The subject is called upon to account for his percepts so that they may be scored according to the symbols. The tester must be tactful and nonleading in eliciting the requisite information from the subject. The Inquiry has been accepted by all Rorschach workers because it affords the tester an opportunity to ferret out the formal components of the subject's response as well as the ideational content. These data usually become available when the subject is asked to account for and elaborate upon his concepts. Beck (1950, p. 5) writes, in regard to the Inquiry, "This is as important a procedure as the free association itself. Without the information obtained in this inquiry, E cannot know how to process the responses and is not in position to pattern out the personality structure."

The Inquiry serves another purpose which might become more important than the primary one of having the subject account for his percepts. This second purpose is to give the testee an opportunity to augment the protocol with responses which he was reluctant to verbalize in the free association range. This affords the testee further opportunities either to conceive anew or to complete previously educed associations more satisfactorily. Neurotics, especially, take advantage of this second chance to supplement an impoverished protocol, since they feel more comfortable as they become more familiar with the testing situation. When this occurs it indicates the extent to which the subject has been able to recover from the original emotional disturbance of the Main Stage and is once more relatively free to respond to the inkblot situation. It is not unusual for normal subjects to increase their responsiveness during the inquiry phase. This is not surprising, since most persons are somewhat concerned when subjected to any psychological test. The amount and quality of inquiry responses are really significant as differentiating factors between the adjusted and the maladjusted individual. The former may elaborate more fully on responses and may add a popular percept here and there, but no dramatic changes will be evident as a result of the Inquiry. The anxious subject, one who in inhibited, emotionally blocked, sexually ambivalent, insecure, and functionally inefficient, will interpret the Inquiry as less threatening with consequent relaxation of defenses that yield to the permissiveness of the Inquiry climate. The flexibility of these adjustive mechanisms in the altered atmosphere is a favorable sign for positive therapeutic prognosis.

The technique of the Inquiry differs among Rorschach workers. Rapaport, Gill, and Schafer (1968) recommend inquiry immediately after the completion of each plate. This is necessary because the inkblot is removed from the subject's sight as they carry out this phase. The majority of Rorschach workers, however, enter the Inquiry phase after all ten plates have been administered. Mons (1950, p. 25) summarizes the prevailing attitude in this statement: "While the test is in progress no question should be asked, because it would convey an element of suggestion which would affect further responses.

The only permissible request is one for the part of the blot in question to be indicated, and this should only be done on rare occasions."[1]

If the Rorschach protocol is to reflect the personality structure of the subject, it is important that the tester remain as neutral as possible. However, experimental evidence indicates quite conclusively that there is a significant element of examiner influence in the free association stage and in the Inquiry. The complete Inquiry calls for a great deal of skill and insight into the examiner's own influence on the testee's responsiveness. It is reasonable to assume that a tester may elicit any desired Rorschach determinant if he questions persistently enough. Gibby (1952, p. 449) studied "the stimulus value of the examiner as it relates to Rorschach inquiry." His findings revealed definite differences in the obtained Rorschach elements in keeping with the individual examiner bias with both standard and nonstandard Inquiry.[2]

Only guiding cautions can be given; testing experience will build up the store of positive techniques for adequate Inquiry. It is essential that the Inquiry be complete for *all* responses, even those that may be obvious to the experienced tester. The temptation to pass over commonly produced and popular responses without inquiry may lead to a serious error in scoring and interpretation, in addition to poor testing habits. If too many responses are taken for granted, it may become a ques-

[1] Rapaport, Gill, and Schafer (1968, pp. 279-281) feel quite strongly in this matter of the place of the Inquiry in the test sequence. They brush aside the possibility of strong suggestion that their method would have upon the subject's responses in the free association stage. The student is urged to read their point of view.

[2] Gibby's conclusion is amply supported by Lord's (1950) investigation. An interpreter is not completely free to accept the protocol as if it emerged *in vacuo*. He should be certain that he has not influenced the final scoring (a function of the individual location, determinant, and content categories) by projecting himself as little as possible into the testing situation. At best, a test is administered and taken in a social, interpersonal situation, with the give and take that inheres in such circumstances.

tion of who the tester is testing—the subject or himself. The seriousness of overlooking a full Inquiry is evident in ascertaining the determinants of the percepts. It is simple logic—errors in scoring or omissions in the Inquiry lead to errors in interpretation. It is much too easy to assume scoring factors for the subject. The beginner should develop the habit of Inquiry into *all* responses, bar none.

The interpretive value of the Inquiry lies in the supplementary information regarding some percepts of the testee and his ability to verbalize them after an earlier period of inhibition. Modifications, clarifications, elaborations, and new additions to the cards call for individual analyses. Several plates seem to be more prominent in eliciting the additional responses or elaborations of previously given concepts. Since plate I is a novel experience and is, therefore, conducive to throwing the subject off balance, it is not unusual to find the subject producing popular and other responses during the Inquiry. The production of acceptable responses during the Inquiry of plate I, after a rather impoverished free performance, should not be considered as an adverse sign unless this picture is repeated in the other cards. The ability to improve performance after the first card has been exposed is one earmark of the adjusted, but cautious, person. In the Inquiry the subject shows the results of "warming up" to an unusual situation. On the other hand, continued paucity of responsiveness in the Inquiry reflects adversely and emphasizes the continued need for defensiveness in order to function in the social milieu.

Card VI, because of its sexual connotation, will result in a more favorable production in the Inquiry phase, especially for the neurotic person. Occasionally the examiner will find the subject stating that a response just given (during the Inquiry) was originally seen in the free association stage, but for one reason or another (it is essential that the tester attempt to ascertain this reason) it was not forthcoming at that time. While it is desirable to obtain additional response for scoring, it is more important, from the point of view of understanding the perceptions of the testee, to consider these delayed responses from their contextual frame of reference.[3] Plates IV, VII, and IX should also be given careful attention in the Inquiry. The first two cards may show recovery from the parental authority situation, while the last may indicate a return to efficient intellectual functioning. Failure to see the populars or to produce effectively mirrors low recoverability.

In the method of sequential analysis for interpreting the protocol, the responses which are forthcoming in the Inquiry stage are regarded as being significant for the trends in the personality structure which are not completely on the level of awareness, i.e., the adjustive mechanisms and the modes of expressing these mechanisms. The subject has to "dig" in order to give overt manifestations of these facets. A favorable indication of recoverability from exposure to disturbing experiences is seen in the productivity during the Inquiry phase which brings the protocol within normal limits in so far as the various computations are concerned. This is also reflected in the nature of the contents as they reveal the movement toward a more wholesome and constructive responsiveness.

It is helpful to write all of the Inquiry data with red pencil or other colored medium to differentiate these data from the pen or pencil recording in the Main Stage. During the Inquiry the testee must work from the plates and not from the black and white reproductions that are part of some record forms, if one of these is being used. The only exceptions are the occasions when the subject is requested by the examiner to circle on the reproduction the exact blot area used in a given concept. The tester should direct the questioning into three areas: Where? How? and What?

---

[3] Most Rorschach workers do not include the scores obtained for the Inquiry additionals in working up the computational data. Such computations are confined to the responses given during the free association phase.

WHERE IS IT?

This query may be introduced by, *You did very well on the first part. Now we will consider each response separately. I'll read what you said for each card, and I'd like you to show me where you see each concept and what gave you that impression.*[4] An inspection discloses that some of the plates are more easily organized into wholes and details than others. The Rorschacher is obliged to ascertain exactly the areas of the card that include the entire response. This may be accomplished in three steps, depending on the testee's descriptive clarity. The subject may be queried as follows:

1. *In this card you said: this reminds me of a bat. Could you please show me exactly where on this card you saw the bat?* An adequate delineation of the blot area for the response would be one in which the subject states, "The whole card" (if that is the location for the impression of the bat). Some subjects go on to say, "The whole card, here are the wings, and this is the body," at the same time pointing to the essential features of the percept. This is not the usual response, however. Or the subject may not verbalize at all, but show the tester the complete blot area. If the testee is vague and does not delineate the blot area

---

[4] Some Rorschach workers return the cards individually to the testee and ask for recall of the responses given in the Main Stage. In this method the variable of recall becomes involved—and the Rorschach is not intended as a test of immediate or delayed memory.

Other Rorschachers make inquiry immediately after each plate has been completed. The disadvantages inherent in this technique is that detailed questioning may unduly influence the free association to the subsequent cards. The rejoinder that the early Inquiry in the standard method will most certainly influence the subject's explanatory date in the later Inquiry only begs the question. In the standard method the free associations are exactly that—free from the suggestions that a sensitive subject may pick up from the tester's questioning. There can be little doubt of the effect of early Inquiry upon later explanation, but there is no way of accurately gauging the practice effect of suggestibility. But the tester knows that the Main Stage data in the standard method are as free from contamination as possible.

for the response with any degree of exactitude then the examiner should proceed to step two.

2. *Please circle with this the exact area that you are including in your concept of a bat.* (Give the testee a small pointer or a pencil making certain that the subject does not use the lead end as it will mark up the plate and destroy its further usefulness.) The examiner should follow the subject's circling movement carefully and then reproduce it on the small design on the record form. The subject should be asked to observe the tester's circling of the blot area to make certain that there is no error.

3. Sometimes the second step fails to elicit the exact area covered by the response. The examiner may then say, *Look at the plate; now, with this pencil* (a red pencil) *and on this copy of the blot draw exactly around the parts of the design that reminded you of the bat.*

The progression from step 1 to step 3 indicates the degree of psychological pressure required to obtain a full accounting of the given concept. Note those responses and areas wherein this difficulty appears, especially if the testee can account more easily for other responses. If the subject has denied or rejected a response during the Main Stage the tester should go back to this in an effort to obtain scorable elements: *You saw a woman in this card, can you see it now?* The elements, if found, should be scored as additional factors and placed in parentheses in the scoring column. Each response should be read to the subject and its location (as well as determinants and content) pursued. At no time should the examiner use leading questions or phrases. Ask the testee, "Where?", and not, "Did you use the whole card or part of it?", "Is it here?", "Is this the area you used?" Steps 2 and 3 preclude leading questions. After the subject has accounted for all of the responses recorded for a particular plate the examiner then states: *Is there anything else you see now which you did not see before?* If the subject gives more concepts, they are to be written in the Inquiry portion of the record sheet, in red pencil or any writing medium different from the Main Stage recording, and in parentheses. They are to be scored in the same way as other responses but placed in parentheses in the Scoring column and considered as additional factors.

Figure 9 shows the Main Stage (free association) and Inquiry completed for cards I and II. The reader is to regard all entries in the Inquiry and Scoring columns as if recorded in red ink. In the first response the subject indicated, "the whole blot," in reply to the usual location question. The tester requested the

Name: J. Smith		Date: 8-15-65		Ex. by: R. M. Allen
Card & R No.	Pos'n & Time	MAIN STAGE	INQUIRY	SCORING
I 1	10″ ∧ ∨ ∧	this is a bat, flying	1. W blot (? parts) wings, body, black (? flying) up in air	W FM+, FC′ A P
2	∨ 73″	1.1. officer's cap insignia	2. W blot, eagle, wings	W F+ Emb
			(1a. now I see a woman's figure, holding up hands, body, hands over her head)	(D M+ H P)
II 1	3″ ∧ ∨ ∧	a btfly here	1. it's shaped 1. one, wings, and feelers	D F+ A P
2	<∧ 38″	two clowns play'g pat-a-cake	2. W blot, colored costumes	W M+, FC H P

FIGURE 9

Main Stage and Inquiry Recorded for Plates I and II

testee to name the parts of the bat, an acceptable procedure in order to check on the form-level accuracy. The examiner's questions are enclosed in parentheses preceded by a question mark—(?parts)—while the testee's answers are recorded after the queries. After each response-Inquiry has been completed a line is drawn underneath the entry to separate it from the Inquiry data for the next response in the card. The writing in parentheses in Figure 9 illustrates the recording of an additional response given during this phase. Note that it has been scored in the Scoring column in parentheses. When the subject is through with a card, a line is drawn completely across the recording sheet beneath the last Inquiry and Main Stage data for that card. In this way the tester will always be able to keep the responses and the cards clearly separated. The recommended use of the separators between responses and cards will help the beginner, especially since it is difficult in the Main Stage to estimate proper space requirements between responses in the Main Stage and the amount of space that will be required for recording the Inquiry for each response. In addition, each Inquiry must be identified by the same number as the response in the Main stage. *Scoring should not be done in the presence of the subject.* This should be accomplished at a later time[5] when the examiner can study the protocol and consult scoring lists and other references if necessary. It should be kept in mind that the Inquiry starts with the Location or Where. Once Location has been established for main and additional concepts, the tester proceeds to the second area—How?

---

[5] However, the scoring should be completed as early as possible following the test. In this way the behavior and answers will be fresh and more readily available for supplementing the written data. It does not look professional to score in the presence of the subject. Besides, the testee may become curious and even disturbed over the hieroglyphics in his record.

Chapter 7

INTERPRETATION OF
LOCATION — WHERE

The Rorschach Inkblot Psychodiagnostic Test may be considered as a problem or series of problems which the testee must solve. The amorphous nature of the stimuli permits the subject a great deal of freedom of responsiveness. Whether or not a person has the capacity and functional efficiency to utilize this freedom is significant in evaluating the total personality picture. The testee must approach a problem in order to address it. The manner of approach is evaluated in these terms: (1) how much of the blot is encompassed in the response(s); (2) the relationship among whole, detail, small detail, and space areas of the blot used by the subject; (3) the extent of card turning.

The first of these will be considered in this chapter: How much of the blot is encompassed in the response(s). In this phase the inferences regarding the manner of organizing responses and the approach to problems are obtained from the subject's use of the whole blot, W, or parts of it, D, Dd, and S.

THE WHOLE RESPONSE

W: The concept built around the total blot reflects richness of associative activity and the ability of the individual to deal with the over-all problem, i.e., the potentiality and willingness

71

to size up a total situation. However, the manner of reaching a W is important in determining the organizational value of the whole response.

The easiest W, which is actually not a whole response, is one in which the testee refers to one half of the blot and then "doubles" the concept to include the entire plate. This is known as a borderline W and is scored D-W, D leading to a W (this should be differentiated from the confabulated whole response, DW, a pathological response). Card II, "An old maid sitting at a table, the same on the other side." Scored: D-W M + H P. The subject has responded to one half of the plate and proceeded to build up a W by merely pointing out the other half of the plate. This is actually a D concept and does not imply the organizational ability of a good W. (For the subject to have been credited with a good W the response would have to be, "This looks like two old ladies sitting at a table." In this both halves of the plate have been integrated into a unified concept.) In some ways it is similar to a symmetry type of response in which the subject feels he must include as much of the blot as possible in his response. This "doubling" is the most easily attained method. D-W responses spring from the need to outshine, to produce on a high level, without the intellectual efficiency required for a higher level of W organization. The lowered efficiency, of which D-W is characteristic, may be due to primary retardation or emotional factors or a combination of both.

If the W is built up by means of adding distinct portions of the blot to each other, thus arriving at a W, the organizational ability is quite concrete and is not as qualitatively creative as the W in which a total configuration is verbalized at once and completely. Plate X, "Here is a bug, there's another germ, all of these are small bugs and reminds me of a microscope like in technicolor." Scored: W CF Biol. This whole response was put together in piecemeal fashion and not by encompassing the total as a unitary idea. The reasoning or organizational activity is inductive but not originally creative. The person who approaches and handles problems in this manner functions mainly on the descriptive and functional levels, but appreciates the need to relate the various parts of a problem to each other. However, he somehow misses the boat and emerges with only faint insight into the entire problem and its over-all implications for him.

Higher on the continuum will be found those readily integrated W concepts which are not taxing in so far as organizing effort is involved. In this category are found the popular responses to plates I, III, IV, V, VI, and VII. In addition to these readily perceived and practically self-organizing whole associations, the minimally effortful W's which have not yet attained the status of popular responses may be considered in this "readily organized" category. These are elicited most easily in plates V, VI, I, and II; less easily in IV, VII, and III. Whole responses with good form accuracy are most difficult to create in cards VIII, IX, and X (Ranzoni, Grant, and Ives, 1950, p. 128). It is in connection with the latter groups of plates that well-organized, highly creative (perhaps original) whole percepts may be elicited. This should not be construed as a generalization that the last three plates in the inkblot series give rise only to the best W's or that excellent wholes cannot be given in the other plates. But interpretation must reflect the testee's ability to produce differently from the main stream. Basic to W evaluation is the form accuracy of the percept. A W + reflects a good organizational ability that can assimilate the parts of the situation and synthesize them acceptably and constructively. The W — is the product of the intellectually inferior and/or disturbed individual.

The W response, then, may range from poor to excellent; from additively integrated through readily organized to the creatively original whole response. The extent to which the subject organizes the total blot suggests the maximum level of potential efficiency. It is to be expected that a testee will function on several organizational levels in the course of a lifetime and during the brief Rorschach test period. Achieveing an o-riginal creative W with good form accuracy indicates the po-tential efficiency. The current functioning efficiency may be deduced from the range of intellectual organization and the predominant W level. It is important to know the maximum capacity and the functioning ability of the subject, and the variability of performance. The difference between these two discloses the functioning efficiency. Should the subject show instances of a high degree of intelligence, creativity, and or-ganization, yet continued productivity on this level is being in-terfered with, a clue to personal difficulty may be obtained from the specific responses in which there is lowered efficiency reflected in the poorer W concept(s).

With specific reference to the level of intellectual func-tioning, there is agreement among investigators that the W re-sponse is a useful indice. Blatt and Allison (1963) have shown that much of the contradictory results obtained in research relating W to intelligence stems from a failure to evaluate the *quality* of the W percept, and a tendency to rely solely on *quantity*. These authors reported that the relationship does hold, but that the complexity *and* number of W responses had to be considered, not just the "simple sign approach." In their study population the more intelligent subjects produced a sig-nificantly higher number of W + and W + + percepts as com-pared with amorphous, vague, and mediocre Ws (Allison and Blatt, 1964, p. 257).

Closely related to intelligence is the drive of the individual to achieve satisfactorily. This is seen in the associative and organ-izational efforts resulting in W percepts of varying quality. Zulliger (1956) suggests that the quality of the W response (form accuracy, presence or absence of movement, spontane-ity, and whether it is popular, original, or simply banal) does reflect the person's "energy drive" — the greater energy expen-diture being necessary (and manifestly available) to produce good to better results. This is an important contribution to the estimate of intellectual efficiency.

THE LARGE DETAIL RESPONSE

D: The large or usual detail reveals the subject's capacity for dealing with the larger essential aspects of a problem. These responses form the core of the protocol and give some insight into the subject's practicality, i.e., to see the obvious and to utilize it in problem solving. D conceptualiztion has been referred to as the "common-sense" approach, the ability to deal with the everyday aspects of a situation. This is related to form accuracy, the contact with and interpretation of reality. Poor form details relate to distanciation or misperception of reality ascribable to limited intellectual ability or impairment of external or internal control by emotionality or fantasy living.

THE UNUSUAL DETAIL RESPONSES

Dd: In order to obtain a complete picture of a situation, the perceiver must give some attention to the small details so essential to filling in gaps. These are the infrequently used portions of the inkblot, symbolized by Dd. Complete absence of Dd responses is not pathologic, but does disclose an inability to deal with minute details, perhaps a dislike for minutiae which can be irksome to the person of better than average intelligence. Its presence is healthy if optimal, unhealthy if maximal. A well-rounded protocol will contain an acceptable percentage of Dd responses.

Dr: This category has other designations which are interpretively differentiated. Dr, rare detail, is usually the product of a fertile imagination, one that can break across natural lines of articulation to produce something different. The Dr-producing testee can get out of a rut and be original. The wholesomeness of this creative ability is a function of the form accu-

racy. The mentally retarded will give Dr's but of F— quality
rather than F +. This is the originality of the poorly endowed
which need not correlate concept to stimulus except vaguely
and inadequately. On the other hand, the easily stimulated,
readily distracted hypomanic individual with little time to relate blot area to blot-associated concept will give poor form responses to the rarely used area. Thus, Dr may be obtained
from the retarded, the highly intelligent, and the emotionally
disturbed testee. The quality of the Dr response, its relation to
the blot area, in short, the concept and its referent, helps determine which of the above characterize(s) the subject.

De: A testee who prefers to remain on the periphery of a
problem may utilize only the edge of the blot to give a response. In the De—edge detail—approach, the subject is revealing his desire to be outside looking in. For some reason he
does not wish to become personally involved. The edge detail
offers an easy escape from immersion, from the probability of
"getting in beyond one's depth." By employing only the outline
of a blot area, the testee plays safe. Used to excess, it may disclose a barren, overly cautious person.

Di: The opposite of the edge detail is the inside detail, Di.
The subject ignores the usual approach and literally "dives
into" his problem without regard for the surrounding area or
context. Such responses as "eyes" usually fall into this category.
It may be related to the easy distractability of the elated or hypomanic individual who jumps from one stimulu to the other;
to the person who is overwhelmed in a situation and seeks surcease and support in disregarding the full impact of a problem
as a source of help. This person is evading by selecting a pica-
yune, nonessential portion of the problem to deal with. Of
course, it may be related to the projections of the paranoid
who sees "eyes" as an overt manifestation of his own suspiciousness. A record with more than one Di need not be considered
pathologic since it may indicate a precise, overly methodical
manner of viewing situations. However, Di responses should be

regarded as pointing to possible areas of personal difficulty in relation to the remainder of the protocol.

Do: Finally, Do, or oligophrenic detail, must be considered. This is usually a pathological sign. To perceive part of a human or animal where it is much easier for most persons to organize a total human or animal figure is significantly deviant from the usual response. This type of association is elicited from among the mentally retarded, the psychotic, and the encephalopathic individuals. The person lacking intellectual ability is unable to deal with universals, i.e., he cannot conceptualize on a level above the concrete, consequently only specific parts are seen where less concretistic persons are capable of producing better organized total figures. The psychotic and severely anxious person may give oligophrenic percepts because of an inability to make full identification with humans, an unwillingness to accept certain sexually significant portions of the human figure (rejection of the lower part of the usual human figure in plate III), and/or impaired ability to concentrate on the stimulus blot long enough to encompass the normally delineated area in a usual percept. The brain-damaged patient, like the intellectually inferior subject, cannot abstract and must be satisfied with highly concrete concepts. He does not want to increase his failures in a situation and so latches on to a part which he can handle in preference to a larger portion of the stimulus blot which might be too much for him. Involved in this may be true inability and an unwillingness to become involved beyond one's own estimate of ability to produce successfully.

DW, DdD, Contaminated R: At this point special types of concepts must be pointed out: the confabulated and contaminated responses. In the former the subject uses a smaller area of the blot to describe a larger portion of even the whole blot, viz., DW or DdD. These responses are pathological and the product of a severely disturbed individual who finds himself unable to account fully for the product of his disturbed thinking. Occasionally an encephalopathic or retarded patient will give this type of response. The spoiled or contaminated response is definitely the result of fuzzy thinking with markedly poor judgment as the main factor involved. Contaminated productivity is the hallmark of the psychotic person.

Space Response

S: The use of the white portions of the plate surrounding the blot or within the blot constitutes an important qualitative element in the protocol. Rosen (1952, pp. 287-288) states, "4. It can be concluded, therefore, that despite several paradoxes in the results some evidence has been obtained to support the hypothesis that use of white space on the Rorschach is associated with oppositional tendencies, insofar as the Pd Scale may reflect oppositionalism. . . ." Rorschach (1942, p. 199) avers that, "Space responses always indicate some sort of oppositional trend." "More than one S concept," he continues, "gives reason for suspicion." Fonda (1960) has tested this hypothesis in a unique and interesting experiment and concludes that his findings are a "partial confirmation of Rorschach's hypothesis that white space responses indicate some sort of opposition tendency, insofar as the criterion measure reflects indecisiveness or contrariness." Brussel, Hitch, and Piotrowski (1950, p. 48) soften the impact of S: "Persons with many S are not obstinate for the sake of being in opposition. They seem to have a need for independency, and their latent obstinacy and argumentativeness make their appearance when others try to sway them from their chosen paths." Research findings support the original postulate of Rorschach that space concepts spring from the tendency to go against the tide; it is related to the inclination of the individual to reverse the figure-ground relationship.

The direction of this oppositional bias is a function of the subject's experience balance (M:Sum C). In an intratensive setting, M greater than Sum C, the testee channelizes this opposition inwardly against himself. It manifests itself as self-deprecatory, self-critical, and self-devaluating behavior. The extent to which this obtains depends on the nature of the S-delineated percept. The milder the nature of the response, the less inclined the person is to be "hard" on himself. Concepts of an aggressive to violent nature may hold the seeds of severe self-recriminaion. Zulliger (1956) supports this notion, pointing out that in the M-greater-than-Sum-C context, the testee may have, or is at least disclosing the presence of a tendency to suffer from, feelings of inferiority. These are close to engendering self-doubt and lack of self-confidence. If the human movement responses (contributing to the M to Sum C ratio) are hostile, aggressive, or violent, then the energy involved is turned inwardly so as to render the testee less accessible to a healthy relationship with his social surround.

The space response occurring in an extratensive context, Sum C greater than M, reveals an obstinacy that may be directed against the subject's surroundings. This may manifest itself in negativism to violent opposition and stubbornness in interpersonal relations. The degree to which these manifestations are mild, moderate, or severe, may be derived from the tone of the concept. This may range from a passive, inhibited reaction, on the one hand, to marked oppositional behavior, on the other. Further personality interpretation, according to Zulliger (1956), suggests that the individual in this setting is "opinionated," "strong minded," and one who would not hesitate to express himself when necessary. Furthermore, the predominance of pure C (color) responses would seem to indicate that the testee is "irascible." Ray (1963) tested the hypothesis of oppositional trends in the behavior of low and high S perceivers. He reported that the subjects who produced more than ten per cent white space responses (high S) in an extratensive setting (Sum C greater than M) showed definite oppositional tendencies to a much higher degree than the low S producers.

Fonda (1960) affirms the general significance of white space as reflecting some sort of contrariness which is related to Bleuler's (1912) concept of negativism. The presence of an S-located percept should not automatically denote an unhealthy personality. The frequency of its occurrence is important here, as with the other Rorschach Test elements. Fonda suggests four per cent or one in 25 S responses as an acceptable baseline. The S response of a psychotic is different from that of an obsessive-compulsive person, so that only the number of such percepts is not sufficient for interpretation. The difference may lie in the dynamics of the response — the former mirroring the delusional process while the latter revealing the need to be complete in responding to the Rorschach Test plate.

Summary

To this point, the extent of the blot area encompassed in a percept has been considered. From this discussion the nature of the inferences regarding the personality under observation should be confined to: (1) The approach of the testee to the problem at hand. (2) How the subject organizes his attack on a situation, i.e., ability to deal with it in an over-all (abstract) manner yet give due consideration to the larger aspects within the general over-all view. (3) Having brought to bear a common-sense practical analysis of the problem, can he detect and utilize the minute essential facets that are part of any problem-solving situation in life? (4) Cautiousness, anxiety, rashness, pathological thinking — all of these may be determined from the manner in which the testee approaches the problem and integrates the parts, either separately or together, into meaningful, realistic concepts. (5) Finally, the subject's ability to express opposition and the direction that this tendency may take can be inferred.

This is a small segment of the total picture — other parts of the puzzle must be fitted together to give a vital personality description. The relationships among the W, D, Dd, and S factors are the next pieces to be considered.

Chapter 8

LOCATION RELATIONSHIPS

It is rare for a testee to use only one area of the blot in all of the percepts.[1] There is usually a distribution of the location symbols indicating the use of two to four of the blot areas. The relationship between and among these is significant for protocol interpretation. As indicated in the previous chapter, each of the area symbols has a basic meaning. However, this is modified by the context within which each one occurs. In Rorschach interpretation the main problem is that of determining *optimal* relationships among factors rather than emphasizing maximal production of factors.

Beck (1950) and Klopfer and Kelley (1942) have evolved acceptable criteria for the usual allocation of W, D, Dd, and S in the protocol of the normal personality. On the basis of 32 responses Beck indicates the following distribution: W-19%, D-72% and Dd-9%. It is assumed that the Dd category includes the usual small details (Dd) plus all other details (De, Dr, Di, Do) and primary S. Klopfer and Davidson (1962, p. 130) give the following percentages for location: W-20-30%, D + d-50-70%, Dd + S-less than 10 per cent. By adjusting the ranges this would give the following Beck equivalents: W-25%, D-65%, Dd + S-10%. A third distribution is given by Brussel, Hitch, and Piotrowski (1950, p. 48): "In a

[1] The one major exception to this is the approach of the young child who usually deals with the blots as a whole; see Allen (1951a).

81

record of average length, of 20 to 40 responses, the expected distribution of area responses is: 25 per cent W, 65 per cent D, 6 per cent d, and 4 per cent S. Since the W cannot be increased as easily as the D and d, the foregoing distribution does not hold in longer records."

There is quite a discrepancy in the expectancy figures of Beck and others. Beck and his co-workers base their latest data on a recently completed study, the Spiegel Sample. Allen (1951b) obtained this distribution of location areas with a group of college students: W-17%, D-64%, Dd + S-19%. The increased Dd + S per cent is much above that found by Beck, Klopfer, and Rorschach. It may be that the training received by College of Arts and Sciences students prepares them to look for more minute context-filling data and thus raises the percentage of Dd and S responses. Buehler, Buehler, and Lefever (1948, p. 17) find the following allocation: W-22.6%, D + d-53.6%, Dd-23.8%, and S-3.1% for normal subjects. By far the most different proportion of location symbols was published by Cass and McReynolds (1951, p. 181) who found 48%-W, 45%-D + d, and 8%-Dd + S, based on main responses only. Their study population included 100 male and female subjects ranging from 20 to 75 years of age and from 7 to 16 grades completed. There is no explanation for the equivalence of W and D + d percentages. An analysis of Roe's data (1950, p. 395) indicates an average of 45% W for her group of eminent biologists, much higher than any of the percentages in Table 1 with the exception of Cass. She agrees with Cass and McReynolds' findings, yet the population in the latter group in not made up of trained persons as in her own group. She continues, "That half of the subjects used more than the usual number of rare details (usually Dr) is of considerable interest," and goes on to explain that this response location is a function of the training of these scientists who are accustomed to seek out "different aspects of a problem, to see things in a little different way."

TABLE 1

Comparison of Location-Area Percentage Distributions of
Normal Populations

	Allen	Beck	Buehler	Cass	Klopfer	Pio-trowski	Ror-schach	Roe
W	17	19	23	48	25	25	25	45
D(+d)*	64	72	54	45	65	71	65	
Dd+S	19	9	27	8	10	4	10	
	100	100	104	101	100	100	100	

* Included in Klopfer's scoring system.

It seems that the only tenable conclusions to which the Rorschach interpreter can come is that generalizations with reference to the application of Rorschach location factors cannot be made rigidly. As in all handling of Rorschach data, interpretation is a definite function of the testee's age, training, social status, occupation, etc. With due awareness of this caution, it is recommended that as a basis for departures in interpretation of location expectancy the following interrelationship should be considered as a flexible criterion for a normal protocol: W-20%, D(+d)-65%, Dd+S-up to 15%. Slight departures should be permissible in this direction, e.g., there should be some give and take with reference to W and D percentages, but Dd+S percentage above 15 does reflect a meticulous, overly detailed manipulation of the situational stimuli beyond the ordinary demands of problem solving. An overemphais in any one area impairs this optimal approach to, and evaluation of, a problem. Too much W may disclose the over-ambitious, hasty, impulsive, or highly intelligent person, depending on the form accuracy, and the presence or absence of supporting creativity.

Under- and overemphasis of D suggests the manner in which the subject deals with the larger and obvious aspects of life that are so necessary for a constructive appraisal of a problem. A predominance of W, or D, or Dd + S is at the expense of the other area symbols. Thus, by finding the percentages of each it is possible to ascertain how the subject approaches problems and deals with them.

Another application of location data is the succession of blot-area usage from one response to the next, i.e., the shifts in area(s) of the blot(s) encompassed in the subject's percepts as he goes from one response to the next. The succession of areas, both within a given plate and from one plate to the next, suggests the degree of orderliness of approach to problems. The W-D-Dd order within a plate discloses the logical attack in which the subject obtains an over-all view of the situation and then proceeds to fill in the parts, the obvious and subtle details, the deductive reasoner. The Dd-D-W sequence is also a regular order or succession characteristic of the individual reasoner who builds from concrete events into an appreciation of the total situation. This regular order may be exaggerated to the point where logic gives way to rigidity so that the personality structure may be described as having a pathological facet. Underattention to a regular approach in analyzing and/or synthesizing problems may lead to the other end of the continuum—irregularity and confusion. The point on the Rigid-Confused continuum may be obtained quite objectively by following the procedure discussed in the chapter on computations.

A rigidly fixed approach in which the subject deals with situations in one way only, or predominantly with one sequence, points to the inflexible, compulsive person who needs order of a high degree to get along in his milieu. Not even the most efficient scientist approaches *all* of his problems in a purely inductive or deductive manner. Thus, a fixed succession is pathological and reflects a defensiveness necessary to ward off impending and ever-threatening anxiety. In the obsessive reactions, rigidity and adherence to straight facts (high F per cent) are the last resorts for warding off psychotic onslaught.

The confused, irregular sequence is seen in the protocols of the retarded, more frequently in the schizophrenic, and in the manic-depressive, manic reaction. These persons seize any stimulus, respond, and go on to the next with little or no concern regarding the whole or the parts. Distractibility mirrors this confusion of responsiveness.

The logical order of succession is characteristic of moderate neurotics and adjusted individuals who can appreciate the forest, the trees, and the surroundings. Not only is there a logical order of dealing with life, but the normal person can deviate from logic to indulge himself in whim and personal predilection on occasion. It is this admixture of order and some departure from fixed succession that typifies the individual who is not hidebound by defenses and rituals in tasting of and meeting life's adventures.

Protocols showing a confused succession of selected blot areas require an intensive analysis within plates and between plates. This is done to obtain an accurate picture of the testee's apparent use of logic or order in handling a problem. Jumping from W to Dd or S and then to D, etc., may reflect the locus of the testee's disturbance, especially if in the earlier plates the procedure from response to response was quite orderly. The plate, or engram within a plate, in which there is a departure from the usual order calls for analysis and intensive study. The starting point is the response with which the interruption of succession makes its appearance. The analysis would be aided by the content, form accuracy, and other determinants in the response(s). This is particularly true in the evaluation of the protocols of normal and neurotic persons. Within the plates certain areas may arouse disturbing engrams in the subject's efforts to deal with them, viz., sex symbols (directly, indirectly, or in an effort to evade such associations), areas usually associated with male and female figures (plates I, II, III, IV, VII), or those areas which hold highly topical (personal) meaning for the testee. Where logical succession is impaired, the tester is in an excellent position to hypothesize emotional involvement on the part of the subject.

The extent of card turning is the third significant bit of test behavior that should be noted. A testee who does not turn any of the plates during the entire test is easily satisfied with a routine manner of viewing and handling situations. He may not be unimaginative, but he denies himself the privilege of adding points of view to his perceptual position. The less routine person, who can feel free to manipulate his problem in order to see it from different angles, usually turns the card. Frequently it may be observed that a subject will turn his head from side to side in an effort to obtain a slightly different view. This person is not sufficiently free from the ordinary method of attack yet feels that the old method is not enough, that he is missing something by keeping both plate and himself fixed. He feels that he can change the situation by constant manipulation of himself rather than the situation. Excessive turning of the plates is pathological — an inability to concentrate, to settle down to the task of thinking through a problem. Extreme irritability may be the main causal factor. Sometimes a patient will "edge" the card, i.e., look at it by holding the edge of the plate up to the eye level. Another type of behavior may be the tendency to look at the back of the plate while giving responses or between responses. This is characteristic of the disturbed individual who either wants to make certain that all possible aspects of the situation have been covered or is suspicious of what is being hidden from him when given the plate in the usual position. He is going to check on his suspicions.

Part IV

IMPOSED DETERMINANTS—HOW?

Chapter 9

FORM—SYMBOL AND INQUIRY

INTRODUCTION

The greater part in *formal* interpretation comes from the manner in which the subject perceives the responses of the protocol. It is not enough for the testee to report: "it 1.1. a black bat flying," the subject must account for the determinants which give the impression of, "a bat," "a black bat," and "a black bat flying." The factors that enter into this engram may be scored in accordance with several widely accepted systems.[1] Actually it should make no difference which scoring scheme is used. The interpretive outcome which stems from a knowledge of the dynamics of behavior and projection theory should lead to similar evaluation of the personality under consideration even though the manner of arrival differs.

How the subject perceives his various responses is divided into three broad categories, i.e., the determinants may be viewed from three positions:

1. Form;
2. Projected or imposed determinants; and
3. Inherent determinants.

Each of these will be discussed in detail.

[1] Here too the beginner should be aware of the differences among Rorschach workers. Rorschach laid down the basis for scoring determinants (1942, pp. 19-51) and has been followed rather closely by Beck (1950, pp. 92-145). Klopfer and Kelley (1942, pp. 82-182) introduced many scoring refinements which have found acceptance in this country. For a detailed comparison of determinant scoring symbols with an international flavor see Bell, (1948, pp. 84-97) and Toomey and Rickers-Ovsiankina (1960).

Form Symbol

A form-determined response is one in which the shape of the selected blot area is the only factor that gives it meaning. This determinant is scored F. The F percept is related directly to the stimulus situation as represented by the blot-area and interpreted by the testee. Another way of expressing this is that a form-determined concept is closest to the objective stimulus or reality situation as perceived by the subject. Nothing but the outline or contour of the selected area determines the response (see Figure 10):

Card: this is a bat, here are the wings, the feelers, and the body in the middle. Scored: W F + .

Card VIII: these are two animals, like a wolf. Scored: D F + .

Card VII: there is a Turkish minaret, shaped just like it. Scored: Dd F + .

this 1.1. a flower vase. Scored: S F + .

Card VI: coastline of Spain. Scored: De F + .

this 1.1. a btfly. Scored: W F − .

Some of the F symbols above are followed by a plus (+) or a minus (−) sign. This sign refers to the accuracy of the form-level, i.e., how well the concept fits the blot-area selected for the response. F + is ascribed to those concepts which may readily be related to the blot area. F − score is given to the response which is perceived in a blot area whose contour does not fit the concept. For example, in Card VI above, the testee indicated seeing a butterfly in the entire blot. An inspection of the design discloses the inaccuracy of such a concept. It would indeed be an odd butterfly which has the shape of the entire blot design in Card VI.

The neutral F symbol (F followed by neither + nor −) is usually assigned to percepts which are not sharply accurate but the area is sufficiently delineated to cover the percept in a broad sense. This type of symbol finds most frequent use with

FIGURE 10

Examples of F +, F −, and F Concepts

By courtesy of Hans Huber, Publishers, Berne, from Rorschach,
Psychodiagnostics.
W, D, De, S refer to the location; + and − indicate the accuracy of form.

evasive and vague concepts such as maps, bugs, insects, land-scapes, and islands. The rationale for this is that these percepts are sufficiently fluid in shape to be seen in any of the plates.[2]

Kimball (1950, p. 144) discusses the two main methods of determining form-level: the quantitative (Hertz, Beck) and the qualitative (Klopfer, Klopfer and Kelley, Klopfer and David-son, Rapaport, Gill, and Schafer). The beginner may obtain a great deal of help by referring to Beck (1950, pp. 155-195), Hertz (1970), and Small (1956) for F+ and F— values.[3] Ran-zoni, Grant, and Ives (1950, pp. 128-132) have indicated the "card pull" for F. They conclude that cards I and V elicit the most pure form responses, followed by IV, IX, and X. Cards II, III, and VIII evoke the least percentage of F responses.[4] The wisest course is, as Korchin (1960) sug-gests, for the examiner (in this instance, the student) to learn to rely on his own judgment regarding the level of form accuracy.

---

[2] Neutral F is also used by some Rorschach workers in those instances where there is ambivalence between F+ and F—. This should be kept to a minimum as it solves nothing.

[3] There is a reservation to this suggestion. It would be best for the neo-phyte to keep these references handy for consultation, but an effort should be made to evaluate form-level accuracy without such aid at first and to use these references for checking one's decisions made independently. In order to save the reader puzzlement, it must be indicated that there is disagreement among authors, and one author contradicts himself at times. In addition, the responses given in these lists may not contain the exact response the tester receives from the subject. It becomes a matter of subjective judgment to compare the obtained response with its nearest analogy.

The subjective evaluation factor enters into form-level consideration. The lists of responses and their form level are the result of testing many persons. However, these lists do not indicate how the author arrived at the F+ or F— designation for a particular percept. Even if the general method is known for each author, there is no way of determining the role of the examiner's judg-ment in this process.

[4] This finding leads to some highly theoretical speculation. Note that the cards that are most and least productive of form-determined responses con-tain color.

INQUIRY

Since the blots are splotches of ink, any meaning or organization ascribed to them must arise from two sources: the creative ability imposed by the subject and/or the objective stimuli inherent in the structure of the blot. The task of teasing out the basic determinants contributing to the unitary organization of the blot area into a meaningful gestalt ranges between very simple and the extremely complex. While the general purpose of the Inquiry is to demonstrate those factors which comprise the determinant portion of the scoring scheme, the search for each type of determinant — form, movement, shading usage, and color — and its components requires special interrogative techniques.

The general question asked first is, *What gave you the impression of a—?* Or, *What considerations entered into your calling this a—?* This is written in the Inquiry as (?impression). A simple answer, "It 1.1. it," carries no hint of determinants involved. Press with, *Yes, but what in the blot gave you the impression of a—?* Or, *What do you mean it looks like it?* This will in most instances evoke a reply referring to shape, outline, or contour of the blot area giving a basis for an F symbol. Once the subject has mentioned the shape or outline (or some synonym for it) the tester may pursue further if there is reason to believe that there is another component in the determinant. This may be accomplished by a question such as, *Is there anything else besides shape that gave you this impression?*—recorded in Inquiry as (?a'g else besides shape). *Do not mention shape (or color, or any other determinant) until it has been given first by the testee.* Nor should the tester state, "What else besides shape?" It is apparent that the formulation will influence the subject's answer. Suggestions or questions that might give the testee any idea of what the examiner is seeking introduces an unmeasurable variable.

Responses determined by form alone are relatively simple to

establish. Occasionally a testee will produce a response in the Main Stage and elaborate on it in the Inquiry. It is difficult for the tester to cull out what has been added during the Inquiry alone and what was present directly and inferred in the original response. Therefore the entire response has to be scored, elaborations and all. If the form-level accuracy is in doubt, the tester should resort to the technique of requiring the subject to point out the parts of the concept, e.g., to the side detail of card I the subject gives: "This is a donkey." In the Inquiry the testee indicates that the shape of the blot area gave that impression. The examiner may then ask of the subject, *Show me the parts of the donkey,* or, *Where is the head and the rest of the animal?* If the subject has organized a + concept he will have little or no difficulty specifying the parts. In this connection it is suggested that the testor ask general questions first, e.g., *Show me the parts of the donkey*, before going on to specific queries like, *Where is the head of the donkey?* In this way the testee will be able to anticipate the nature of the information desired by the examiner.

Chapter 10

INTERPRETATION—REALITY TESTING

The degree to which one is in contact with reality and the extent to which impersonal control is introduced into the interpretation of this real world is reflected in the form determinant, F. A form-determined concept is one in which the shape or contour of the selected blot area is the only factor that has contributed to its meaning for the testee. It is a direct relationship in which contour leads to concept. While a premium is placed on reality testing and objectivity, there is a point beyond which a too critical interpretation of the external world interferes with adaptive living.

In the use of F + the subject reveals his perceptual control, the extent to which he can make decisions based on the objective aspects of the situation. Beck (1948) describes these decisions as having been made in the highest cortical centers. He points out that the poor form accuracy (F−) of the schizophrenic reflects the ego's preference "to desist from measuring the self with one's fellows (reality)," while the poor form of the encephalopathic discloses the "loss of tissue doing the criticizing." It is in these ways that form accuracy should be considered as mirroring the patient's perceptual control and the degree of critical interpretation of the biosociophysical field in which the individual is functioning.

In the analysis of a protocol the examiner must consider the "goodness" of the subject's reality contact. Formally, F and F + (conversely, F−) precentages are the data from which the quality of reality testing may be inferred. In an optimal distribution there should be between 30 and 60 per cent F, with approximately 90 per cent of this in the F + category.

In a seven-year longitudinal study of two two-year-old children, the author noted the same phenomenon as reported by other investigators with regard to the development of form-level accuracy. The progression in the number and quality of form-determined responses (from F— to F +) is slow and fluctuating over the years. But the frequency of F + increases and becomes somewhat stabilized from a low of 40 per cent F + at four years to close to 100 per cent (but not regularly so) at nine years (Allen, 1957a). In adolescence the protocol reflects the usual upheavals of this turbulent period, thereby lowering the form accuracy which, however, subsequently settles down as adulthood is approached. Deviations from optimal F + productivity are a function of emotionality at all ages.

The contribution of the form determinant to personality is evaluated in terms of its basic meaning as modified by the context within which it occurs, i.e., the location, accuracy, content, and its relationship to other determinants. These are the factors that give quality to the skeletal structure.

An overemphasis of form, 65 to 100 per cent, is characteristic of the pedantic, meticulous, unimaginative person. The testee, in this instance, is extremely defensive, so much so that there is need to resort to stern objectivity as an aid in fending off the impending anxiety that might be engendered by indulgence in nonobjective ideation. Furthermore, the testee may fear emotional reactivity to, and involvement with, the social milieu. What better adjustment (defense) than to shut oneself off from inner promptings and external stimulation which might elicit these ego-alien associations? Thus, the F per cent discloses the degree to which the person is critically examining problems and relating them to the real world in which he lives and behaves. Too high F reveals that the subject is too critical, too afraid to "let go" of objectivity.

An underemphasis of F, 0 to 30 per cent, is pathological in that the testee is responding to other than the "objectiveness" of the blot stimulus. Reduced F percentage means high "some other" percentages, such as movement, shading, and color (see Klopfer and Davidson, 1962, p. 133).

With reference to F, Beck (1950, p. 154; 1952, p. 131) has devised a Lambda Index (L.I.) which is the ratio of all non-form-determined responses to all concepts utilizing F (all non-F: $F + + F + F-$). In this way the degree of "adhesion to control" may be estimated. There is an inverse relationship between L. I. and the extent of control, or rigidity or resilience, of the individual. The higher the L. I., the greater the number of non-F determinants and, therefore, the lower the degree of adherence to objective reality as represented by the inkblot stimulus. Interpretively the subject is somewhat resilient. The same reasoning applies to the greater amount of pure form-determined concepts as compared with the nonform percepts. In this instance the ratio is low and discloses a greater dependence upon stark, unembellished reality. This suggests the rigid person. Beck states that the norms for his L. I. have not been established. However, on the assumption of 30 to 60 per cent F as optimal, the L. I. should range between .68 and 2.2 in order to be considered within normal limits with regard to flexibility of dealing with the objective features of the environment. An L. I. below or above these limits respectively reflects rigidity and resiliency of the individual's rational processes.

The quality of this reality responsiveness inheres in the quality of the form, i.e., its accuracy, F, F +, F —. Good form, F +, reveals excellent use of the stimulus and acceptable contact with reality. This is seen in the highly intelligent person, the realistically thinking individual. The usual expectancy of F + is 90 per cent or more. Percentages below this minimal level raise the question of the tenuousness of the testee's ties to reality, i.e., how close or distant are the concepts with reference to the objective stimuli. The closer the relationship the more accurate is the subject's ability to relate himself to reality. The more distant, inaccurate, or distorted the percept in terms of the objective nature of the stimulus, the more incapable is the testee of making constructive use of his objective world. Poor level of form accuracy is the product of the brain-damaged person quite consistently, while the psychotic vacillates markedly between good and poor form usage. In the organic, F— stems from two sources: (1) the inability to synthesize multiple stimuli and to deal with abstract concepts so that the effort to go beyond concrete stimulus interpretation results in a poorly synthesized resultant percept, F—; and (2) an excellent form percept given to an earlier card may be perseverated so that F + (which solved the problem in that instance) in one plate proves to be F— in a subsequent plate.

The hebephrenic and simple schizophrenic patient functions irregularly and therefore interprets what he sees and thinks in an irregular manner. The resulting productivity fluctuates between good and poor, sometimes bizarre, application of form in determining percepts. The tenuous hold on reality is inferred from this alternating between F + and F —. The paranoid schizophrenic is capable of a higher degree of control, and F + percentage will therefore remain fairly high. The degree of health may be implied from the F + , with deterioration positively related to increase in F—. Even with 30 to 60 per cent F, a clue to possible pathology lies in the F + and F— distribution, which reveals the subject's mode of experiencing and responding to the real world.

In the affective psychoses, the phase of the cyclothymic reaction will be reflected in the quality of the form usage. The depressed phase shows high F percentage due to the constriction in emotionality. At the same time form quality is not consistent because of the inability to sustain effortful attention on the stimulus. In the euphoric period F percentage is low and F + is extremely low in light of the subject's easy suggestibility and low threshold of stimulation. These two factors result in part stimuli giving meaning to large areas. The bizarre productions (contaminated and confabulated) of the excitable patient are the outcome.

In the neurotic, F percentage holds up, but with crucial stimulation eliciting ego-alien thoughts F+ becomes F—, definite indicators of an area of conflict. Such changes are assumed to be the result of neurotic shock, i.e., color, sex, and shading shock. Haan (1964) suggests that F— productivity helps differentiate between coping and defensive behavior. For those psychologists who are interested in this kind of dichotomy, Haan characterizes coping behavior by its flexibility, purpose, reality-orientation; he describes it as "differentiated" (this term is not defined). Defensive behavior is "rigid, compelled, reality distorting, and undifferentiated" (p. 430). In her futher elaboration of this concept, Haan believes that the role of form in inkblot perception is significant. The defensive testee, she claims, has a need to elaborate his percepts and strives for accuracy of reporting. This yields a high F per cent and an especially high F+ per cent. Her description of the "defensive" behavior (p. 438) comes close to suggesting an obsessive-compulsive-ruminative personality picture, which is in accordance with the dynamics and overt manifestations of this character structure. The converse of this, a lesser degree of accuracy drive, may not denote coping as much as it points to the nondefensive nature of the behavior.

The mentally retarded person is usually unimaginative so that the use of form is quite high, but its accuracy is contrastingly poor. This stems from an inability to utilize the contours of the blot adequately due to limitations in creativity, in organization, and in the breadth of experiences upon which to draw and which are important in concept formation.

In sum, the subject's use of the contour or shape of the blot reflects the ability to relate himself to the purely objective aspects of reality. This means the manner in which stark, unadorned, and unelaborated reality is adhered to in an effort to deal with problems. From this is inferred the adequacy of the problem solving, one aspect of intelligence, and ties to reality or the ability to remain in healthful contact with the environment. The sources for these inferences are not only the percentage of form-determined responses but also the accuracy of these percepts, i.e., F, F +, or F—.

Chapter 11

IMPOSED DETERMINANTS—MOVEMENT SYMBOLS AND INQUIRY

INTRODUCTION

The term imposed determinants includes those factors which are projected onto the plates by the subject and do not exist as objective stimuli in the blot itself. While the shape, or color, or achromatic character of the blot stimulus may initiate the percept, the total concept transcends these objective values of the blot. The "more-than-the-objective-stimulus" that gives meaning to the blot area comes from the subject himself in that there is imposed on the blot area a subjective element.[1]

MOVEMENT SYMBOLS

Look at any blot; obviously the designs are permanently printed and stationary. Yet the subject may report motion or a feeling of movement:

Card I: a woman holding her hands over her head. Scored: D M + .

a bat in flight. Scored: W FM + .

Card II: (bottom middle detail) flames shooting up. Scored: D mF.

[1] It is appropriate to recall Stern's, "*Keine Gestalt, ohne Gestalter,*" and urge the student to center on the perceiver *and* the percept.

These illustrations indicate three different movement scoring symbols—M, FM, m(F). The symbols describe the "transcendental" quality which the subject has projected into the objective blot stimulus. From where does this attribute come? From the subject himself—his inner resources, creative ability, originality, and ability to fantasy. Most important, the impression stems from the testee's ability to go beyond the objective stimulus as printed on the plates.

1. Human Movement

A concept that revolves around the human figure, or derivation of the human figure, or it parts, *and* is seen in motion or doing something is scored M. This includes concepts in which animals are engaged in purely human action or activity. It is a general principle of Rorschach scoring that M contains a twofold assumption: muscular tension and form, F. Therefore, M derives its qualitative interpretive value from the direction and extent of kinesthetic sensation, on the one hand, and its + or − accuracy from the form-level (or F), on the other. It must be remembered that all human movement impressions are scored M and *not* FM. Many beginners overlook this simple fact.

Card I: 1—woman holding hands up in prayer. Scored: D M + . (The Inquiry reveals human muscular tension and the form-level is excellent, therefore the combination of human movement and accurate form becomes M + .)

Card II: two Teddy bears doing the Charleston. Scored: D M + . (The animals are engaged in human activity while the accuracy of the form is good, therefore the symbol M + .)

Card VII: 1.1. a cartoonist's sketch of two ladies busy gossiping with each other. Scored: D M + . (Even though the percept is a derived human detail, it is considered in the human category, and the human-like activity makes the scoring M + .)

Human movement responses appear most frequently in

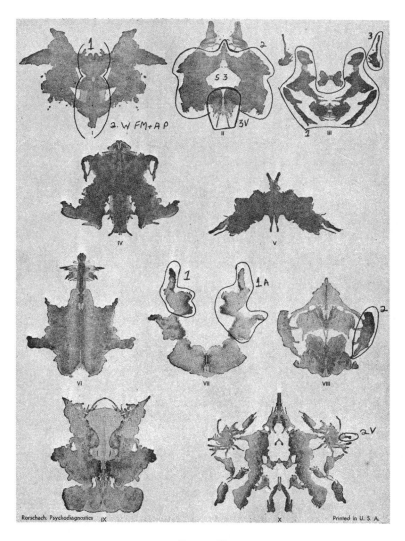

FIGURE 11

Typical Movement, M, FM, and m Responses

By courtesy of Hans Huber, Publishers, Berne, from Rorschach,
Psychodiagnostics.
The numbers refer to types of concepts as indicated in the text.

cards III and VII, less so in IX, II, and I. The remaining cards present some difficulty in eliciting human movement. This is inherent in the blots and requires either much originality and creativity or a great deal of distanciation from reality to produce human movements in plates VIII, VI, and V.[2]

A persistent and unsettled problem is the scoring of facial expressions. Do they reflect true tension or kinesthesis? Or are they the result of shading or darker lines giving the impression of facial grimacing? The answer to these questions will determine scoring of M, F. or Fc.[3] It is recommended that facial expressions—smiling, laughing, talking, grimacing—of human figures be given M consideration if the protocol shows a tendency toward the production of other M's. Careful inquiry will usually disclose the presence or absence of muscle tension.

2. Animal Movement

This is a contribution of Klopfer to the refinement of the scoring technique. The symbol FM is assigned to the concept that has the element of animal, or derivation of the animal, figure in purely animal activity or action.[4] Here, too, muscle tension or kinesthetic impression should be clearly indicated by

[2] This is in support of Ranzoni, Grant, and Ives (1950) who contend that not all M's are the product of a very fertile imagination. Therefore, because of the frequency of occurrence, an M in plates III and VII will not have the same qualitative interpretive significance as an M in cards IX, II, or I.

[3] Klopfer and Kelley (1942, pp. 116-117) suggest scoring facial expressions as Fm or minor movement: "The expressive descriptions do not give these (M and FM) properties to the projected concept. These grotesque faces, or threatening images, or masks, are not imagined as if they, by themselves, could actually express any emotions or do any harm. They serve only as a screen, onto which the subject projects certain of his own feelings or emotions." Beck, on the other hand, states: "Laughing, smiling, and similar facial activity are in some instances M" (1950, p. 105).

[4] If a Disneyesque animal clearly represents a human character, or has the attributes and qualities of a human, its action may be considered human movement and scored M. For example, Figure 11, Card VII: 1A—Bugs Bunny's girl friends having a gab-feast. Scored: D M + .

the subject. Examples of this type of percept are shown in Figure 11:

Card I: a bat in flight. Scored: W FM + . (Inquiry elicits animal movement and the concept fits the blot area accurately, therefore the FM + .)

Card II: 2 — two bears rubbing noses. Scored: D FM + .

Card VIII: 2 — an otter about to spring from a rock onto something(s'g). Scored: D FM + .

Card X: 2 V — a trotting horse. Scored Dd FM − . (The animal movement is there, but the blot area does not fit the concept given, therefore FM − .)

It will be noted that the F precedes the M in all animal movement scoring. The + or − quality of the FM is taken from the F portion of the concept. In animal activity scoring the form appears in the symbol but the assumption of tension or kinesthesis is present as in human movement. Cards V and VIII evoke FM percepts most easily, followed by plates X and II.[5]

3. "Minor" Movement[6]

Some concepts contain the element of motion or movement but it is not of the human or animal variety, i.e., it is not the kind of action that is characteristic of a living organism. Activity or movement that is imposed upon the person or animal from a source external to the organism is symbolized by an m determinant. An object that is activated by an external force is always scored m. See Figure 11:

Card II: 3 — an explosion with sparks and flames shooting

---

[5] An examination of the plates will disclose the reason: animal responses are popular for plates V, VIII, X, and II. Card I also has an animal popular concept, bat or butterfly, but the frequency of movement is higher for the first four cards listed.

[6] This term is taken from the contributions of Klopfer and Kelley (1942, p. 116). It is also known as inanimate movement and motion due to natural forces.

upward V. Scored (in part): D mF. (This illustrates an inanimate force in action.)

S3 — a spinning top. Scored: S Fm + . (Illustrates an object in motion.)

Card III: 3 — a monkey falling down, probably missed his hold on the branch. Scored: D Fm + . (Animal motility, but the source of motion is an external force — gravity.) If the monkey is seen bent over or struggling to right itself then the movement factor is true animal movement and requires an FM, changing the scoring to: D FM + , Fm + .

> (usual side detail) — two men being whirled round and round. Scored: D Fm + (Human motion, but coming from an outside source, therefore Fm.) If the men are causing the whirling activity, such as in a dance of some sort, the scoring then becomes D M + . At times the men are seen in a wild dance with their coattails flapping in the wind. This would be scored: D M + (for dancing men), Fm + (for the coattails flapping in the wind, inanimate movement.)

Usual minor movement percepts are: objects or bodies falling or coming apart, whirlpools, explosions, smoke rising, moving clouds, flames shooting skyward, spinning objects, and forces that bring together and separate. The latter is illustrated by the testee's perception of any midline area in any of the blots as a force that attracts, binds, separates, or divides actively the symmetrical halves of the design. In short, any impression of motion or kinesthetic sensation that is not characteristically human or animal is to be considered under the minor movement and scored as m.

The form element may be present or absent. Responses may be pure m, Fm, mF, depending on which factor is primary. Pure m is assigned to concepts which do not use the contour of the blot area in any way. See Figure 11.

Card VI: the middle is like a magnet that attracts the water on both sides forming a whirlpool. Scored W m. The mF and

Fm concepts are illustrated in Figure 11, Card II, 3 ∨ and S3 given above. If the movement is primary and form secondary the symbol is mF, the converse calls for Fm. Which element in the percept is primary and which is secondary is not always an easy matter to define. A guiding principle is this: if the form-level accuracy is good and the percept is of such a nature that it has definite form (and is generally accepted as such), the F is primary and m secondary. In S3 of card II (Figure 11) the form is very definite and accepted so that the concept of "spinning top" is scored Fm +. In those instances where F and m are utilized, the combination (mF and Fm are considered a scoring unit) derives its form-level accuracy from the shape of the blot and how it fits the concept. Therefore Fm + or Fm − do not refer to the movement aspect of the concept but to its form-level.

A last word of caution: in all movement responses the tester must be reasonably certain that muscular tension and/or kinesthetic impression are established before considering the M, FM, or m symbol.

INQUIRY

A response containing a verb which terminates in "ing" is not automatically a movement percept. In card III: a man wearing a tuxedo, is not scored M since no tension or kinesthetic impression is involved in the concept of "wearing." Humans seen as talking may or may not involve M. It depends on the sharpness or the impression of muscular tension or kinesthesis involved in the talking figure. Cards III and VII are usually most productive of human movement responses, while plates V and VIII evoke animal movement most easily. Despite the popularity of these movement concepts, the Inquiry must establish beyond a reasonable doubt the presence or absence of F or FM. Not infrequently the subject may give what appears to be a pure form or form plus some other nonmovement description of the percept, and in the Inquiry the movement may be added. Unless the subject admits that this movement was not present in the original percept, the M, FM, or m must be scored in its proper order of preference. If the movement is the product of only the Inquiry, then M, FM, or m should be scored additionally despite the aforementioned[7] order of preference of determinants. At best this matter of additional determinant-scoring for elements given only in the Inquiry is difficult to handle adequately. Suggestions for movement queries are given below:

Card I: this is a fly'g bat.

Inquiry: (*?impression*) the shape, (*?fly'g bat*) the wings are spread out[8] (*?wings spread out*), it's gliding in the air. Scored: W FM + A P. If the last response is not forthcoming the examiner should follow with (*?a'g else besides shape, fly'g bat*). If this is unsuccessful add, (*?bat on exhibit in museum*). The affirmative answer precludes movement, but a negative reply does *not* establish movement. As a last resort to ferret out FM the tester may ask (*?alive or dead*). If "alive," then pursue with a query as to the reason for being alive. After each question beyond the original (?impression) or (?) the tester must interpose the same query in order to take advantage of the additional information.

The same process is required to establish the human movement. For example, Card III: this is two men lift'g s'g. Inquiry: (?)[9] here are the two men (S circles both side details with

[7] For what it may be worth, the tester may ask the subject whether or not the Inquiry elaborations were present when the percept was first given in the Main Stage.

[8] "Wings spread out" is not a priori evidence of action.

[9] During the course of recording the Inquiry it is not essential that the questions put to the subject be reported verbatim. A first (?) usually indicates "What gave you the impression of a—?" Only those questions beyond the usual one for establishing the presence or absence or an uncertain determinant-component are recorded. When this occurs it is suggested that these queries be put down in some shorthand system, e.g., "and what gave you the impression of lifting" could be (?lift'g), and so on.

finger)[10] bending over these pots, (*bending*) well, they look alive. Scored: D M + H P.

The "minor" movement responses also run the gamut of scoring expediency. Explosions, falling bodies or objects, and balancing rocks are readily established as m. Running water, a force that divides, or grinning faces may offer difficulty in scoring. The question (*?impression*) must be pursued carefully in order to justify the presence of m.

Card I: this is a cat's face, it's grinning.

Inquiry: (*?*) whole t'g, eyes, ears, mouth, (*?grinning*) the way the cheeks puff out and the mouth curves upward at the corners. Scored: WS Fm + Ad.

this is a cat's face, grinning.

Inquiry: (*?*) whole t'g, eyes, ears, mouth, (*grinning*) the shape of the mouth here, (*a'g else besides shape*) no. Scored: WS F + Ad.

An over-all caution with reference to the inquiry into movement responses is emphasized by Allen and Dorsey (1954). In a study of the effect of suggestion on human movement productivity, they found that a set to report movement increased the number of such responses to a significant degree. The tester must be careful not to suggest the desirability or the possibility of seeing movement in the percepts. This restraint should be exercised in the main and the inquiry stages of the Rorschach Test administration.

[10] Behavioral and observational notes should also be placed in parentheses in the Inquiry column to differentiate them from the testee's responses. If these notes become prolific, the tester should use a separate piece of paper for this purpose.

Chapter 12

INTERPRETATION—THE MEANING OF MOVEMENT

This nonobjective response symbolizes an imposed perception. Rorschach (1942) did not include in his scoring scheme the three different kinds of movement that are in general use today. These modifications were introduced by Klopfer and Kelley (1942): human movement, M; animal movement, FM; and inanimate movement, m, mF, Fm.

Human Movement: *M*

Objectively the stimulus is stationary, i.e., from the point of view of the observer. So far as the testee is concerned, therefore subjectively, the stimulus is part of a process which initiates kinesthetic feelings that are interpreted as movement or kinesthetics. Basically, the use of the movement determinant in an engram reflects the capacity for imaginative living beyond the confines of the stern realities of life. The key to enrichment of living is contained in the ability to project onto static inkblots humanlike movement. Klein and Schlesinger (1951) offer an interesting *process* postulate with reference to movement: "By this hypothesis, then, the range of apparent movement is an index of a person's readiness to accept a compromise solution to a task in visual organization, how much tampering he permits with things as he knows them to be for the sake of expedience or comfort, or, more generally, how well he can tolerate an unstable or ambiguous state as a solution to a perceptual problem. Reciprocally, it tells us the degree to which one's personal stability requires that things be maintained as they are known to be, to what extent reality testing demands the stability and immobility of known stationary forms." Form boundness as against form lability or tolerance for instability is mirrored in the subject's ability to impose movement. This freedom from the rigid realism of the stimulating environment may serve as a source for adjustment in view of the flexibility of "moving" about the facets of the problem so as to seek new insights with new interrelationships. This, of course, must be within the context of reality itself, otherwise control is below optimum and fantasy living may take over. Some imagination is necessary and healthy, too much of it is autistic and even bizarre. More simply stated, these writiers seem to express the beliefs of most Rorschach workers, viz., in the experience of human movement responses may be found the sources for actual and potential adjustment, tolerance for accepting change, and extent to which the subject can compromise. All this must be considered in the light of reaiity contact.

To the genius of Rorschach is ascribed the basic meaning of the movement response as indicating the individual's potential for "inner creation" and how the subject relates himself to his social milieu. The projection of one's "role in life" (Brussel, Hitch, and Piotrowski, 1950), or self-percept, is drawn from the "extensor" or "flexor" nature of the movement responses. This flows from the rationale that the self-percept and body image is projected from the testee's sensations or feelings continually assailing him as a result of internal and external stimulation. Schachtel (1950, p. 98) calls this the "tendency in the individual to view others and the environment in an *automorphic* way, in his own likeness." The basic meaning is modified by the context within which the M determinant occurs. No one determinant can be singled out as being unique in its effect upon M interpretation. All play a role in addition to the form accuracy inherent in the human movement percept and scoring symbol. The latter is important in differentiating wholesome and constructive productivity from conceptually poor (perhaps bizarre) autistic fantasy. The M response contains the self-perceptions that are usually on the level of awareness, the active role which the subject is currently playing. This does not imply acceptance of the role by the person.

The direction of movement, extensor or flexor, requires further discussion. Briefly, the flexor movement ascribed to the human figure is toward the center of the plate. Extensor motion is away from the center. In the flexor percept, the testee is disclosing passive and submissive tendencies, a sort of reinforcement of introversive, nonsocial preference in attitude and/or behavior. The basic meaning of the M-determined percept is strengthened in that it indicates a desire to be left alone, to be permitted to reflect on life's problems.

The extensor M response, on the other hand, is given by the person who is more active and outgoing. When this occurs in the presence of color-determined percepts, the M's are considered to be sources for emotional stability. The acting-out potential (seen in the color determinants) is tempered by the ability to think, to seek inwardly and reflect, and then to respond to the stimulation from the social surround. Taulbee (1961) reports that extensor M is positively associated with "continuation and improvements in psychotherapy."

The meaning of flexor and extensor movement responses was evaluated by Hammer and Jacks (1955). Their investigation supported the "extensor-assertive" and "flexor-submissive" hypothesis. However, efforts to relate flexor and extensor movement to femininity and masculinity have been unsuccessful (Wetherhorn, 1956; Taulbee, 1961).

The optimum number of human movement-determined concepts has not been fixed. In general, the higher the intelligence level the greater the number of *good* M's. Altus and Altus (1952, p. 533) conclude: ". . . the curvilinear regression

of M on intelligence is, apparently, a function of the unstereo-
typed M." The reference here is to M + that is not of the popular variety usually elicited in plates I, II, III, and IV.[1]

The presence of M-determined responses indicates the capacity for human identifications. As postulated by Piotrowski
(1942b) in an interesting series of assumptions, the tester may
derive the subject's self-percepts, acceptable and alien, and his
attitudes toward human figures in his environment. Deroga-
tion of human figures, e.g., witches, clowns, animal-like
human responses, reveal unacceptable interpersonal relationships. This is especially true in the production of the schizophrenic who sees depersonalized and/or deteriorating human
content. Since form is assumed in the symbol for human movement, M, the level of form accuracy gives insight into the
degree of contact with reality that is inherent in the percept.
Thus, M + and M — reflect the ties to reality expressed in the
testee's human associations. Disturbed interpersonal relationships, when M is expressed, will eventuate in M —. Yet the neo-
phyte in the Rorschach method requires a basis for beginning
interpretation. In a record of 30 responses, normal expectation
is two M responses. Less than two is suspicious of a lack of richness of inner living and acceptance of self. Singer, Meltzoff,
and Goldman (1952) in a study of the relationship between M
and motor activity, found that an individual experiencing
motor inhibition will express this demurral in an increase of M
responses, while the "motor" active subject gives fewer M's.
The subject, then, who has a high degree of self-restraint will
experience and express this energy in ideational motility (M,
FM, and m). Movement-determined percepts may be a substi-

[1] This is similar to the interpretation of whole responses in which some are
readily organized by virtue of the structure of the blot. Such easily formed
whole percepts, as in cards I, II, IV, and VI, are usually the popular responses. Thus, while they indicate an ability to deal with abstractions they
contribute less to the implication of intellectual function than the more
rarely formed W percepts.

tute for actual living out or acting out one's needs, desires, and aspirations.[2] By the same token, the protocol with a dearth of movement may reflect the active subject with less need or capacity for self-restraint.[3] Logically, if not psychologically, the M producer has greater potential for adjustment because of greater tolerance. This holds up to the optimal point; beyond this, tolerance for adjustment or compromise may be so malleable as to take the shape of a wall (defense) around the subject behind which he lives so completely that he has little need for external reality. This condition dramatically illustrates the extent to which the patient (for patient this person is!) is accepting his inner life as the more satisfactory guide to adaptive living.

ANIMAL MOVEMENT: *FM*

In this type of response the subject associates with the more frequently perceived aspects of the blot and ascribes movement to it. Because of the plethora of possibilities for animal responses, the interpretation of the intellectual functioning in the higher direction is not expecially enhanced. Quite the contrary, a high number of FM responses contributes interpretively in the opposite direction, viz., the testee is not handling his drives maturely, but is channelizing this *Gestaltungskraft* or mental energy in a manner characteristic of performance at an earlier chronological level. The mode of adjustment ascribed to the animal movement response is *as if* cortical control has been removed (in the adult through the use of alcohol or drugs or by some trauma) and the person is freer to indulge in less inhibited behavior permissible at an earlier age. Of course children are not expected to be as repressed and restrained as

---

[2] Especially when color responses are few or absent.

[3] The color total will usually be high and indicative of acting-out tendency.

adults. Therefore a higher number of FM responses is expected, and observed, in the protocols of children and teenagers. Gradually, however, as the socialization process unfolds and takes root in the growing personality, FM becomes less prominent and M is on the increase. This process symbolizes the growth in intellect, experience, and acculturization (all adding up to maturity) of the individual in a social milieu.

The FM response is potential M, i.e., the imposition of movement stems from the same subjective ability to experience kinesthetically when exposed to a static stimulus. The description of FM as immature resources for adjustment is based on the association with an animal figure instead of a human percept. Children live in a world of fact and fancy intertwined. Thus, the capacity for imagination, for subjectively imposing a process that is not present in objective reality, is more readily attached to animal forms by children. This is normal for children but not typical of adults. Therefore, FM discloses the child's good adjustment resources for *his* interpretation of *his child world*. In the adult it mirrors a less mature channelization of inner creativity.

The direction (flexor or extensor) and intensity vectors of the animal concept(s) define(s) the degree of passivity or assertiveness of the primitive, basic drives which are coming to the surface and which are seeking expression as representatives of the "most instinctual layers within the personality" (Klopfer and Kelley, 1942, p. 278). The value of FM is not entirely negative; basic drives, sources of physical energy, are necessary for meeting the needs of everyday living. It is the *relative* presence of FM in the context of other modes of experiencing that will contribute to the appraisal of personality. The absence of FM-determined percepts, according to Klopfer and Davidson (1962), reveals a tendency toward repression of "primitive impulses" (sex drive, hostility, aggression) because of their unacceptability to the testee, It is necessary for the tester to observe rather closely how this repressed energy expresses itself in other aspects of the Rorschach Test protocol.

INANIMATE MOVEMENT: *m, mF, Fm*

If the human movement derives from the conscious aspect of living, i.e., the projection of one's self-percept derived from one's awareness of kinesthetic feelings, then the inanimate movement is least acceptable because it originates in associations furthest removed from the subject's awareness. The m concept symbolizes forces most likely to engender anxiety if permitted direct expression; therefore, they represent the most repressed forces in the personality structure. The intensity and direction of the m-determined concept reflect the magnitude of the internal kinesthetic sensations and, by inference, the extent to which the subject is open to psychological trauma. Halpern (1953) believes FM and m responses represent the least acceptable and most unconscious conflictual drives of the individual which are almost completely repressed. The nature of the m production reveals to the tester: (1) the strength of this repressed—actually hostile—material; (2) the nature of the repressed material—which has to be "worked through" with the testee; and (3) the amount of emotional disturbance which would be incurred should the conflict come to the level of awareness. The degree of control over the intensity of the disturbance is manifested in the form element introduced into the percept. Explosions, squirting blood, shooting flames, disclose an uncontrolled, acute disturbance potential as contrasted with the m involved in the concepts of a gently flowing stream or of a leaf falling down. Another factor is the level of form accuracy (mF + or mF—, Fm + or Fm—). Like other form-involved responses, the accuracy reveals the extent to which ties to reality are affected by an emotional upheaval, or how the subject experiences disturbing associations.

This determinant is usually a sign of poor mental health.

However, in a context of M and some FM, its adverse meaning is modified somewhat so that the testee's inner life may be considered less chaotic than would obtain if m outnumbered M and FM or occurred in a picture of FM alone.

The absence of m-determined percepts in a conflicted person, according to Klopfer and Davidson (1962), may be a "danger signal" in that repression is too complete. Thus, the presence of m in responses calls attention to the existence of the emotional upheaval.

INTERRELATIONSHIPS

In the protocols of adults it is usually expected that there will be more M than FM, and that m (m, mF, Fm) will occur not at all or not more than once in a record. In the younger years the M determinant should emerge gradually with increase in age. This implies sources of healthy growth toward emotional stability. M that appears too early may suggest a precocious maturity and a loss of some of the adventures of childhood life stemming from lack of affection and acceptance, thus forcing the child to fall back on himself as a source of security and satisfaction. Concomitant with the appearance and increase of M, the initially emergent and predominant FM begins to decrease and continues to do so. However, even in the most mature and stable adult there should be FM present to reflect the basic drives that remain part of everyone's biological make-up. Absence of FM discloses a lack of drive necessary for carrying on everyday activities. By 40 years of age, in males especially, the M should be much higher than FM, to mirror the attainment of stability in personal and career activities. For by the time the person reaches this age, there should be less seeking and a higher degree of "settled" stability requiring less expenditure of energy.

In an intratensive setting (M greater than Sum C) the subject will require more M than in an extratensive (M less than

Sum C) picture (Klopfer, 1949). Much more mental energy is required by the intratensively inclined person to meet bifurcated needs: (1) those involved in his autistic propensity, to imagine and fantasy, thus using up some M; and (2) those originating in his external world, press which require solution and/or satisfaction. This is in contrast to the extratensive individual, i.e., more sensitive to external stimulation, who does not have as much demand for overcoming autistic needs and therefore can channelize most, if not all, available energy toward the solution and/or satisfaction of these motivating urges. In both experience settings the nature of the content, viz., the liveliness or forcefulness of the movement, will disclose the extent to which the sources for adjustment, the mental energy, are available for use. Again, the intensity and direction of movement are useful indices of the submissiveness and assertiveness of the self-concept (M), the basic drives (FM), and deep-seated, anxiety-producing conflict (m).

Other relationships discussed below will acquaint the student with the significance for Rorschach interpretation of determinants considered as part of a pattern rather than a series of isolated factors, each with an independent meaning unrelated to the other elements.

(Primary) Experience Balance

M: Sum C refers to the personality, the experience balance (E. B.), or the *Erlebnistypus*. This reveals the conscious and current mode of experiencing and responding to stimuli in the phenomenological field. The major modality that serves the testee as a source of motivation and as an outlet for behaving may be inferred from this ratio. M greater than Sum C denotes the intratensive personality, the manifest prevailing response is to inner urgings, the thinker rather than the doer (although the possibility of tendency and ability to "act out" one's affective responsiveness is not precluded entirely). Since the subject is reacting on the level of awareness to both internal and external stimuli, the ratio is interpreted as the current mode of responsiveness.

The Experience Balance is one of the more objectively obtained yet more inconsistently interpreted Rorschach Test variables. Allen, Richer, and Plotnik (1964), investigated the relationship between the E. B. ratio, on the one hand, and the scores on the Social Introversion-Extroversion (Sie) Scale of the Minnesota Multiphasic Personality Inventory (Hathaway and McKinley, 1951) and the B3-I(ntroversion) Scale of the Personality Inventory (Bernreuter, 1935), on the other. Introversive and extroversive groups were established on the basis of extremely high and low scores on these inventory scales. The M:Sum C ratios for both groups, on the individually administered Rorschach Test, divided the two groups in a manner consistent with their separation by the introversion-extroversion scales scores obtained on both inventories. This dichotomy was beyond the .02 level of confidence.

In a second criterion study, the same authors submitted E. B. data to Rorschach Test authorities, requesting a rank ordering of the protocols from most to least introversive. The judges' rankings agreed significantly with the outside criteria (psychometric test scores) for classifying the subjects along the introversive-extroversive dimension. Further, the interjudge concordance on the interpretation of the M:Sum C ratio was significantly high. The interpretation of the Experience Balance as an indication of the direction of ideational and/or behavioral experiencing (depending on the extent and intensity of the movement-color perception) is well supported. The nature of the testee's adjustment stands apart quite distinctly from the introversive (M greater and Sum C), ambiversive (M equal to Sum C) or extroversive (M less than Sum C) quality of the *Erlebnistypus*.

Other findings reported by Allen, Richer, and Plotnik (1964) were:

(1) The ability to maintain controlled social ties is characteristic of adjusted college students regardless of *Erlebnistypus*. However, the extroversive individual stands apart quite distinctly from the introversive and the ambiversive person with regard to the ability to make warm interpersonal ties.

(2) All segments of the sample population are capable of emotional swings. The extroversive group is more prone to make warm interpersonal ties and act out emotional responsivity than introversive persons. This supports the Rorschach Test stereotype of the extroverted individual.

(3) The Rorschach Test stereotype of the introverted person is not completely borne out. Mentally healthy introversively inclined persons are not necessarily incapable of responding to the social surround or of making social ties. Continued normal growth to maturity is essential for the fulfillment of the introversive portion of the M-stereotype. It is time to lay aside the social stereotype of the introverted personality when dealing with persons not mentally ill.

(4) Introversion-extroversion groups placement on the basis of personality-inventory and Rorschach Test data are consistent with each other. The dichotomy between ideational and behavioral phenomena is tenable in view of the significant introversion-extroversion placement concordance between the psychometric personality inventory and inkblot test group subjects.

They also reported that extroversively inclined individuals were much more easily differentiated and classified than persons in the ambiversive categories.

(Secondary) Experience Balance

$FM + m:Fc + c + C'$ discloses the latent and less accessible personality characteristics. Both sides of the ratio are modifications of the more conscious personality facets, e.g., FM and m are related to M; c and C' are akin to C, color. As such, this ratio indicates the experience balance at a chronologically earlier period of behaving. FM and m emphasize potential M or how closely the testee approaches the more mature method of dealing with inner drives; while c and C' signify potential C or how closely the testee is able to relate himself fully to the external world yet demur or delay actual motor activity. Thus, in terms of possible responsiveness, it may be assumed that the FM + m:Fc + c + C' ratio discloses a chronologically earlier, and therefore currently less mature, mode of behaving. It is *as if* cortical control were removed and the testee is perceiving and reacting with a lesser degree of inhibition.[4]

If M:Sum C gives the current mode of living, then FM + m: Fc + c + C' reveals the previous (childish, less controlled) mode of dealing with the stimuli in the life space. If both ratios are in the same direction, i.e., M is greater than Sum C and FM + m is greater than Fc + c + C', there is no change in the direction of *Erlebnistypus*. This does not preclude a change in the *intensity* of mode of experiencing and responding within the internal or external segments of the ratios, e.g., M:Sum C = 5:1, FM + m:Fc + c + C' = 3:2. In these proportions there is no directional change, but there is a decided decrease in intensional thinking and an increase in acting-out potential under less inhibited conditions. One might hazard the opinion that at an earlier age (and currently when less on guard) this subject was still predominantly intratensive, but his affective experiences were (and could be when less inhibited) more labile and more responsive to the environment. In growing up, this subject has become, for a variety of reasons, more responsive to inner promptings and less willing to relate with the social milieu. Did this person pay a price for growing up?

---

[4] This interpretation is especially helpful in the manner indicated by Brussel, Hitch, and Piotrowski (1950), viz., that it will reveal the direction and intensity of reaction by an individual who is under the influence of alcohol, drugs, or some other traumatizing agent, all of which are capable of removing or interfering with cortical control.

On the other hand, M greater than Sum C with FM + m less than Fc + c + C', the present manner is intratensive but under stress and concomitant loss of inhibitory restraint the subject would most likely "act out" or seek satisfaction for more basic drives in the external environment. A change in the personality has taken place. The previous (younger) E. B. discloses an outgoing make-up, this is at variance with the present mode of experiencing and behaving. Whether the testee's reactions would be violent, aggressive, assertive or submissive, passive, meek is dependent on the nature of the content within which the movement or shading determinants are given. The opposite ratio has the same meaning: current reaction may be predominantly extratensive (M less than Sum C), while, in a disturbing situation or with cerebral dysfunction, the testee may disclose a withdrawing type of behavior (FM + m greater than Fc + c + C'). Again, the intensity of the reactivity depends on the liveliness of the determinants in the concepts. Another interesting inference stems from the following: in the M:Sum C ratio, intensity may be assertive, aggressive; this may or may not be true of the FM + m:Fc + c + C' ratio. If the action is energetic or phlegmatic in both ratios then the presence or absence of restraint will make little or no difference in the person's manner of responding to the forces in his life space. If the former (M:Sum C) is passive or assertive, and the later (FM + m:Fc + c + C') is passive or assertive, the overt behavior will differ in the indicated directions under conditions of control as contrasted with lack of control.

Alcock (1963) has designated the FM + m:Fc + c + C' ratio as the "Interior Balance" as a complement to the "Experience Balance," in that M:Sum C and FM + m:Fc + c + C' juxtapose the conscious and unconscious aspects of the testee. She further points to the "child within the man" significance of the latter ratio in contrast to the adult's awareness of his role inherent in the M:Sum C responsivity. The implication in her interpretative description is that the wishes, urges, attitudes represented by the Internal Balance perception are unaccessible to the adult. There is a dearth of research with this particular ratio. Klopfer and Davidson (1962) devote very little space to a discussion of this phenomenon, while Piotrowski (1957) disagrees with their interpretation of the minor movement interpretation. This is one of the Rorschach Test variables which should be subjected to further construct validity study.

Intimately tied up with the above two ratios is a third one, the color ratior (C.R.) or number of responses to plates VIII, IX, and X. This is usually expressed as a percentage and is also known as 8-9-10 per cent. On the assumption that responsiveness to the chromatic hues of the plates reflects the ability and nature of the person's experience of emotional stimulation from the environment, the higher the number of emotional stimulation from the environment, the higher the number of concepts given to the last three colored plates the more sensitive is the individual to external stimulation. Thus, the C.R. is compared with the M:Sum C and FM + m:Fc + c + C' proportions.

Chapter 13

IMPOSED DETERMINANTS —
SHADING SYMBOLS AND INQUIRY

INTRODUCTION

Attention is now shifted to another type of determinant which derives its character more objectively from the blot-stimulus that does movement. At the same time, though, the interpretation of the determinant adds a transcendental quality of expansiveness or distance to the entire percept. This is achieved by an impression of diffusion which is imparted by the shading in the achromatic and chromatic areas of the blots. In the psychograph of Klopfer and Davidson the diffusion-vista type of determinant is a triad: k, K, and FK. Each of these determinants stems from the shading quality of the blot-stimulus. The distinction among these factors lies in the use the subject makes of the shading, in addition to the contents of the response. Carried one step further, the distinction between k, K, on the one hand, and FK, on the other, is the extent of depth or expansiveness imposed by the subject.

SHADING SYMBOLS

Shading as Depth

The symbol k is used when the testee ascribes depth to the flat-surfaced design. The variation of shading tones in the blot are interpreted as differences in depth, thus giving rise to a two-planar impression.[1] Some examples of this determinant are presented in Figure 12:

Card I: 1—this is an X ray of the back. Scored: W Fk—. Inquiry reveals that the lighter parts of the blot are the lungs and ribs while the dark line in the center is the spinal cord. An X ray because the testee has seen X rays in his doctor's office. The form-level is poor, therefore Fk—.)

Card VII: 1—a map of an island. I can see the mountains and the slope down toward the sea. Scored WS kF. (Islands are not particularly definite in form and therefore secondary to the description of the mountainous and sloping characterr of the island. This is a concept with two planes. The WS indicates that the whole blot is used primarily and S for the sea is an additional use of space in the total concept.)

Card III: 1—a very good X ray of the chest area; the darker spots are lungs and these here are the ribs and bony structure around the lungs; this is the spinal cord back here. It's a front view. Scored: D Fk+.

Card IX: IV—this is a map of some country showing the valleys and mountains. Scored: W CF, kF. (Inquiry reveals that it is a geography book colored map of some region unknown to testee. The two-planar impression of mountains and valleys is invoked by the variations in the shading of the colors. The latter adds kF to the determinant scoring.)

As with the other determinants, the form-level accuracy contributes the + or — to the Fk or kF unit.

The use of shading as depth is usually given in topographical concepts such as map and X ray. Occasionally a two-planar response due to shading tones may be of a different nature:

Card IV: 1—a man in a fur coat sitting on a tree stump. Scored: W M+, Fc, Fk. (Inquiry reveals that the Fk determinant is appended additionally because the tree stump is seen in

---

[1] The imposed additional plane giving the illusion of depth confers on the shading determinants their transcendent quality and justifies their inclusion in this chapter on *imposed* determinants.

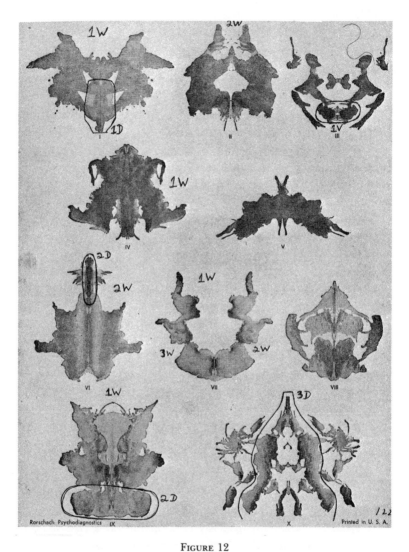

FIGURE 12

Shading concepts of the k, K, and FK Variety

By courtesy of Hans Huber, Publishers, Berne, from Rorschach,
Psychodiagnostics.
The numbers refer to the type of response indicated in the text.

back of the man and the subject attributes this to the difference in shading of the blot areas.)

Card I: 1D—this is the lower part of a girl's body, she is wearing a thin dress and you can see the shape of her body below the hips. Scored: D Fk +. (Ordinarily this would be considered a surface texture response of the transparency variety, but inquiry reveals that there is an element of distance between the skirt of the dress and the body within it, therefore an Fk is justified.)

Shading as Diffusion

When shading is used to introduce the impression of diffusion or expansiveness into the concept the symbol is K or KF. The former symbolizes the absence of blot contour in the percept while the latter utilizes the form of the blot with its concomitant level of accuracy. Essentially the K determinant is space occupying but in a nebulous intangible manner that reflects the rationale of the personality dynamics which imposes this quality on the blot-stimulus. The K determinant is usually applicable to cloud, smoke, fog, and light concepts such as those in Figure 12:

Card VII: 2—clouds, the whole t'g 1.1. fleecy clouds. Scored: W K.

2—these 1.1. cumulus clouds. Scored: W KF. (Both shading and form used.)

Card II: 2—a forest fire with smoke choking out the flames. Scored: W C, K. (Smoke is scored as an additional determinant in this particular response, and requires K.)

Card IX: 2—1.1. the cotton candy you buy at the circus, you know, the pink kind. Scored: D CF, KF.

Card VI: 2—I see a lighthouse tower with the light on, these (upper wing detail) are the rays from the powerful lantern. Scored: W KF, F +.

2D—a newel post, it's so highly polished that there is a light reflection on it here. Scored: D K, F +.

The determinants discussed in this chapter show a shift in the direction of objectivity so far as the blot stimulus is concerned. The scoring symbols suggested are based on those introduced by Klopfer and Kelley (1942, pp. 119-137). Beck covers these determinants under "The light determined response: FV and Y" (1950, p. 126).[2]

Shading as Distance

There are occasions when the subject perceives something off in the distance. Not only is there expansiveness but it assumes a linear perspective such that the testee reports the impression of distance between self and the percept on the plate. This phenomenon is scored FK. The classical example taken from Klopfer[3] is shown on plate X, Figure 12, 3D—this is the Champs Elysees and that (grey top detail) is the Eiffel Tower. Scored: DS FC, FK. (In the Inquiry the subject avers that the pink details are the flowered borders of the roadway leading off into the distance to the Tower.) Airplane views also contain an element of distance that is scored FK—Card VII: 3W—this is an airplane view of an atoll in the Pacific. Scored: W FK. The prime requisite for FK, then, is the impression of distance and that the percept be far off, above, or below the perceiver.

A parting caution: The shading determinants are most controversial because the degree of subjective imposition possible ranges from impressions of distance, through expansiveness, to a single-plane surface-concept of complete objectivity. In view of this, the interpretative dynamics are subject to wide discussion and critical examination in Rorschach circles.

---

[2] For the sake of completeness: Beck, 1950, pp. 126-145, assigns V to our FK and Y to our k and K concepts. This is placed here to emphasize to the beginner that the formal techniques of scoring may differ among Rorschach workers, but the interpretations remain essentially the same.

[3] In the past 28 years of testing with the Rorschach the author has received this response only once.

INQUIRY

Shading

The effect of shading, alone or in combination with forms, offers difficulty because of the several possible determinants — c, k, K, FK. A continuum may be set up with these determinants in order to facilitate the Inquiry and scoring problem. Use of shading as:

one plane	two planes	diffusion	expanse
or	or	or	or
surface	depth	nebulous	distance
c*	k	K	FK

* This determinant will be discussed in Chapter 15.

with this as a guide content may give a clue as to the determinant since the continuum shows determinants merging from c to k to K to FK. Texture responses — c; X ray, topographical maps — k; clouds, smoke, fog — K; vistas, scenes — FK. However, the beginner is cautioned not to assume a particular shading determinant on the basis of content alone. All components of scoring must be the result of an Inquiry:

Card VI: this 1.1. an animal's skin.

May be scored: W F+ AObj P, or

W Fc+ AObj P — this second scoring is given if the testee indicates that the skin impression, either fur side out or skin side out, is due to something else besides form, viz., the difference in shading elements of the blot area. The following illustrates the questioning to elicit this in the above percept:

Inquiry: (?) the shape of it and it 1.1. fur, (*?fur*) it's darker here and lighter there 1. you see on a hide, (*?darker and lighter*) the shading. Scored: W Fc+ AObj P. If the subject indicates that only shape entered into the animal skin concept, then: W F+ AObj P is justified.

The same procedure must be followed for the other shading-determined factors. The caution regarding "animal skin" concept in cards IV and VI applies to "clouds" in plate VII and "vista" in other plates, especially II and X. In short, though the tester may feel that certain determinants are definitely assignable to a response, *the subject* must be the source of scoring and not the opinions of the examiner.[4] The interrogation should also be channeled to ascertain whether the form component enters into the response, e.g., c, Fc, or cF. Some examples of shading inquires follow:

Card II: (upper middle detail) this l.l. a castle off in the distance.

Inquiry: (?) it's shaped l. it, a pointed tower, (*?distance*) features are not sharp, gives me a feeling of distance, (*?where are you standing in relation to the castle*) it's way up on a hill and I'm below it and far away.[5] Scored: D FK + Arch (Vista).

Card VII: this card gives me a feeling of s'g fleecy, cotton candy at a circus.

Inquiry: (?) it's so fleecy and fluffy l. being in the clouds, (*?fleecy and fluffy*) the coloring, (*?coloring*) I mean the way it's shaded, uh . . . light-like and has no body to it, l. cotton candy. Scored: W KF Fd.

Black, Gray, and White

If the subject describes his percept with one of these three adjectives, the use of C' is simple to justify, provided white is not a space-determined response.

Card I: this l.l. a flying black bat.

Inquiry: (?) shape, wings open as if in a long glide, (*?black*)

---

[4] In the final analysis the tester is the scorer and his experience and training will influence the scoring; but the testee should be the symbol-initiator.

[5] In all FK responses the position of the perceiver in relation to the percept should be obtained. In a sequential analysis the testee's position above, below, or on a par with the object perceived has interpretive significance.

all bats are this color or a bit lighter, grayish-like, (*?this one*) it's definitely black. Scored: W FM +, FC' + A P.

Card IV: (side detail) this is a large heavy boot and there's another one on this side.

Inquiry: (*?*) it's shaped just l. one, same with this one here; I'd say a pair of boots, (*?heavy*) looks large and heavy, (*?a'g else besides shape*) yes, it's massive and dark which gives me a feeling of heaviness, (*?dark*) it's black. Scored: D FC' + Clo P (Sym).

The Inquiry for this determinant should establish the achromatic use of color, and such responses as "dark," "light," and "shading" must be followed up until C' or some other determinant is confirmed.[6] A recognition of form in the percept will indicate the need to define the role of F, as secondary or primary. For example:

Card IV: this is gloomy blackness, night.

Inquiry: (*?*) the darkness and it spreads all over the card, (*?darkness*) black, grayish black color makes me feel queer, (*?a'g else besides grayish black*) no, only the darkness. Scored: W C' Sym(night).

Card IV: this is l. s'g evil.

Inquiry: (*?*) it's huge and black, (*?further*)[7] seems to be looming up towards me, (*?a'g else besides size and black*) it has the shape of a monster, a large gorilla like Gargantua in the circus, (*?looming*) it's coming toward me with arms (S spreads own arms apart) like this. Scored: W FM +, FC' + A (concept given definite shape, gorilla, thereby justifying FC' +).

---

[6] Another technique in the Inquiry which may be used as a next-to-last resort is this: If in card I the subject used a determinant whose authenticity the tester is unable to settle, it is well to wait until a similarly determined and more readily scored response given to a later card is reached. Once the scoring for the latter response has been set the tester may turn back to the doubtful concept in card I and ask the subject whether he was using the same determinant in this plate (card I) as in the second response.

[7] This is a shorthand symbol for "Can you explain this a bit more?" or "Would you please go further into this response?"

Card IV: a drawing of a human anatomy, 1. in an uncolored biology book.

Inquiry: (?) 1.1. a pencil drawing, (*?a'g else besides pencil drawing impression*) no . . . but I can't see the body parts clearly except for the head area here (points to top center), arms, and legs. Scored: W C'F At.

Chapter 14

INTERPRETATION—THE MEANING OF SHADING

The use of shading to formulate a response has been accepted quite readily. The differential use of shading tones has been recognized and discussed by practically all investigators who have worked with inkblots. Hertz reviewed the shading response and traced it to Rorschach and Oberholzer: "A shading response, or, as it was originally called, a 'chiaroscuro response' is one determined by the shadings and the light-dark values within the black and colored areas . . ." (1940, p. 123). Agreement does not seem to be prominent in regard to scoring symbols and the means of determining how to score a particular shading response. Also, the rationale for the different kinds of shading symbols seems to be at variance. Binder (1937) writes of two types of shading responses, "Those involving (a) dysphoric emotional tones where the 'darkness' and the 'shadowiness' are employed, and (b) euphoric emotional tones, where the ligher shadings and the fine gradations of grey tones are stressed" (Hertz, 1940, p. 128). Diffusion is also noted by Binder under the name of *Helldunkeldeutung*. Beck (1950, pp. 126-145) speaks of the "light-determined response: FV, Y, T." The latter, T or texture determinant, is an addition to the family of Rorschach scoring factors used by Beck.

The Klopfer system (Klopfer and Kelley, 1942, pp. 126-145) is more widely used in this country and will serve as the basis for interpretive elaboration. Before considering each of the categories separately, it is advisable to refer to the general meaning of the shading determinant as summed up in a paper by Rorschach and Oberholzer (1942, pp. 245-246): "Chiaroscuro responses showed something of the ability to manipulate spatial dimensions, hence ability to apperceive space, depth, distance. . . . More important, this category revealed significant aspects of the affective life of the individual." It is related to the "capacity of adaptation in the affectivity; it reflects an anxious, cautious, and unfree kind of affective adaptability to the will to master oneself and especially to an inclination to a depressive fundamental disposition (*Grundstimmung*) which one tries to master in the presence of others." Unfortunately, little is actually known regarding the dynamics of the shading-determined concept. "The evidence such as we have it," states Balloch (1952, p. 120), "is based on clinical observation, and quite a large amount of it is purely speculative."

Shading as Diffusion: *K, KF;* and Vista: *FK*

In this type of percept the subject employs the shading tones as an unlimited expanse best characterized as diffusion. Actually this reflects the diffuseness of the testee's anxiety. The "unboundness" of the anxiety state manifest in a K or KF concept proclaims the subject's inability to focus on the nature of what is troubling him. Interpretively this determinant reveals a free-floating type of anxiety. Pure K concepts, e.g., smoke and fog, symbolize pervasive and overwhelming diffuse anxiety. The KF response, such as a "cumulus cloud," suggests that the subject is making an effort to introduce some semblance of reality (F) into his struggle to cope with the anxiety. This is usually a futile, or at best a partially successful, assay to come to grips with the pervasive threat to the integrity of the personality structure. The nebulous, vague intangibility of the K-determined response (despite the introduction of a secondary form element) stems from the inadequately assimilated forces within the personality—forces which the testee is unable to handle properly. Every such concept lays open to inspection the chaotic condition of the individual's inner feelings from which anxiety and distress arise. The degree of distress may be inferred from the number of $K-$ (and $k-$)-determined percepts. Binder (1937) suggests the presence of depression.

In connection with K and KF it is necessary to turn to a consideration of FK, vista or distance. This three-dimensional expanse or perspective shows that the testee is making some effort to disperse the noxious and pervasive intangibility of the inner anxiety. In a manner of speaking, the vista-perspective concept stands as a safeguard against the intolerable buffetings of anxiety-laden conflicts from within the individual. They reflect an attitude of wary watchfulness of the ego over threatening inner impulses. (In psychoanalytic terminology and conceptualization, these FK percepts mirror the attempts of the ego acceptably to relate the inner strivings and instinctual drives to reality or to the external world.) Thus, FK is a representation of an introspective attitude and a desire for self-appraisal, i.e., the person is attempting (1) to come to a realistic, intellectualized (F) appreciation of his problem, and (2) to understand relationships and to trace them to the etiologic agent(s). The latter may be inferred from the testee's report of the position of the percept, viz., is the subject above, on the same level with, or below the observed engram. The position of the reporter is tantamount to an expression of superiority, equality, or inferiority with reference to the given concept. The presence of one or two FK concepts in a protocol discloses the individual's introspective tendencies. The absence of FK does not necessarily mean that the subject cannot introspect, it may very well be that the testee is utilizing some other means of achieving some measure of self-appraisal and adjustment, e.g., through healthy, or unwholesome, M. But the use of more than three FK-determined associations in a record is suggestive of a marked tendency for an unhealthy type of introspection in which the individual feels inferior and the self-evaluation tends to be self-critical rather than wholesomely constructive. This effort at personal insight when tied up with M concepts may point to a suspicious make-up, the type of structure that one sees in the paranoid patient whose introspections are related to fantasies about the self rather than being rooted in external reality. The patient has become too aware of his anxiety and needs to search for causes outside of himself. This is unhealthy.

On the other hand, diffuse shading associations with CF or C (presumably in an extratensive setting) represents agitated anxiety, i.e., distress that is reinforced by emotionality. Another way of stating this is that the subject is "taking out" his anxiety "on" his external environment; he may be noisy and obstreperous. However, in an individual who is extremely frustrated, who is unaware of or unable to accept the frustrating material, the protocol will disclose K or KF with m and/or FM. The built-up tension is quite marked in this instance, and there will be a need to find some outlet for the discharge of this energy. If the client cannot cope with the anxiety that might develop from his acting out his needs in the external environment,[1] then there are two possible directions these pressures may take; which one prevails is a matter of the degree of stress and past experience.[2] Basic to both alternatives is the

[1] Another way of putting this: some testees are unable to accept the consequences of their reactions or behavior which might ensue as a result of seeking avenues of tension release in a social milieu. The expression (of the need-motivated energy that is directed outwardly) may lead to hostile and/or aggressive behavior against significant persons who are in a position to retaliate or who have the prestige of social mores and cultural taboos to enforce direct punishment or reinforce guilt feelings. These, in turn, increase feelings of insecurity which give rise to further intense anxiety.

[2] It would be well to consider Hooke's (Lehmann and Dorken, 1952) "*ut tensio, sic vis*" — freely translated: strain is a function of stress — which has been put into a formula: $S = Es$ (S is stress, s is strain, and E is an elastic property). Lehmann and Dorken (pp. 387-388) point out, "The more elastic a mechanical system is, the smaller the strain which develops in it under the

complete absence of color responses (Sum C equals 0), or, at most one or two FC responses (Sum C equals 1), revealing the subject's inability to relate the satisfactions of needs with socially acceptable modes of behaving: (1) The person may turn this energy inwardly to the extent that a psychophysiologic reaction will ensue — conversion, dissociative, or somatized reaction — indicating that the energy has found an outlet through one or another organ system of the body; or (2) there may be a flight into total fantasy living because of the threat-laden external world; in this logic-tight self-constructed world all is serene and any external stimuli that pierce this autistic barrier are apperceptively distorted for the comfort of the perceiver.

In any instance, diffuse and vista associations are interpreted on a continuum: K is a disclosure of uncontrolled distress, an inability to alleviate the anxious state; as form is introduced, the individual is signalizing his attempts to deal with it. KF shows a modicum of awareness on the part of the subject in that an effort is being made to insinuate some rational appraisal into the conflictual situation. Inherent in the FK concept is the imposition of limits or appreciable dimensions on the expansiveness of the free-floating, unbound anxiety. While not quite successful, the testee is *trying* to "compensate for his anxiety, at least on an imaginative level, if not in concrete reality" (Brussel, Hitch, and Piotrowski, 1950, p. 75). The effort to come to grips with one's difficulties, to indulge in self-evaluation, is healthy in some contexts, unhealthy

---

impact of stress. . . . Hooke's law applied to a living organism would simply state that the strain suffered is in direct proportion to the stress imposed upon it and in inverse proportion to its capacity for homeostatic regulation." For the Rorschach interpreter the application of this principle lies in the search for predictive signs of behavior. In addition to the inferences available from the Rorschach responses, the estimate of elasticity, which will increase or decrease strain, must be derived from previous (learning) experiences of the subject. It is this last which gives the flexibility to the "E" phase of Hooke's law.

in others. The interpretive continuum of the shading response
is continued in the toned-down shading effects that are utilized
in formulating a concept.

SHADING AS DEPTH: *k, kF, Fk*

This is the experience of three-dimensional expanse projected onto a two-dimensional plane such as "X ray" or "topographical map" percepts. The subject is attempting to objectify and give some context to his anxiety by reducing the vagueness of intangible distress. Klopfer and Kelley (1942, p. 242)
write of the k-determined percept in this vein: "In all these
cases the attempt to intellectualize anxiety is merely more obvious," i.e., more obvious than in the use of the K and KF
determinants. The dynamics are rooted in the organism's
effort to meet the threat of an idea or situation symbolized by
the shading components of the selected blot area. The effort to
reify is reflected in the giving of limits, or definite dimemsions,
to what could otherwise be a diffuse, boundless use of the
shading tones of the stimulus as in K. The difference between
K and k, respectively, is the difference between unbounded
diffusion and limited diffusion.

The use of form with shading, better if the form accuracy is
good, is interpreted as the introduction of a higher degree of
intellectual reality to account for the insecurity due to anxiety.
More specifically, the testee is adhering as best he can to the
real situation in the hope that it will serve as a prop for
handling his distress and personal discomfort. Thus k reflects
limited concern, but no saving graces are in view as the situation is perceived by the subject. In kF and Fk respectively, the
ties to reality become more pronounced so that anxiety is
under increasing intellectual control. (The quality of the
mastery is related to the F + and F − component in the scoring
unit.) This determinant occurs often in neurotic states. The
presence of two or more k, either alone or in combination, sug-

gests anxiety beyond the normal limits (Klopfer and Kelley, 1942, pp. 14, 260). A record with one or even two Fk-determined concepts manifests the distress which seems to be the usual burden of most individuals in our culture. The absence of k does not imply that the subject is anxiety free. It would be necessary to examine the entire psychograph of Rorschach determinants and response contents to ascertain the subject's mode of expressing the feelings of insecurity and other indices of anxiety that are part and parcel of everyday living.

SUMMARY

There is no general agreement among Rorschach experts with regard to the scoring of shading responses. More common agreement is found in one oft-repeated statement exemplified by this excerpt from Brussel, Hitch, and Piotrowski's introduction to a discussion of the shading response: "In this sphere of percept-analysis reigns the greatest discrepancy of views. Both the symbols and their psychological implications vary from author to author" (1950, p. 149). The shading-diffusion and shading-depth responses are to be interpreted with the caution they are assumed to reflect.

Part V

INHERENT DETERMINANTS—HOW?

Chapter 15

LIGHT-DARK DETERMINANTS

Introduction

The elements in this and the following chapter differ from those previously discussed in that they are inherent in the physical make-up of the blot. The determinants revolve around the chromatic and achromatic characteristics of the designs.[1] The imposed determinants have a transcendent quality which is elicited subjectively and exists only in so far as the perceiver evokes them in forming a percept. This holds more for movement (M, FM, and m) than for shading (k, K, and FK). Any person can justifiably deny the presence of movement and two-planar concepts even under the extreme pressure of testing the limits.[2] The inherent determinants will be seen by a subject even if they are not used in the course of the Main Stage or Inquiry because they are objective qualities of the plates put there by the printer's ink and press.

[1] This does not imply that the testee *must* use the black-white or colored features of the designs in formulating a response. It should be kept clearly in mind that form alone may be the major determinant in some instances, with a complete or partial absence of achromatic and/or chromatic factors.

[2] This is a postinquiry technique for applying psychological pressure to elicit further responsiveness to the plates. See Hutt and Shor (1946). See also Chap. 23, this book.

143

Surface Texture[3]

The subject's use of the variations in shading as *lighter and darker* to form a concept is the basic guiding principle for the assignment of the texture determinant, c. This determinant admits only of single-plane or surface percepts. It is found most frequently in card VI, followed by plate IV. The use of this determinant in other cards is less facile so that the interpretive value of a c response in the latter cards is significant. Generally, the type of concepts that include c as either the main or additional determinant are: rocks or rocky surfaces, fur, dirty mess, eyes, and "tangible" feeling of tactile impression, e.g., smooth, rough, velvety. Examples of these are presented in Figure 13:

Card II: 1 — this is a cave, here is the entrance and around the opening is the rocky cliffside. Scored: DS Fc.

Card IX: 1 — four boulders, large, round rocks, sort of worn away in some spots. Scored: D cF. (In both of these percepts, Inquiry discloses the surface quality as due to the difference in shading of the colored and noncolored portions of the blots.)

Card VI: 1 — a fur rug spread out in front of the hearth. Scored: W Fc + . (Inquiry reveals texture or feel of fur as due to light and dark differences in the blot.)

1W — a dirty mess, l.l. vomit. Scored: W c.

Card IV: 1 — the head of bull with prominent eyes here. Scored: D F + , Fc. (The eyes are an additional percept to the total bull's head. In the Inquiry the testee states that the darker shading gives the impression of prominent eyes as standing out from the lighter surrounding gray area.)[4]

As with some of the other determinants already treated,

---

[3] Beck (1950, p. 128) has admitted this determinant to his family of Rorschach factors: ". . . I am adding a new scoring category, T, for texture."

[4] Eyes can easily be seen in any of the darker spots in the plates. The tester must be certain that the subject is making use of the differences in shading and not just form alone to score c.

form may or may not play a role. If form is present in the percept, the F symbol is placed in front of, or after, the c in keeping with the primacy of the shape in the organization of the total concept. In addition, + or − is always in terms of the accuracy of the blot area for the concept.

BLACK, GRAY, AND WHITE

This is the last of the still controversial determinants − C'. A concept which is described somewhere along the black-gray-white continuum is scored thusly; in a manner of speaking C' is a color determinant, i.e., an achromatic color determinant.[5] Employing the delicate variations of the shading as black or gray or white is a response to the objective stimulus-character inherent in the blot. This type of response does not usually appear in cards VIII and IX. Occasionally it is seen in X. The remaining plates readily lend themselves to the use of C', especially IV, V, and VII. Plates II and III may elicit achromatic responses, particularly when the popular "men" are seen in card III: (Figure 13) 2 − live waiters wearing black tuxedos. Scored: D M + , FC' + .

White as a determinant usually refers to the space-area of the plates. The principle in differentiating S from C' is this: if the subject actually uses the color white to describe the property of a percept, score C'; if white locates the concept on the blot area, score S. For example, Figure 13:

Card II: 2 − this white is a spinning top ∨. Scored: S Fm + . (Inquiry elicits the impression of a top that is spinning and is evoked by the spatial portion of the blot area; the term "white" delineates the area, it is not a white top.)

2 − a ballet dancer in a white costume. Scored: S M − , FC' + . (The Inquiry for this response discloses a concept

[5] Brussel, Hitch, and Piotrowski consider C': "The C' category contains all interpretations of the very dark nuances of the inkblots . . ." (1950, p. 45).

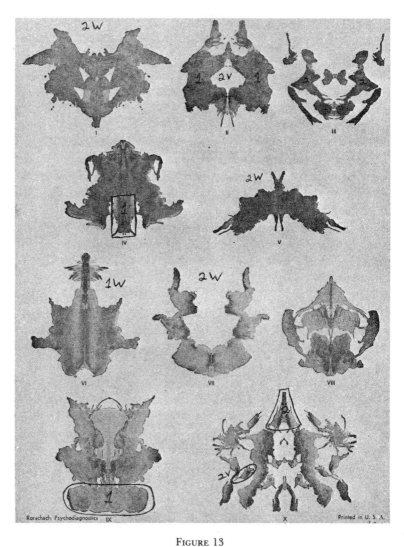

FIGURE 13

Responses Using c and C'

By courtesy of Hans Huber, Publishers, Berne, from Rorschach,
Psychodiagnostics.
The numbers refer to the various responses indicated in the text.

built around the human figure — a ballerina holding one of the ballet positions. Further, she is wearing the costume of the ballet, a white short-skirted dress. In this response white describes rather than locates. The human figure is poor form level, hence M —; the costume concept does fit the blot area giving FC' + .)

It is absolutely necessary that the subject identify the concept as employing achromatic value (black-gray-white) in order to score C'. Whether responses such as "lighter," "darker" contain C' is contingent upon the subject's definition of these terms in the Inquiry. Since this determinant carries some wholesome as well as negative personality attributes, the presence or absence of achromatic usage must be reasonably well established when it appears in a concept. Figure 13 offers some instances of C' responses.

Card I: 2W — this a black bat, flying. Scored: W FM + , FC' + .

Card IV: 2W — this reminds me of a gloomy scene, it's dark. Scored: W C'. (Inquiry draws out the impression of blackness related to a morbid feeling.)

Card V: 2W — another black bat, it's clearer than the first one. Scored: W FC' + . (Inquiry reveals no movement, a museum exhibit.)

Card VII: 2W — there are gray clouds. Scored: W K, C'.

Card X: 2 — two gray field mice gnawing at a cornstalk. Scored: D FM + , FC' + .

2 — this l.l. a grayish beetle. Scored: D FC' + .

The chief difficulty a beginner may encounter with the shading and achromatic elements of a concept is to have the testee account for such terms as "lights and shadows," "lighter and darker," "black," and "gray."

The Inquiry into these determinants is presented in Chapter 13.

Chapter 16

LIGHT-DARK ACHROMATIC INTERPRETATION

Attention now turns to a consideration of the meaning of the variations in achromatic and chromatic values of the blots: c, which may be employed in both the colored and noncolored plates, and C', which ordinarily appears in connection with the achromatic plates.

These particular determinants have found much wider acceptance than the ones discussed in the two previous chapters. They are found on the "external" side of the Rorschach psychograph in the Klopfer and Davidson Individual Record Form. The rationale is that all light-dark experiences have the same basic meaning as color in that they represent the sudden impact of emotional feelings. They are symbolic of something other than pure intellectual control (or intellectualizing of stimui) as represented by the F determinant. A light-dark response implies that the testee is aware of experiencing through modalities other than the intellect.

Shading as Surface: *c, cF, Fc*

In general, the use of the shading tones as surface texture involves a tactile quality or feeling. This is most frequently

148

supported by the subject's rubbing his fingers over the blot when responding to plate VI with the popular "'animal skin" concept. Pure c reflects a mode of experiencing which indicates that the individual is trying to make contact in the real sense. He is trying to touch and to hold on to something. It stems from a feeling of insecurity from which is derived a need to fasten on to something for security. In the language of behavioral dynamics it reveals the testee's desire for close contact with aspects of his external environment in order to gain assurance of acceptance of himself (Alcock, 1963; and others). Pure c is not common in the protocols of healthy persons. It should not be assumed, however, that the absence of c in a record is a favorable sign. In the undifferentiated state, viz., pure c with no form element, this light-dark reaction may be interpreted as indicated above, a need to remain in contact, and, therefore, a search for affection and attention. When this reasoning is extended further, the c-determined percept may be considered as a sign a egocentricity mirroring a drive to bring all within the purview and control of the subject. The absence of stabilizing human movement concepts is suggestive of the subject's vulnerability to overwhelming sensuality. Combined with undifferentiated or poorly differentiated color percepts (C or CF) the sensuality is crude, gross, and may symbolize aggression directed against the environment and people in it.

Efforts at adjustment, to control the crude awareness and tactile sensuality, are concomitant with the imposition of form on the elements of the percept, viz., cF and Fc. The latter is, of course, healthier than the former and is expected to be present in an amount that exceeds c and cF in the protocol of an adjusted person. Cass and McReynolds (1951, p. 181) found a median of two Fc-determined percepts for their standardization population. Other investigators state directly or imply the desirability of form-shading concepts. Brussel, Hitch, and Piotrowski (1950, p. 72) write: "The Fc and c suggest that the subject tries to sacrifice (abandon, postpone, or modify) his important goals of external achievement in order to appear less assertive and thus more acceptable to the world; *the individual then is said to value his relations with the environment too much to jeopardize the respect, affection, and protection which the environment can give . . .*" (italics added). The central theme of pure c does change if it is in a more socialized context (Fc) — sensitivity to social amenities and the desire to inhibit emotionality so as to be acceptable. The subject is tactful or cautious, depending on whether the E. B. is extratensive or intratensive.

In an extratensive setting the individual is relating well with his outer world and the Fc emphasizes the careful manner in which he reacts to this external stimulation. The desire to remain in good contact and satisfy his dependency needs brings with it the requisite of so behaving as not to offend. This is social tact and characterizes the subject's manner of "securing" himself in this social milieu. On the other hand, in an intratensive setting the awareness is channelized inwardly so that the inner promptings are obeyed with caution. The testee is not totally free to lose himself in unbridled autistic behavior, M, because of his awareness of external stimuli (c) which temper the tendency toward abandonment or complete avoidance of the external environment.

An excess of c and cF points to gross sensuality; the superfluity of Fc is somewhat akin to this, with the element of intellectualized control, i.e., supersensitivity toward the deeds and words of those in the environment (in an extratensive setting) and extreme criticalness of self in a intratensive context. Klopfer and Kelley (1942, p. 287) describe the use of light-dark as texture: "Both texture and C' [see below] responses may be considered as an intermediate category between form and bright color which can serve two purposes: they may serve as shock absorbers for too strong emotional stimuli from without, or they may facilitate a still broader influx of impressions." If Fc exceeds the use of color in forming concepts, the interpretation is modified to indicate a desire to avoid emotional conflict. The use of Fc, cF, or c is, then, a shrinking away from the complete and spontaneous identification with the outside world. This is one indication of how this determinant fulfills the function of a shock absorber as defined above by Klopfer. In the presence of C'-determined (see below) percepts, the possibility of depression or dysphoric mood must be entertained. It is interesting to note the kind of situation in which a testee can become involved insofar as his emotional life is concerned: the use of shading as surface mirrors a necessity for remaining in contact, ranging from the lover who must touch his loved one continuously in order to reassure himself of her love, to the socially conforming person who has marked dependency needs (love, security, acceptance) which must be satisfied in the outer world. If the subject does not react to color, it is because of an inability to act out these needs. Where shall he turn to find satisfaction for them? Not to the social milieu. Can he find satisfactions within himself? Yes, if good M's (or even poor ones, if out of context) appear in the protocol. It has been felt by Rorschach workers that the presence of Fc in an otherwise poor protocol is a favorable sign — that the individual wishes to remain in contact, is aware of amenities, is still concerned. In a poor personality picture this looms as a hope for a favorable prognosis in therapy.

Like the other shading-determined engrams there is an element of anxiety present, but it is not the vague, intangible concern of K, or the "effort at limiting" of k. In the surface texture of c the anxiety is tied up or "bound." Thus, this determinant reveals the presence of a deep-seated experience of, and reaction to, threat from the testee's apperception of the environment. A more overt manifestation and reaction to threat is implied in the subject's use of black, gray, and white to formulate an association to the inkblot stimulus.

BLACK, GRAY AND WHITE: *C', C'F, FC'*

On the Klopfer and Davidson psychogram (1962) this determinant is but one step behind the color responses. Its psychological meaning is analogous—one step removed from open affectivity or relation with the external environment. This is interpreted as denoting a cautious approach in responding to the stimulation of others in making interpersonal attachments. Ordinarily, one or two such responses, preferably of the FC' type, may be expected in a protocol. This is an expression of the individual's controlled or intellectualized lack of self-confidence that leads to an attitude of suspicious caution. They may be tinted with hostility (depending on the context and the nature of the white association) or morbidity (the use of C' and C'F). Piotrowski (1950, p. 78) quotes from Binder: ". . . c'-shock or dark shock makes its appearance only when the neurotically depressive mood is chronic, and it reveals stronger emotional disturbances than does color shock." Brussel, Hitch, and Piotrowski develop the hypothesis that c' and Fc' (Piotrowski's use of the symbol) response discloses the ability to demur, the tendency to "give up, if necessary, many emotional gratifications which the environment can give, [but] to save the subjectively important ideals and individual goals" (1950, p. 73). Furthermore, the c' response "is a valid sign of a serious emotional disturbance associated with an attitude of expecting the worst." The C' person is tending toward acting out, more so than the c person who has already shown a greater ability to inhibit overt behavior. This interpretation finds support in the prevalent interpretation of black, gray, and white as the "burned child" complex, viz., the subject is basically responsive to emotional stimuli from the outside, but having experienced what Goldstein (1939) calls a "catastrophic" disappointment, the person prefers to withdraw from "hot, bright colors" to the safer nuances of the black-white continuum. This determinant also implies its shock-absorber role between the impact of affective external stimulation and the reality role of the individual, inherent in the F-determined experience.

SUMMARY

In consideration of all the chiaroscuro determinants, anxiety is at the basis. Its methods of expression, how the subject will cope with this psychological phenomenon, is important for the Rorschach interpreter. The engendered anxiety revolves around the testee's affectional needs, the desire to be "in contact with" the social surround, and how well these can be handled.

Each of the shading and/or achromatic-determined percepts reflects this affectional hunger and mode of satisfaction in somewhat different ways. In the K or diffuse determinant the testee is revealing the presence of free-floating distress, unbound anxiety which he is unable to fathom. At best the subject can try to put dimensions on it, i.e., give it some semblance of a beginning and an end. This moves the subject from K through KF and FK. The next portion of the continuum, k to kF to Fk, is the repository for anxiety that is not as pervasive, but its presence is not considered favorable for good adjustment. For the neurotic, however, it discloses the fact that the subject is struggling, is resorting to defenses to cope with his personal difficulties. Moving further to the right (on the continuum of shading-determined responses) are the toned-down associations of a tactile nature which bring the subject closer to external responsiveness, closer to potentially healthful interpersonal ties—c, cF, and Fc. Here the testee is attempting to relate to external reality in terms of affective attachments. For this assay to be effective the testee should have some capacity for acting out in order to satisfy dependency needs for love, esteem, and recognition from interpersonal relationships. Finally, the handling of anxiety through doing something, inability to sit out stress comfortably, is revealed in the extreme end of the continuum — C', C',F, FC'. These persons suffer from intermittent depressive moods with some agitation because of the pressure to act, yet at the same time there is an unwillingness or inability to become actively involved with the environment.

The chromatic use of achromatic blot areas is to be interpreted as abortive sublimation, viz., the testee is unable to control his impulses, he cannot live in the manner he would like to, he wants to act, to achieve; the conflict is resolved in an unrealistic, highly topical projection of the pressure to act out — the subsequent response contains the color determinant. The projection of color onto an achromatic blot is a pathological response and, when present, is in a psychotic context — either as a hallucinatory or illusional experience, or as an expression of the need to escape from overwhelming depression.

Chapter 17

COLOR SYMBOLS AND INTERPRETATION

INTRODUCTION

The final determinant is the use of color in the concept. While there may be some questions regarding the movement and shading factors, color is not prone to such doubting. The different hues are objective and recognizable in all cultures where there are names for them.[1] Kouwer (1949) discusses the background of color in different societies, cultures, and in psychological testing. An understanding of the dynamics of color plays an intrinsic role in color interpretation.[2] These introductory remarks with emphasis on the physical and physiological objectivity of the color experience should not becloud the issue with reference to the psychological aspects of color in the responses.[3]

[1] A lack of color responses does not controvert this point. Color-determined concepts may not be given by subjects who respond quite readily to color naming in a non-Rorschach situation. This brings up the possibility of color blindness. It is wise for the tester to ascertain whether or not the testee has normal color vision. One clue would be the absence or distortion of color-determined concepts. It is suggested that a color blindness test be administered *after* the Rorschach has been completed and not before it. There is the possibility of influencing the testee with regard to color in the responses.

[2] Some of the affects of color phenomena form-level accuracy, consistency of responses, and other issues have been reported by Allen (1951b); Allen, Manne, and Stiff (1952); Allen, Stiff, and Rosenzweig (1953); Lazarus (1949); Loosli-Usteri (1950); Schachtel (1943); and Wallen (1948). These should be read.

[3] Would it be mere rhetoric or idle speculation to indicate that this holds true for the c and C' determinants as well?

Color Symbols

The use of a bright hue in describing a percept introduces the color symbol C into the scoring scheme of the particular response. The many color-score combinations are illustrated in Figure 14. Each will be presented separately.

1. *Form-color (FC):* when form and color are blended into one concept with form the primary element of the percept —

Card II: 1 — this is a red btfly. Scored: D FC + .

Card III: 1 — a red bowtie. Scored: D FC + .

Card VIII: 1W — this l.l. the coat of arms of a royal family, the coloring is exactly as I expect it to be. Scored: W FC + .

Card IX: 1 — this reminds me of the cherry trees in Washington V. Scored: D FC + .

Card X: 1 — a collie dog lying down and resting. Scored: D FC + , FM + .

In all of these examples, Inquiry elicits the definite form and color aspects of the responses. The form-level accuracy gives the + to the FC unit. An example of FC — is:

Card X: 1 — a gold fish. Scored: D FC — .

2. *Color-form (CF):* in this the color is primary in forming the concept while form is a secondary factor.[4] The decision as

---

[4] Klopfer introduced a more refined scoring technique to supplement these form-color (and color-form) symbols (Klopfer and Kelley, 1942). These are known as F slash C (F/C) and C slash F (C/F). A beginner would most likely encounter difficulty in deciding between CF- and C/F-determined responses. The same is true for FC and F/C. The guiding principle is included in this excerpt from Klopfer and Kelley (p. 146): "There is one further combination of form and color, scored F/C, in which the color, while used, is actually used in a colorlesss sense, in that it merely marks off or designates certain areas but has no color value. Such a 'colorless' use of color would be found in those map responses in whic color is used to mark off certain areas or sections, but where the choice of a particular color has absolutely no significance.

"What has been said about F/C applies equally to C/F." The same scoring symbols appear in Klopfer and Davidson (1962).

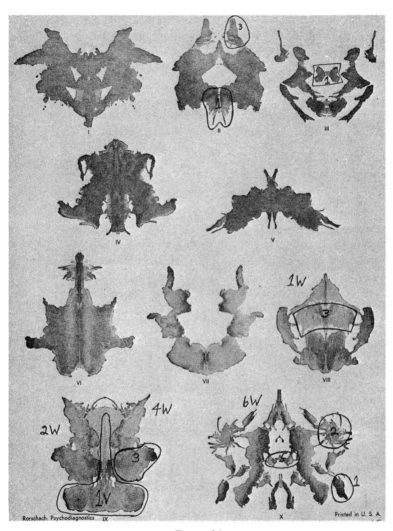

FIGURE 14

Color Concepts
By courtesy of Hans Huber, Publishers, Berne, from Rorschach,
Psychodiagnostics.
The numbers refer to the different responses indicated in the text.

to which is primary, F or C, is easily made in some concepts and more difficult to determine in others. Basically the testee must account for the percept and so give sufficient ground for a proper differentiation. If, however, the percept is one that is generally accepted as having a blend of form and color, then FC is most usual, viz., a flower may be CF but a Rose or Violet is FC.

Card IX: 2W—a map in a geography book. Scored: W CF.[5]

Card X: 2W—a micro slide in technicolor like you see at a science show. Scored: W $\overline{\text{CF}}$.

2—this blue part is a spider. Scored: D F+. (Inquiry reveals that blue is used to locate the percept on the card. The testee denies "blue spider."[6])

3. Pure color (C): the contour of the blot area has no part in the organization of the concept. Pure color may be used in a variety of ways—

a. C—color alone determines the quality of the concept. See Figure 14:

Card II: 3—blood. Scored: D C.

3—dried blood. Scored: D C,c.

1—an explosion, fire and flames. Scored: D C,m.

Card VIII: 3—this reminds me of the ocean off Miami, it's so blue. Scored: D C.

b. C_n—this refers to color naming. The testee uses the color but not in an assimilated manner, i.e., the subject is not

---

[5] Students of the Klopfer method would score this C/F.

[6] This example is cited to emphasize an important point, one that weighs heavily in the interpretive aspect of Rorschach. The tester must determine the presence or absence of color in the response *as the testee perceives it.* This particular response might possibly be scored under the Klopfer system as: D F/C. At first this may seem quibbling over trifles. But it is not. F/C responses are totaled in the FC column and contribute to the M:Sum C ratio, one of the more important computations used for protocol interpretation. The author suggests the score, D F+, and in the qualitative notes due consideration be given to the subject's awareness of, and responsiveness to, color (indirect as it may be).

integrating the color of the blot area in an organized manner.

Card IX: 4—this is red, green, and orange. Scored: W C_n.

c. C_{des}—color description, a response in which the subject describes the colored component of the percept.

Card X: 5—this l.l. a washed-out blue like you see in a water color painting. Scored: D C_{des}.

d. C_{sym}—in color symbolism the testee makes an "abstract" use of color. The subject ascribes to color a quality that is symbolic of an event, object, or idea.

Card X: 6W—this is a picture of Spring and Gaiety. Scored: W C_{sym}.

e. Color denial—is symbolized by $\overline{C}$, $\overline{CF}$, or $\overline{FC}$ and is revealed by the testee's reference to color but his inability to assimilate it into a percept.

Card III: (the whole plate)—there are two men doing a vaudeville act, but I don't know what these red spots could be. Scored: W M +, $\overline{CF}$.

This scoring category was suggested by Brussel, Hitch, and Piotrowski (1950, p. 68) and minimizes the possibility that the Rorschach interpreter will overlook the significance of this type of response in his evaluation of the protocol.

Color-determined responses are obtained most often in cards VIII, IX, and X. Plates II and III contribute to color conceptualization but less frequently. The importance of color is aptly expressed by Kouwer (1949): " The significance of these chromatic colors is assumed to be particularly in the emotional sphere; interpretations based on the chromatic color rather than shape of the blots supposedly indicate a strong emotional component in the character of the subject" (p. 144). It is essential, then, that the use of color and the primacy of color or form be established during the Inquiry. There is an occasional projection of color into one of the achromatic cards. This is regarded as a serious sign and should not be overlooked by the disbelieving beginner.

Color

The same vital problems that crop up in other determinants appear here despite the strong supposition of a definite symbol on the tester's part. The question of C, CF, or FC must be answered satisfactorily:

Card II: these are two clowns.

Inquiry: (?) they l.l. clowns, head, hands, costume, and feet (S points to these parts as named), (?*costume*) they're wearing red hats, even their faces are painted red, and you can see the bright coloring down here (pointing). Scored: W FC + H P.

Card IX: l.l. the insides of a person.

Inquiry: (?) l. you see in a biology book, (?*parts*) not exactly, the lungs are about here, intestines and stomach down here (pointing). Scored: W CF At.

Card III: (center detail) this is a bowtie.

Inquiry: (?) it's shaped just l. one, with the knot in the middle and these two ends, (?*a'g else besides shape*) no. Scored: D F + Clo P.

(center detail) this is a bowtie.

Inquiry: (?) it's shaped just l. one, with the knot in the middle and these two ends. (?*a'g else besides shape*) yes, the color, it's a red bowtie. Scored: D FC + Clo P.

Card IX: (green detail) l.l. a meadow.

Inquiry: (?) it's green l. in the country, (?*a'g else besides the color*) it's green and reminds me of the country. Scored: D C N.

Chapter 18

THE MEANINGS OF COLOR

This has long been a controversial area — all the more so, since a great deal regarding the interpretation of the color-determined concept is accepted somewhat uncritically. Wallen (1948), Dubrovner (1950), Barnett (1950), York (1951), Allen (1951, 1952, 1953), Lazarus (1949), and Meyer (1951), have investigated, in one way or other, the influence of color on various aspects of the Rorschach productivity. The results are indefinite, even contradictory, with reference to the effects of the presence and absence of color in the Rorschach plates (see Baughman, 1958). It is difficult to adopt a point of view other than the clinically verified one with regard to the influence of color in the Rorschach Test. This means adhering to the basic classical interpretation of Rorschach and his followers.

The role of color in human behavior has been explored in every culture in which there are language symbols for the color experience. Kouwer (1949) has studied the color vocabulary of different societies and cultures. Among his conclusions the following loom quite significant: "2. The relations between color and the other phenomena . . . . can never be fully explained rationally. . . . 4. The characterological value of the colors appears to be inextricably connected with their nomenclature in the language. . . . 7. The designation of the colors in the language proved largely dependent on the psychological effect of the colors. . . . 9. Psychologically the characters of the colors are given as an *a priori*. They may be analyzed and described

161

but psychologically they cannot be further reduced or explained. . . ." In the Rorschach Test, "color is seen in a special relation to emotional life" (p. 42). In discussing color and the Rorschach method Kouwer seems to summarize the current thinking: "The significance of these chromatic colors is assumed to lie particularly in the emotional sphere: interpretations based on the chromatic color rather than on the shape of the blots supposedly indicate a strong emotional component in the character of the subject" (p. 144). Schachtel (1943), a profound student of the Rorschach method, essentially agrees with Kouwer. He reiterates Rorschach's point of view when he asks the question: "What has the color experience in common with the experience of affect?" The answer lies in this hypothesis: "Color is essentially a phenomenon of the surrounding world, of the *visible world.* . . . Colors draw people into extroversion, as Rorschach once remarked, referring to the vivid colors of a carnival or a military parade. And the extratensive type is characterized by the urge to live in the world outside oneself and by a labile affectivity. All these qualities commonly emphasize the responsiveness, *the reactive readiness to respond and adapt to the environment and its affective stimuli*" (pp. 397, 407-408). The reader is referred to Beck's (1950) discussion of color (p. 113).

Color, then, has two interwoven qualitative components: responsiveness to external stimulation, and affectivity. Therefore, the manner in which the subject handles color-determined associations mirrors the characteristic mode of dealing with the emotionally tinged aspects of everyday life experiences. [1] The basic meaning of a color concept is related to the emotional life of the personality structure; this is modified by the context within which color is employed; e.g., pure C, CF,

[1] The serious student of the experimental work in the problems of color and emotions is referred to Kouwer (1949), Schachtel (1943), and Norman and Scott (1952).

or FC. For a developmental picture of color perception, see Shapiro (1960).

PURE COLOR: *C*

The first of these is the use of pure color in the formulation of a response. Of this determinant, C, Rapaport, Gill, and Schafer (1968) write: "the pure color response represents either the extreme of impulsive and wild affectivity, or an abandonment of all control" (p. 380). Responses such as "blood," "fire," and others that might utilize only the bright hue are characteristic of the manner in which the individual copes with the emotional stimulation by other persons in his social milieu. This is an unhealthy way of dealing with emotionality and reflects an inability to make an acceptable emotional identification. The person is literally and figuratively speaking the servant of his emotional upheavals when this pure color determinant is the dominant one. Such a person is usually considered to be unmindful of others because of his self-involvement. He is so engrossed in his unthinking reactivity to the experience of the bright-hue stimulus that he does not consider his fellow man. The derived interpretation, then, is that of an ego-centered individual who is unable to relate well in his social contacts when markedly disturbed. It occurs rarely in the protocols of well-adjusted persons. In those instances where it is found in the records of mentally healthy subjects, it will be in the context of a richly variegated productivity. It adduces the *range* of the individual's capacity for emotional experience and not the *characteristic* mode of emotional responsiveness. It is at this point that a frequently overlooked aspect of the color response must be considered, viz., the specific color involved in the percept. Brussel, Hitch, and Piotrowski (1950, p. 65) and Kouwer (1949) are especially strong proponents of the point of view that each color has its own unique meaning, interpretively, with regard to strength or weakness of the feeling involved, its positive or negative value, and the singular nature of the colors themselves. An example: "Blood, especially when it appears as early as in Plate II, was recognized even by Rorschach as a sign of fear of others; destructive fires, anatomical and sex responses implying violence, wounds, or dissections of organisms, are other examples of negative CR" (p. 65). Positive feeling is expressed in "ethereal" color responses and constructive anatomical or sex concepts.

The mentally retarded and excited subjects give pure C because of the primitive, infantile emotionality which does not yield to reason and is uninfluenced by inhibitory cortical control. This is equivalent to the "I lost my head" type of response or behavior. In the neurotic it reflects the volatile affectivity in the personality structure. The testee finds difficulty in maintaining an evenness of function in the face of stress from the environment (as one directional source of distress) with consequent loss of emotional control. For the schizophrenic it discloses the inappropriate affect. Should pure C occur in an otherwise healthy record, it reveals the extent of emotionality with which this person may react.

In general, the presence of C without the stabilizing influence of accurate form level (F+) in a quantity to yield C greater than CF and FC, is a sign of danger. It strongly suggests acting-out tendencies (Brady, 1953).

Shapiro (1960) writes that pure color percepts given by the *deteriorated* schizophrenic and the brain-damaged person represent *not* affect discharge but a "concrete report of a sensory experience" (p. 173). It is as if the testee were merely reporting just another experience in a passive, perhaps helpless (because of stimulus impact), sort of way.

Elaboration of Color: $\overline{C}$, C_n, C_{sym}, C_{des}

The color response is complex. In order to help the interpreter of the inkblot test to differentiate levels of emotionality, the pure color-determined percept has been subcategorized. The testee at times may be unable to assimilate the colored portions of the inkblot properly, yet he cannot avoid these stimuli which are impinging upon him. There are available several modes of handling the color stimulus, each of which is in keeping with the subject's characteristic way of dealing with the color-associated engrams.

A rather weak but effective defense against emotional involvement with the external environment is the denial of the influence of the color in the plates in forming a percept. This is called color denial and symbolized by $\bar{C}$. Brussel, Hitch, and Piotrowski (1950, p. 13) state: "$\overline{FC}$—color by denial ('I don't know what this red could mean . . . .'), indicating a weakness of integration, yet a lack of ability to reject the pertinent "emotional stimulation." Color denial is not necessarily a pathological indicator. The subject is cognizant of his environment and rather than resort to apperceptive distortion he "nods" in its direction, gives it credit, but passes it by. He is announcing to the world that for good reasons (unknown to himself) he is in the world but wants little or no part of it. It has been observed that color-denial responses are usually accompanied by a high CR (color ratio-8, 9, 10%) percentage which supports the $\bar{C}$ interpretation of sensitivity, but reluctance, to respond to the environment with positive feelings.[2]

A more pathological manner of handling affective stimuli from the outside is to name the colors as they are encountered in the plates. This emotional defensiveness is one means of isolating oneself from the environment and its concomitant press for making interpersonal identifications. Thus, the subject deprives, as if by magic, the threatening import of external forces. By resorting to color naming, C_n, the subject is giving insight into the extent of emotional disorganization that has

[2] The denial concept and symbol may be useful to record the denial of any response or any part (location, determinant, or content) thereof. While it does not enter into scoring, it adds to interpretation.

taken place. It reveals the magnitude of the feat that the testee's carefully built-up autistic world will be shattered by these aggressive representatives of a hostile outside world. For it is from this world that the subject is fleeing and against which he must protect himself. Color naming is one way of neutralizing these threat-laden forces, for in doing this the testee is relieved of the necessity for assimilating and organizing these unwelcome colors that symbolize threats to the self-concept, and therefore repressed, associations. This is more so if the repression is inadequate. Color naming seems to have a magical function and takes on the semblance of Klopfer and Marguiles' (1941) "magic key" formula for meeting difficult situations that is usually seen in the young child. The C_n response is found in the records of the schizophrenic, the epileptic, and the brain-damaged patient. The last shows more clearly the effects of cortical disorganization and the desire to retreat from a difficult and unmanageable field. How simple it is to denote concretely rather than flounder in the face of complexity, which might induce awareness of inability to deal with problems, which increases anxiety, which . . . . ad infinitum! In resorting to color naming the patient has given up the struggle. Brussel, Hitch, and Piotrowski (1950, p. 67) write: "C_n is a measure of superficial affectivity which causes sudden mood changes: The patient is easily irritated but easily calmed, his feelings being strikingly shallow and fleeting." The literature is unanimous in the consideration of color naming as a pathological response. (An important caution: the presence of this determinant, and many others, should not be interpreted unfavorably when dealing with the protocols of children.)[3]

Another type of pure color response is the C_{sym} percept in which the stimulus elicits an abstract or symbolic use of color, viz., "This red reminds me of Spring," or in plate X: "This is the spirit of Gaiety." The artist is more prone to give

[3] For this particular point, see Allen, (1951a, 1954, 1955, 1957).

this kind of response than the individual who is less sensitive to the abstract-cultural interpretation of color. For an artist (with supporting pathological signs not in evidence) this is a banal response equivalent to the popular concept of the nonartistic person. For the latter individual the symbolic use of color is pathological in that it represents a contamination in the two spheres of the subject's life, the external and internal. The testee is not readily inclined to react to the external emotional stimulus, yet he feels he must. Instead of organizing and assimilating the color intelligently he confuses this external stimulus with his inner ideational fantasy. The result is a highly topical (personal) abstraction. Interestingly enough, much of the interpretation is also a function of the nature of the symbolism. "This red is Spring" is certainly less pathological than, "This red is Murder and Death." Color *plus* content lend meaning to the interpretive inferences regarding the subject's affective life.

One more generally accepted type of pure color response is C_{des}, color description. In this, the testee describes the attributes of the colored portion of the blot as he views it. This represents a commonplace use of color and places the subject closer to reality and the world about him, but he is "watering down" or diluting the impact of emotionality. As a defense against uncontrollable subservience to affectivity this is quite effective. Klopfer and Kelley (1942, p. 284) believe that this use of color belongs "to the CF combination, since the impact of pure color effect is mitigated by some rational element." Usually a testee who describes the color stimulus utilizes a difference in the shading tones (c) as one descriptive attribute. By doing this the testee discloses the effects of demurring or the ability to inhibit the impulsivity characteristic of a pure color concept.[4] One response to Card X is: "This looks like a

---

[4] In the writer's experience this has usually been considered a favorable sign.

washed-out blue like you see in a water color painting."
Scored: D C$_{des}$, c Ptg. (Inquiry reveals that the testee is using,
not only the blue color, but also the differences in the shades of
blue in the selected blot area, i.e., the lighter and darker portions of the blot.) In this concept the subject reveals his sensitivity to external stimulation, impairment of ability to relate
well emotionally with his world, with, however, the saving
grace of the tendency to control a possible outburst not by
introducing intellectual control, F, but by actually inhibiting
motility, c.

COLOR FORM: CF

The introduction of reality ties in the effort to cope with the
affective aspects of social living and responsiveness focuses attention on the combined color-form determinant, CF. The favorable interpretive aspect of the CF concept is its reflection of
the subject's willingness to make warm emotional ties with
others in his external field. This is usually found in subjects
who are fairly well adjusted. It represents a high degree of
spontaniety of affective association with the element of control, albeit secondary, present. It represents restraint that is
tied to reality. Cass and McReynolds (1951) are in agreement
with Beck et al. (1950, p. 259) who wrote that: "Of most
interest is the weighting in the direction of CF and FC, in that
order; and the comparatively small instance of undiluted C.
The population of which this sample is representative may,
therefore, in respect to affectivity, be described as having
made some progress towards maturity and towards capacity
for social rapport. Yet they are slightly more labile than fully
stabilized. . . . Again, one may speculate as to implications for
our society generally; unstable, easily excited, but resisting un-
disciplined violence; and also reaching for a friendly, mutually
sympathetic, rapport." Beck and his co-workers implicitly attribute to CF an "unstable, easily excited, but resisting undis-

ciplined violence" quality. Nor does their statement indicate that CF greater than FC (discussed below) is an acceptable optimum. The experience of other investigators (Shapiro, 1960; Alcock, 1963) has led them to deduce the fact that CF should be present in the record of a well-balanced personality in minimal quantity; one or two at most, balanced by a larger number of healthy form-color (FC) concepts. The absence of CF would indicate an inability to make emotionally warm and close personal ties with people in the social environment.

The above holds true for the adjusted person. In other personality pictures, the CF concept gives insight into the method of coping with affective responsiveness to external stimulation. The manic manifests his elation and easy distractibility. Thus, since he is so readily attracted by any and all stimuli, he cannot introduce intellectual control, F, as a primary factor in his associations. This accounts in great measure for the evident lack of self-control seen in the reactions of the euphoric patient. This patient usually responds with C and CF concepts, while FC percepts are lacking. The presence of well-formed CF associations, as compared with CF—, introduces a favorable element. In the neurotic the presence of CF mirrors the instability and the degree to which the testee is "emotionally suggestible." In children CF may represent a step in the direction of growth toward maturity, FC as contrasted with C; but it also points to their affective lability with growing awareness of the intellectual aspects of coping with life's problems. One more word to round out the CF concept; in the superior individual it discloses the emotional sensitivity and range of affective responsiveness of this personality.

Form Color: *FC*

The final color-determined response is the one in which the form (intellectual tie to reality) is primary and controls the secondary affective responsiveness. Thus, FC suggests the controlled intellectualized or rational approach to emotionally stimulating situations. FC also points to social adaptation. It is expected to be present in optimal, not maximal, quantities. As an absolute number the usual expectancy is from two to four such concepts in a protocol.[5] Of more pertinent significance is the relationship that exists between FC and CF + C concepts. Rorschach workers have traditionally accepted a ratio of 3FC: 1CF:.5C. Too much FC, or FC in the absence of CF, discloses a restrained individual, one who is lacking in warmth and spontaneity, since emotionality is consciously overcontrolled.

It should be noted that in the CF and FC percepts the level of form accuracy plays an important role. The poor use of form, in combination with color, resulting in an FC— or CF—, reveals the weakened reality tie in the face of emotion-arousing stimuli. This gives a more pathological tinge to the color responsiveness and even dilutes the positive effects of FC. Thus, if in a protocol the CF lends an interpretation of warm personal ties being within the purview of the testee, the CF— modifies this quality and adduces a meaning of poorly controlled relationships, discomfort in such associations, and an inability to accept such interpersonal external attachments. In FC— the inhibitory effect of the intellectualized control over emotionality is deprived of its positive value. In its place is a distorted apperceptive reaction that bodes ill for the subject. The testee reveals an inability to handle emotionality despite awareness of the need to do so. He is just short of a complete actualization of his capacity for effective interpersonal relationships.[6]

---

[5] Absolute numbers mean very little in this situation.

[6] A very stimulating and advanced discussion of color-interpretation theory is found in Shapiro (1960, pp. 154-201).

Chapter 19

DETERMINANTS — ADDENDA

In this chapter several issues that do not clearly fit into any one definite section are presented.

Multiple Factors

The list of determinants is complete, yet the story of scoring is not. The translation of a simple response into symbols will give little difficulty:

Card I: this is a bat. Scored: W F + .

this is a flying bat. Scored: W FM + .

this is a black bat. Scored: W FC' + .

But: "this is a flying bat" introduces a scoring problem in that more than one factor enters into the determinant column. This response is scored (after Inquiry): W FM + , FC' + . Note that the elements in the determinant segment of the score are in a sequence. Buehler, Buehler, and Lefever (1948) give the following order of precedence of determinants: "Scores are listed as main and additional in order of appearance, with the exception of certain signs which have preference over others, e.g., M scores precede all other signs, bright color scores (not C') rank second, FM third, Fc scores fourth. The other signs follow without discrimination. This rule corresponds to Klopfer's present technique" (p. 64). The order of preference when more than one determinant appears in a response is: M, C, FM, Fc. The remaining: m, k, K, C' are scored as they appear in the response without discrimination, i.e., the temporal sequence in which the testee gives these determinants.[1] Additional examples of the scoring preference scheme are:

Card III: this l.l. two black-suited waiters wearing aprons and doing an Alphonse and Gaston act. Scored: DS M +, FC' +.

Card II: this reminds me of two flashily dressed clowns playing a game. The costumes are black with darker and lighter stripes. Scored: W M +, FC +, cF, FC' +.

here I see smoke and flame, like a terrific explosion. Scored: W C, K, m.

The beginner is urged to score all scorable components of the subject's concepts. The additional determinants may have a cumulative effect in the interpretive process.[2]

SCORING PROBLEMS

At times a subject will give responses which do not lend themselves to scoring because they are either unintelligible or unscorable. The former type of response offers little to the tester except as an effort may be made to have the subject repeat the response during the Main Stage or develop some meaning in the Inquiry. It is more difficult to deal with the second type of response. When a subject exclaims, "What gorgeous colors!" to card VIII, is this a color description concept or is it merely

---

[1] A crude analogy with color may help clarify the thinking in this. The M, C, FM, and Fc determinants may be considered as equivalent to the primary hues while the m, k, K, and C' determinants are the derivatives of the primary determinants much like orange is a derivative (mixture) of red and yellow. The derivatives are special uses of the primary qualities.

[2] Some Rorschach interpreters give additional quantitative credit, such as one-half point, in computing the totals of the various factors in location, determinants, and contents. Whether or not formal recognition is given to additional determinants in terms of partial credits, all Rorschachers agree that the secondary factors must be taken into final account in the qualitative handling of the protocol data.

an aside or remark? The tester is faced with the necessity of determining whether or not this verbalization has behind it the dynamics and portent that are usually associated with color-determined responses. In short, when is a verbalization a response or remark? The answer lies with the testee. If the statement proves to have substance to it, the response is scored, e.g., should a subject verbalize: "What gorgeous colors!", the tester would ask, during the Inquiry, what the testee meant by that statement. If the subject shrugs it off with, "Oh, there's nothing in particular in the card that made me say that, I was just struck by the variety of coloring," it may be considered a remark and assigned a color denial additional $(\overline{C})$. If, on the other hand, the subject replies, "These colors are beautiful and so well balanced," the response should be scored: $W\ C_{des}$. Another technique is available to the tester if the subject should give more than one such borderline response. If it can be established definitely that the subject meant a response instead of a remark in one instance, then the tester may go back to the doubtful response and ask the testee the portent of the doubtful response and compare it with the established color response.

Other scoring problems include elaborations which raise the question of whether or not to score. In the following sequence of responses this problem would arise:

Card III: 1) $\wedge$ these 1.1. two actors bowing after having completed their act. Scored: D M + .

2) $>$ 1.1. a red rooster. Scored: D FC + .

3) $\wedge$ these are white collars that the actors are wearing. (This last response is not scored separately since it is an obvious elaboration of the first concept in the plate. But it is not overlooked, it adds the C' [white collar] determinant to the total scoring of the first response which is now rescored: D M + , FC'.)

Two responses to the same blot area are considered as two

separate concepts unless the subject denies the first and replaces it with the second:

Card I: 1) ∧ this l.l. a btfly. Scored: W F +.

2) ∧ also reminds me of a bat. Scored: W F +.

In this illustration the same blot area evokes two engrams, both scorable and acceptable as responses. In the following sequence the second response replaces the first:[3]

Card I: 1) this middle part reminds of a woman; no, it's not a woman . . . it's a . . . a bug with six legs, black and ugly. Scored: D FC' +. [(D F +) for the denied response of woman].[4]

When two identical concepts are given for the same blot area but with the card held in different positions they are considered as two separate scorable responses:

Card V: 1) ∧ this l.l. a bat. Scored: W F +.

2) ∨ this also l.l. a bat this way. Scored: W F +.

In the course of testing, the beginner will meet with many complex scoring problems. The best method for addressing these problems is to analyze the salient points in the location, determinant(s), and content. When in doubt, it is more desirable to overscore than to underscore.

REJECTED CARDS

If a card has been rejected in the Main Stage, i.e., no response has been given to it at all, the tester should present the plate to the testee in its regular order and ask if any impression can be noted at this time. The examiner shows the cards that have been rejected and says, *You didn't see anything on this*

---

[3] Some testers follow the practice of scoring denied or rejected responses additionally, using their own judgment for scoring location, determinants, and content.

[4] The author suggests that all additional responses be enclosed in parentheses for easy identification.

card before, can you see anything now? All responses are inquired into and scored as additionals.

A FINAL WORD

The importance of an adequate Inquiry cannot be stressed too strongly. Nor can illustrations in any one book cover the variety of experiences and difficulties a Rorschach examiner will encounter in the course of testing. The suggestions given here should serve as starting points for further queries, as guides at best. The goal of each Inquiry should be to establish the presence of a determinant, or its absence. If the response entails a form element in the determinant-combination, then the role of F must be probed. A response which involves more than one determinant places upon the tester the further responsibility of inquiring into these additional factors. As previously indicated, it is better for the beginner to overinquire and overscore than to be satisfied with mediocre and incomplete Inquiry and scoring. Cautions that bear repetition: do not give leading questions, and a determinant should not be included in a question unless it has been verbalized first by the subject. Above all, tact and patience are prime requisites. The testee most likely has not read books on the Rorschach and therefore does not know what is required of him in terms of a neatly organized Inquiry. From the point of view of the subject the Inquiry may be a pleasant or trying experience. If the latter condition holds, it may be due to the pressure that the tester is exerting on the testee. It is no longer a test but a contest situation that threatens the security and integrity of the subject. The examiner must avoid this. But equally important, the tester should attempt to ascertain why this situation obtains. It is by analyzing the entire circumstances surrounding the testing situation that the tester will gain from an experience.

Part VI

CONTENT — WHAT?

Chapter 20

CATEGORIES OF CONTENTS; THEIR SYMBOLS AND INQUIRY

INTRODUCTION

The contents of the response refer to what the testee has finally achieved as a result of organizing the "where" and "how" aspects of the percept. The value of content for qualitative interpretation has become prominent with the better understanding of behavior dynamics and their verbal expression.[1]

Elizur (1949), Lindner (1946), and Lubar (1948) discuss this from the point of view of neurosis and character disorder.

CATEGORIES AND SYMBOLS

There may be as many content categories as there are terms used by subjects. However, these are the commonly used classifications:

Human

H—entire human figure such as man, woman, female, clown. This category of response is elicited most frequently in

---

[1] The author's experience has led to the conclusion that content analysis within the framework of sequence analysis (analyzing the responses as they occur temporally) gives material aid in teasing out the thought content of the subject. Skillful content and sequential analysis will elicit sufficient information regarding the thought processes of the testee to warrant the extra time and effort required.

cards III and VII, and least often in V, VI, and VIII. This in turn affects the M variable.[2]

(H)—derivatives and derogations of the human figure including witch, monster, statue, cartoon, caricature, Disney-esque animal with human attributes (Mickey Mouse).

Hd—human detail, i.e., surface parts of the human body such as hand, head, nose, foot, fingers, hair. Parts of the body below the skin are scored as anatomical content.

Hdx—oligophrenic human detail, refers to human details given to blot areas where the whole human figure is usually seen, e.g., in Card III a "human leg" response is scored Hdx because the usual human concept in the side of the plate is the entire human figure—man or waiter, etc. This does not apply to the top-third detail of Card VII in which the subject reports the "head of a woman." This is scored Hd.

Sex—a special class of human responses are sexual in nature. These are phallus, penis, breasts, vagina, genital organ(s), coitus, and other responses of a similar portent.

Animal

A—the entire animal figure such as dog, cat, chimpanzee, otter, insect, bug, butterfly. An inspection of the very first pro-tocols the beginner administers will disclose the popularity of A responses in cards I, II, V, VIII, and X.[3]

(A)—derivatives of the animal figure such as Disney (non-human) caricature (Pluto the Pup, Tom and Jerry), cartoon, statue, mythological animals (gryphon, unicorn).

Ad—animal detail that is readily seen on the surface of the animal—paws, nose, head, body.

Adx—oligophrenic detail referring to parts where the whole animal is usually seen, e.g., card II, center bottom: the testee

[2] This is cited to indicate the interrelationship that exists between the various factors of the Rorschach Test. See Hertzman and Pearce (1947).

[3] Since A concepts are quite easy to organize in all of the blots up to 50 per cent A responses in a protocol is considered to be within normal limits.

reports, "the bleeding paws of a bear," yet does not perceive the rest of the blot as the entire bear, scored Adx.

AObj—this special class is reserved for such concepts as fur rug, fur coat, animal hide or skin, hearthrug, and others of a similar nature. These are found chiefly in cards IV and VI.

Others

Anatomy—At—any concept of a body part underneath the skin such as chest, lungs, pelvis, insides of a body, anatomical chart, skeleton, ribs, and the like are scored here.

X ray—because of the interpretive contribution of this response it is accorded a symbol of its own, X ray.

Blood—Bl—this is another special category for a highly topical concept. All percepts with blood are scored Bl: dried blood, menstruation, bleeding, and just plain blood.

Object—Obj—is applied to man-made objects such as lamp, bedpost, bell, bullet, pillow, mask, totem pole.

Architecture—Arch—man-made buildings, castle, bridge.

Design—Des—this class of contents includes drawings, u-shape, numbers and letters, coat of arms[4] and symmetry.

Nature—N—natural phenomena, events, and parts of nature belong here: rain, grass, underwater scene, meadow, sky, cave.

Plant—Pl—botanical responses, viz., flower, tree, leaf.

Geography—Geo—some concept-contents such as map, island, airplane view, and geographical chart belong here. Others may be classified Geo or N according to the testee's usage: "a mountain" is N, "the Rocky Mountains" is Geo. North America, or any continent or country is Geo. The guiding principle is: if the response describes terrain or natural phenomena it is N, it if refers to a named area or portion of the world it is Geo.

---

[4] This concept is sometimes found under a special class, Emblem—Emb— along with officer's cap insignia, badge, flag.

Clouds — Cl — this is another unique category in which the particular interpretive significance of the content justifies the assignment of a special symbol. All Cloud responses are scored Cl.

Other contents may be classified under:

Food — Fd	Vista — Vist
Clothing — Clo	Fire — Fire
Scenes — Scen	Symbolism — Sym
	Artistic — Art

and any other category the tester finds convenient for his use.

INQUIRY

The Inquiry for classifying a response-content should pose no serious problem to the beginner. The percept practically classifies itself, and it remains for the tester to determine convenient categories. The facility in coping with content-scoring, however, should not lull the Rorschacher into a false feeling of complacency. This phase of the Inquiry requires the same skill as "Where" and "How." The answer to "What" the subject perceives is usually found in the Main Stage response: "this l.l. a man," "this reminds me of clouds," "here is another btfly" — scored H, Cl, A respectively.

WHAT IS IT?

Ordinarily it is not necessary to press for the content. An occasional difficulty may be encountered in the response which has several components:

Card II: (upper middle detail) this l.l. a castle off in the distance. Scored: D FK + Arch (Vista). (Inquiry reveals two scorable contents — castle and vista. The response is built around the "castle" and "off in the distance," justifying a main Arch and additional Vista.)

Card IV: (side detail) this is a large heavy boot and there's another one on this side. Scored: D FC' + Clo (Sym) P. (Inquiry discloses the primary clothing content with a secondary symbolism for "feeling of heaviness.")

There is one special problem which may arise in connection with content exploration. This is best illustrated by:

Card III: this l.l. two human figures, they're lifting a large pot between them. Scored: D M + H P. How much does this sequence of symbols directly inform the examiner about the subject's personality dynamics?[5] But to obtain a completer picture the Inquiry should proceed as follows (after the location and determinants have been settled):[6]

Card III: This l.l. two human figures, they're lifting a large pot between them. Scored: D M + H P. (Further Inquiry: (*?sex*) no, they don't l.l. either sex particularly, (*?male lack*). If, however, the testee has answered (*?sex*) with "male," continue with (*?male*). On the other hand, if the subject indicates in answer to (*?sex*) "female," continue with (*?female*). No matter what reply the testee gives to this last question, follow immediately with (*?male lack*).

This procedure may be adopted for any response which requires a more definitive depiction of the contents. Percepts which may call for this are the popular responses which have been omitted or distorted, nonsexed human figures in plates I, II, III, and VII, and those responses where the human figure is derogated or distanciated.

Lindner (1946) indicates that content up to 1946 was the most neglected phase of Rorschach analysis. Since then it has increased in importance because of the manifest and latent meaning contained in the final nature of the organized

---

[5] It has a great deal of inferential value.

[6] The transcribed shorthand reads as follows in order of appearance: Can you identify the sex of these human figures? (?sex); What is lacking for these figures to be males (or females)? (?male lack), (?female lack); Why do they look like males (females)? (?male), (?female).

concept (see Brown, 1953). Some Rorschachers treat content as analysts deal with dream material. No matter what the orientation of the individual examiner, the content cannot be overlooked. It is the easiest of the three scoring components to handle adequately, and therefore more liable to carelessness.

Chapter 21

THE INTERPRETATION OF CONTENT

This phase of the Rorschach protocol contains many possibilities for the interpreter. How the content will be integrated into the personality picture is dependent, in great measure, on the set of concepts which the interpreter brings with him into the Rorschach situation. With better understanding of behavior dynamics, the role of content as the representative of the testee's ideational processes is important and potentially relevant. Most of the research literature regarding the integration of content into protocol interpretation is either completely analytically oriented or strongly flavored with some type of latent and manifest symbolism. Zulliger (1953) and Lindner (1946, 1947) seem to be the proponents of the symbolism of content. In a non-Rorschach setting the contribution of Machover (1947) in her monograph on figure-drawing interpretation may be considered another prototype of this approach. Zulliger's paper is a definite "attempt to highlight the use to which psychoanalytic concepts can be put in interpreting content symbolism on the tests" (editorial note, p. 61). This lead seems to have been followed by the greater number of Rorschach workers. The content of a response, however, cannot be separated from the determinants with which it has been organized. This requires, therefore, that content be considered within the context of *where* and *how* in order to obtain an adequate picture of the subject's method of experiencing and subsequent reactions. In his discussion of the failures of the Rorschach Test, Zubin (1954), in a summary statement, writes that the "atomistic" and "global" interpretation of the contents in the test protocol ". . . as distinct from perceptual scoring, seems to work" (p. 344).

The intricacies of content interpretation are treated at great length by W. Klopfer (1954, pp. 376-402) and Piotrowski (1957, pp. 323-389). The latter, however, has a very broad conception of "content" which includes the formal (location and determinant) as well as the nonformal (specific content) aspects of the protocol in his presentation.

Number of Content Categories

The author has generally applied the rule of thumb that nine or more separate classes of content are indicative of better than average diversification of interests. This is especially true if the nature of the contents is outside of the frequent animal and banal object percepts. The extent to which content may vary for the ten plates is evident in the frequency tables by Beck (1950) and Hertz (1970).

The number of categories should be considered a function of the total number of responses in the protocol. On the basis of 32 items in an average length record, approximately 50 to 60 per cent of the responses should be classifiable into eight or more content categories in addition to the animal percepts, which may include up to 40 per cent of the total productivity. The lower the A + Ad percentage, the more likely will it be that the intelligent mature individual distributes his responses among a greater variety of categories. The mentally retarded usually centers much of his intellectual ability in animal and part human ideas. Occasionally, object concepts and one or two popular responses raise the total to as high as six categories. The limited content reflects the circumscribed experiential background and its subsequent narrowing of ideational processes or the lack of benefiting from experience. In the pseudo-retarded the content may be deliberately suppressed. The constricted associative indulgence is in the expressive aspect rather than in the receptive phase (unless this condition has existed since the early years of the testee.) The pseudo-retarded has a narrowed horizon as a defense against a threatening field. This, of course, is characteristic of the neurotically involved person.

A wide range of contents is correlated with broad experience and personality responsiveness that is free to give full expression to these associations. This is more so if the concepts are creatively original. The excited patient produces effusively, but the percepts are usually ineffective (both as to popularity and originality) despite the extremely high number of categories. Thus, variation in the nature of response contents can be overdone as it is in the case of the easily distracted subject who produces with originality but with highly topical doubtful quality (F−).

In general, the variety of content is an index to the range of the subject's interests, experiences, and the extent to which he has benefited from exposure to the formal and informal aspects of everyday learning and living. The absolute number of content categories is not the major clue to the wealth of association. A fairly wide distribution can readily be obtained with animal, animal detail, animal object, and oligophrenic animal detail percepts, to which may be added anatomy, map, X-ray, and human detail responses. The sole use of these eight categories in one protocol detracts from, rather than adds to, the stability and wholesomeness of the subject's personality picture. Concentration in one area suggests the pervasiveness of that particular thought content, resulting in a narrowing of receptive and expressive processes in keeping with psychic preoccupation. Excessive concentration points to the use of an adjustive mechanism (intellectualization) as a defense against ego-alien material coming to the level of awareness. Possible clues to specific areas of personal difficulty stem from an analysis of the content of a protocol. The self-reference may be quite direct and easily detected by the tester and/or the testee, or the meaning may be so complex and deep-seated that its topical value may escape both. These two contingencies may occur in one Rorschach record. Brussel, Hitch, and Piotrowski (1950, p. 80) warn that, "Unusual content always indicates unusual and significant interests. At times frank individuals openly reveal very important personality traits in the content of their responses. Reserved and shy people sometimes suppress content which is objectionable to them. *Since content may be suppressed deliberately, it is less reliable than the other components of the test*" (italics added). In a less restrained vein Harrower (1952, pp. 51 ff.), in her dialogue with the learner-physician, explains: ". . . . Now, turning to your own answer, What do you think of in connection with a beaver? *Physician:* Busy as a beaver. *Psychologist:* And, a sloth? *Physician:* Why, slothfulness, ease, relaxation. *Psychologist:* Isn't that a rather unusual combination, an extremely energetic and busy beaver and a lazy sloth? It might well raise all sorts of questions in regard to your habits of work and play and your conflicts over relaxation and duty, or perhaps a solution to such a problem...." While this oversimplifies the directness of the relationship between percept and inference, it does illustrate how content *may give clues* to the possible dynamics which determine one kind of response over the many other contingencies. Zulliger (1953) joins Piotrowski in urging caution when interpreting contents symbolism.[1]

CONTENT CATEGORIES

Human—H

Hertzman and Pearce (1947, p. 421) conclude on the basis of their research that "the human responses in the Rorschach

---

[1] The student is urged to read the content analysis Zulliger presents in the cases of Franz and Lotti.

are capable of representing keenly felt attitudes about oneself and the environment." They follow in the very next sentence with a significant caution that human responses should not *invariably* be interpreted as such. Those subjects who are fairly well adjusted will have less need for verbalizing, consciously or unconsciously, their self-percepts and reactions to others. By the same token, those who produce few H percepts may also be in the group of individuals who need to suppress adverse self-percepts or hostile and aggressive attitudes toward others in the environment. The difference between these two types of H-producers will ordinarily be found in the nature of the human percept. The latter, suppressors, will communicate more unhealthy concepts, e.g., derogated human figures (clowns, monsters, witches, and statues), deteriorated figures (falling apart, torn asunder, or body part missing), and depersonalization references. These denote a pathologic attitude toward the self and/or others in the environment, Goldfarb (1945a, p. 8) believes fear and/or avoidance of people is (are) reflected in vague and fearful semihuman percepts. Should the testee produce good human percepts along with unhealthy ones the latter serve as excellent clues to possible areas of personal difficulty; plate III, e.g., may elicit the usual popular male percept while plate VII may result in a derogated female response such as "two old ladies gossiping" (mild), or "statues of two women" (freezing the effect of the feminine aspect of the environment), "these are two dogs, two bitches" (interpretation left to the student!). The total or almost complete absence of H percepts in the protocol of a disturbed subject should alert the examiner to look for another category to reveal the area of conflict, viz., human detail, anatomy, or sex. Wholesome human identifications manifested in good form (F +) disclose "liberated intelligence" (Beck, 1952, p. 62). Much may be derived from the nature of the human figure, but caution is always necessary in regard to the specificity of interpretation. In giving a human response the subject may be referring to a facet of his own self-percept or to another signifi-cant person in his private world. Emphasis on one manner of describing the human engram reveals the pervasiveness of the testee's self-percept or his conceptualization of the role of others in the field. It is certainly desirable to know specifically the patient's attitude toward himself, mother, wife, father, etc. But the presence of a hostile H response cannot be inter-preted quite so definitely. It is much more in keeping with the law of parsimony to recognize that there is less difficulty involv-ing the subject and another significant person than to state that the subject hates his mother. This aversion may or may not be true; the testee may be reacting aggressively to his own femi-nine tendencies, or he may have an antipathy for women in general or for only certain significant females. The answer lies not in the Rorschach protocol but in the life history.[2]

W. Klopfer (1954) suggests that the male figure perceived in masculine terms, e.g., man's clothing or activity uniquely mas-culine in the culture, describes the healthy role concept of the testee as compared with the engram of a male figure cloaked in feminine attributes. The latter may be mirroring confusion in role-playing, or it may serve as an inkling into the latent (or at least not overtly manifested) cross-gender identification. The same holds for the female-feminine and female-masculine pro-ductivity.

The human percept may or may not be seen in the context of movement. Where no kinesthetic sensation is experienced by the subject, form alone may be the basic determinant. The testee's identification of self and/or other people is being made on an impersonal, realistic basis. The nature of this reality in-terpretation is related to form accuracy of the identified

---

[2] This should not make the Rorschach worker feel that he is not contri-buting adequately. At least there is a definite clue to an area requiring fur-ther probing in therapy, or a problem that should be handled with care. This is a contribution since it gives direction to therapy and may deter the therapist from uncovering too rapidly for the unprepared subject.

human figure. The movement-associated human concept discloses the role the subject does or would like to assume in life. The acceptability or unacceptability of self-percepts and attitudes involving others in the field and the extent to which self-percepts and these attitudes are rooted in real conditions may be derived from the form quality of the H concept. Human figure productivity adduces the attitudes toward self and others. Those humans seen in a color-determined context may mirror the subject's mode of making social and interpersonal ties — FC, somewhat impersonal; CF, warm, sympathetic, and emotionally attached; C, impulsive and unwholesome.

With reference to the frequency of H associations, Cass and McReynolds (1951, p. 181) find a median of 2.5 such concepts in their sampling, while Beck et al. (1950, p. 269) indicate a mean of 4.5 (S. D. of 3.62) for their population. Because of the wide variability in the Spiegel Sample (Beck) it would be more appropriate to use the criterion of between 2 and 3 H responses as characteristic of the normal groups studied. In both investigations the frequency of M and H (+ Hd) factors are approximately equal. Therefore, within normal limits the H concepts involve movement, M. In above-average H and M expectancy, the frequency of H accelerates faster than that for M. This demonstrates that with better adjustment and higher intellectuality the testee goes beyond the popular human movement concepts to show other facets of his personality and ability that are distinctive of greater stability and maturity. "Absence of human figures," write Brussel, Hitch, and Piotrowski (1950, p. 79), "indicates that the testee lacks interest in people as distinct personalities independent of and different from himself."

Human detail—Hd

Anxiety, restraint, and intellectual inferiority (primary or secondary) find an outlet in human details beyond the anticipated ratio of 2H:1Hd in the middle range of total responses.

In disturbed persons the Hd percepts approach equivalence and even exceed H, since the intellectual inferiority due to deprivation and/or impairment is pronounced. The mentally retarded, the manic, and the inhibited person will produce more human details than whole human percepts. It is important to note the part of the total H percept that is omitted.

Oligophrenic human detail — Hdx

The perception of a part where normally the entire figure is seen presages a pathological condition. It is entirely absent in the protocol of the well-adjusted person. The excited patient reports Hdx responses because of easy distractability which precludes sufficient concentration on the blot area to produce constructively. The brain-damaged and mentally retarded cannot synthesize adequately to obtain an over-all and integrated engram. The inhibited person reveals the extent of emotional constriction and limited outlook on life in the production of Hdx responses. One such response is pathologic, two are even more so. In an extremely prolific record there may be one Hdx. This is not serious, but does reveal the fact that at the extreme of productivity the testee does become constricted and ordinarily should not be pushed to the limit.

Animal — A

This category has the greatest number of acceptable possibilities, especially of the "insect" variety. The usual expectancy for A + Ad is approximately 50 per cent of the total R. The tendency to devote a great deal of energy to animal associations is one manifestation of intrapsychic sterility. It is *as if* the testee has become barren, constricted, and bereft of ideational diversity. Thus, the end product is a preponderance of associations that are easiest to make, i.e., bugs, insects, dogs, cats, and crustaceans. Before the interpreter hastens to assign a severely pathologic role because of the A contents alone, it is well to consider the following: of 24 (Beck) popular responses

(1950, pp. 280-282) ten are in the A category and the remaining 14 are distributed among six other classes.[3] The animal category offers a ready escape for the subject who feels threatened by stimuli having unacceptable portent. The retarded finds it the easiest type of percept to organize because the multiplicity of shapes and shadings inherent in the blots may be tied to an animal concept however vague or clear, especially multiformed insects and bugs. The brain-damaged need not face another failure or difficult organizing task in view of the almost limitless choices among the genera in the animal kingdom. The absence of A concepts is not unhealthy since it underscores the testee's apparent freedom from rut-like banality.[4]

Several Rorschach Test authorities (Klopfer and Davidson, 1962; W. Klopfer, 1954) develop the notion that the kind of animal reported throws light on the individual's personality. (In its popular form it is the parlor game of "what kind of animal would you like to be and why?") Aggressive tendencies, accordingly, are equated with perceiving "fierce" animals like a tiger or a lion. (This should exclude the popular bears in plate III unless this is surrounded by such characterizations as "bloody," "fighting," or "snarling.") The nonaggressive animals, lamb or sheep, reflect passive and submissive attitudes.

Animal detail—Ad

With increase in anxiety and unfavorable effects on intellectual efficiency, animal detail productivity increases. Ordinarily, these should not be more than one half the absolute number of whole animal concepts. A disproportionate amount of Ad mirrors intrapsychic inefficiency due to anxiety, morbid

[3] For the student's information: the popular responses are distributed as follows—A, 10; H, 4; Hd, 4; AObj, 3; Clo, At, and N, 1 each.

[4] Attention is directed to a paper by Goldfarb (1945a) in which he reviews the psychoanalytic references to animal symbolism.

inferiority, and marked stereotypy in thinking. In the manic reaction this reflects poor reality contact. The protocols of the schizophrenic paranoid who is actively delusional, and the latent, superficially controlled paranoid patient, will show a high Ad percentage. This is the result of marked sensitivity and suspiciousness of the environment which distorts stimuli and channelizes the perception of reality into a self-deluding system of interpretation.

Oligophrenic animal detail—Adx

Here is another pathologic index in the animal genus. This constriction factor is quite rare. Beck's Spiegel Sample gave an average of 0.13 Adx responses per record. Beck considers Adx "to be evidence of an inhibited intellectual living, result of an anxiety state."

Animal per cent—A + Ad/R or A%

This is obtained by dividing the total A and Ad associations by the total number of responses. This percentage presents the extent to which the individual is free from stereotypy in thinking. A low A percentage leaves the subject free to turn to other than banal ideation. However, the interpreter is cautioned to examine other content categories to see whether the A percentage is not being displaced by some other high percentage content classification. Spontaneity in ideation reflects lack of restraint. If the overemphasis is found in a category other than A + Ad it might suggest a trend in personality aberration as well as the nature of the pervasive ideation. The basic amount of A + Ad is 50 per cent. Above or below this ratio reflects more or less restriction in thought content and wealth of association.

(H + A):(Hd + Ad)

The intent of this formula is to ascertain the relationship of whole to part figures. From this computation the interpreter may evaluate the testee's approach to problems, the extent to which his criticalness permits the integration of details, and the degree to which he is free from constricting part views of stimuli.

This ratio usually calls for a 2 to 1 relationship for normalcy, i.e., the subject should be sufficiently free intellectually and emotionally to produce twice as many whole figures as part figures. An overemphasis of whole figure, e.g., more than twice as many H + A as Hd + Ad, indicates the tendency to approach and interpret situations from the over-all point of view, with some, but not enough, attention to the smaller aspects. In the extreme case, all H + A and none or very few Hd + Ad responses, it would seem that the subject is overlooking essential details and therefore would find difficulty in fully appreciating a total situation. Support may be found in the W-D-Dd +S distribution. If the prolific whole-figure producer shows an overemphasis of W, then the implication of reliance on total views at the expense of essential details is justified. Again, due consideration should be given to the level of form accuracy for the H and A concepts. Poor form adduces pathological organizational ability and therefore faulty over-all views. While the use of total figures points to "liberated intelligence," the prevalence of whole figures with little or no reference to details suggests too much intellectual freedom.

The converse ratio, Hd + Ad equal to or greater than H + A, is an unhealthy sign. This subject is overly critical, he is immersed in details and therefore functions in an inefficient manner because of anxiety which interferes with taking the time and making the effort to gain an over-all perspective before reacting to the situation—the approach is limited by a *pars pro toto* attitude. It is well to turn to the W-D-Dd +S allocations for further evidence of this perceptive mode. Should the D + Dd(+S) outweigh the W, the interpretive inferences just mentioned are supported. The optimal relationship is half as many details as wholes when giving human and animal concepts.

Animal Object—AObj

These responses may be considered in the total A productivity. They do not clarify the interests of the subject, but seem to render more vague the determination of his proclivities. AObj contents are found most frequently in plates IV, VI, and VII. It is not usual to find more than two such responses in a record. A protocol with more than two AObj percepts, i.e., fur rug, hearthrug, A skin, reflects an inordinate amount of dependency, and/or sensuality if the differences in shading tones (c) determine the concept.

Anatomy—At

Anatomy concepts lend themselves to easy and superficial interpretation: bodily concern, hypochondriasis, and as a manifestation of a psychophysiological involvement (somatized or conversion reaction). This may be valid in some cases, but the evidence is not yet conclusive. On the other hand, Beck et al. (1950, p. 270) report a mean of 1.55 At responses for the Spiegel Sample. The S. D. is 1.97, indicating a wide variation in the incidence of At. Rav (1951) has made a study of the anatomy responses in the Rorschach Test with some interesting results. The conclusion is: *"Anatomy responses do not indicate hypochondriasis nor intelligence-complex nor sexual fantasies. At is a result of restriction and is formed with a minimum of intellectual strain. This restriction might be in the ability sphere—feeblemindedness, or in the affective sphere—anxiety"* (p. 442). Her study population averaged 1.62 At percepts. Ordinary expectancy for At is between 1 and 2 per subject. An At response is popular in card VIII, and the "pelvic" response in plate I is not quite as popular but close to it in frequency. Rav found that plates VIII, III, I, and II accounted for 67.3 per cent of the 275 responses in her sample. On the other hand, Klopfer and Davidson (1962) find it possible to ascribe "real concern" about the body to the person who produces anatomy responses. This position is supported by W. Klopfer (1954) especially with reference to an X-ray percept. The concern need not be pathological.

This raises the question: When should At responses be considered a morbid sign? The answer is complex: (1) when At total goes beyond normal expectancy of two per protocol; (2) when a stereotyped At percept appears in several plates, usually with poor form; (3) when the At response represents a means of evasion, an intellectual "stalling" device to permit the subject to gather his wits and to organize an acceptable concept; (4) when an At response is determined by minus form accuracy, reflecting the disturbing component of the perceptual experience; and (5) when the At concept is preceded or followed by an unusual response or mode of experiencing, viz., delayed reaction time, break in the sequence, poor level and/or oddity of conceptualization ($F-$, C/F, $CF-$). In this context the At response is a manisfestation of insecurity and threat, eventuating in lowered intellectual efficiency. In the mentally retarded the overproduction of anatomy may be related to limited ability and to the ease with which these percepts are organized. Piotrowski (1957) agrees with Rav that anatomy responses suggest feelings of intellectual inferiority since "vague anatomical associations need a minimum of intellectual strain" (Rav, 1951, p. 439). Moreover, even with physicians, ". . . the symptomatic value would not change . . ." (p. 439).

In general At suggests intellectual inadequacy stemming from limited ability as a response to anxiety. However, if At percentage is high, particularly if perseverated to the extent of 15 per cent or more of the total contents, the tester should regard the possibility of an attitude of concern over body parts as a channel for emotional expression. There is reason to assume

a relationship between At preoccupation and defensiveness
against anxiety.

X ray and Relief Map

It will be recalled that these responses are perceived by projecting a two-planar dimension (spatial) onto the inkblot. The
subject is attempting to objectify by giving a frame of reference
and limits to his anxiety by reducing the vagueness of intangible distress. X-ray responses disclose the experience of
anxiety. Closely tied to this, in terms of the experiential dynamics, is the topographical map percept which also employs
the differences in achromatic and chromatic shading. In the
chromatic plates anxiety is more prominent when the testee
either denies color or avoids its use in formulating the shaded
response. Feelings of insecurity are so pervasive that they interfere with the subject's ability to respond to his external world
with healthy emotionality. In this content category (and the
cloud and vista responses discussed below) the experience of
ambivalence and unattached anxiety limits the richness of
association of ideas in which the subject may indulge himself.
The result is banal, evasive, and intellectually inferior productivity.

Clouds — Cl

This response mirrors unattached, vague, free-floating anxiety. A cloud percept in plate VII is not unusual and therefore contributes less to an interpretation of disabling un-
attached anxiety than a similar percept in other cards. In this
concept the testee is extending his experience of intangible insecurity and unreasoning restlessness into the nebulousness of
an unstructured and "unholdable" interpretation — cloud.
More than one such response is uncommon. The protocol of an
adjusted person may show a Cl response in plate VII. As such it
generally reflects the usual anxiety attendant upon any testing

situation. It assumes significant proportions if given more often in the other cards.

Vista

The introduction of perspective, or distance, into a percept suggests the testee's need to stand off in an attempt to analyze his experience of anxiety more objectively. This rationale, of a more objective and more impersonal approach, reflects the testee's efforts to cope with these feelings. The absence of FK-determined concepts does not invariably imply a pathologic handling of anxiety and/or lack of insight. Unwholesome inwardly channelized thinking (autistic) may be seen in the presence of three or more vista responses.

Blood—Bl

This is a pathological response. It points to an uncontrolled and poorly assimilated use of the color value of the inkblot stimulus. It is an indication of the extent to which the subject is disturbed by emotion-provoking forces in the social milieu. Almost invariably it is a pure color concept with the affective and immature behavioral implications of this type of experience. Usual expectancy is none; one or more blood responses are increasingly unhealthy. Some subjects mask the full impact by qualifying the Bl engram as "menstruation" or "dried blood." The former reveals the sexual concern of the testee, while the latter mirrors the subject's attempt to "bind" his anxiety. "Blood dripping," "blood splashing," on the other hand, disclose the violent nature of the patient's reaction to disturbing associations. Essentially, the affective state has resolved itself into a tension system that is coming to the level of awareness, much to the patient's increasing acute distress.

Object—Obj

There does not seem to be a generalized approach to the symbolism of this category. The bedpost in plate VI, the pillow in card VIII, or the airplane in the first plate do not seem to be topically significant. Again, a totem pole concept in plate VI may be an acceptable symbol suggesting the socially refined manner of dealing with sex concepts. For the analytically oriented this is an accepted truism. It has been suggested (Lindner, 1947) that Obj category is the refuge of those who wish to remain noncommittal.

Architecture — Arch

Percepts of this nature are uncommon. When given it may be in response to the upper detail (D4) of plate II — a castle, and the minaret or spire in plate VII (D8). Religiosity is suggested by the "church" percept or some part of a place for worship.

Design — Des

This category may include artistic productions, insignia, and references to numbers and letters. The latter are not usually the product of normal perception. Distanciation from reality interpretation results in ascribing number and letter forms to portions of the blot. "Dot" responses are described for the many specks in plate I. Since these are minute (Dd) details they are experienced by the meticulous, compulsive testee who is manifesting his need to encompass as much of the blot as possible. The mentally retarded may point to these articulated spots to satisfy his need to achieve in compliance with the tester's directions. The elated patient finds delight in distorting these minutiae and ascribing to them far-fetched meanings.

Symmetry responses may be included in this category. The pedantic person who is concerned with the necessity to see all will usually describe to the tester the symmetrical or assymmetrical features of the plates. When this remark comes first in a card it suggests a device to gain time, i.e., the subject is being cautious and prefers to enter the situation after he has gained some semblance of its fuller appreciation. This approach to a complex and unfamiliar problem is healthy and acts as a deterrent on impulsivity. When it occurs late in a given card it may emphasize the compulsive component in the personality, to make certain that all possible aspects of the situation have been noted and utilized.

Nature, Geography, Plant—N, Geo, Pl

The frequency of these percepts varies. Their significance lies in the determinants of each response. Form, color, shading, and achromatic hues, singly and in combination, reflect the subject's mode of experiencing and organizing the inkblot stimuli. Content interpretation in this category is usually of much less significance than the real carriers of portent—the determinants. Unless there is overemphasis, and therefore pervasive preoccupation, the one or two percepts of this class occurring in a protocol do not have unusual topical meanings per se.

Fire, Explosion

The pathologic nature of this specific percept lies in the lack of emotional control implied in the violent experience of the red areas of the inkblots. This is an excellent channel for expressing aggressive feelings and "world destruction" fantasies. These are not healthy percepts both from the point of view of determinants and personal meaning.

Mask

The dynamic meaning of this response is ascribed to a need to hide, to present a facade to the world. This involves the ability, real or desired, to beguile. Deliberate deceit may or may not be involved. It occurs most often in response to the first plate, and less frequently a mask is seen in the center portion of plate IX. When given in other plates this need is more strongly suggested, especially if it precedes or follows a disturbing response.[5]

Clothing — Clo

This may disclose the pressure for conformity with the demands of society. Elaborate descriptions of clothing point to the testee's emphasis on social living, extraversive and perhaps exhibitionistic trends.

In plate III the absence of clothing, i.e., describing the human figures as lacking in clothing, suggests a mode of handling sexual attitudes less encumbered by social restraint. This does not mean that the subject is actually less inhibited behaviorally, he may be so, but it may reflect the subject's attitude on an ideational level only. The question of "would do or should do" is best answered by life history.

Sex

Shaw (1949) and Pascal et al. (1950) have investigated the problem of sex productivity in the Rorschach. Both generally agree with regard to the inkblot areas which elicit sex-related percepts. With slight differences each study presents a total of male and female genital responses. These percepts emerged either under testing-the-limits pressure (Pascal) or in an experimental situation "with a given mental set for producing sex-content responses" (Shaw, 1949, p. 466).[6] These two studies disclose that subjects are able to give sex percepts when directed to do so.[7] In the main or free-association stage the usual expectancy for sex content is less than one per record. This is

[5] In plate VII, with the card reversed, the testee may see the center dark detail (D6) as a "vagina" and immediately follow with, "This (D4) reminds me of a mask, but there are no holes for the eyes. It might be a sleeping mask to cover the eyes." The implications are somewhat clear!

[6] Actually, this is a form of testing the limits but outside of the standard Rorschach administration context.

[7] Pascal et al. do not feel that this procedure is in any way disturbing to the subject.

Beck's (1950, p. 271) rationale: "The mean for sex content in the normal (Spiegel) sample turned out very low, 0.03. The actual number of overt sexual associations among the 157 individuals was 4. This need occasion no surprise. The censor is operating. This is no doubt an established habit in a normal population sample on the topic of sex. The significance of this low figure will be more apparent when the statistics for neurotic and schizophrenic groups are established."[8]

The value of the sex response is solely for diagnostic classification. The interpreter should look for the manner in which the testee handles these ideas. Predominance of sex-tinged percepts is interpretively similar to the overemphasis of any other content category. If normal expectancy is one or less per record, then two or more suggest an undue preoccupation with such thoughts. Crude and vulgar expressions reflect the grossness of sexual ideation; disguised or more restrained sex references indicate a more mature and socially acceptable way of handling sex attitudes. It should not be assumed that the presence of sexual ideas is a priori evidence of pathologic thinking or activity. The contextual determinants and the level of form accuracy enter into the evaluation of the wholesomeness of these engrams.

Popular Responses—P

The extent to which the testee can relate his perceptions to those of his group reveals his sameness to group experience. In other words, social conformity, compliance with socially established thinking, and the acceptance of this code of reality living, are reflected in the popular responses given to the ink blot stimuli.

A normal protocol, indicating ability to accept the expec-

---

[8] Some of the statistics have been published. Pascal and his co-workers (p. 287) write: "The difference between means for male and female subjects is not statistically significant. The differences between diagnostic groups [neurotics and psychotics] was also found to be not statistically significant."

tancies of the social milieu, should have between 20 and 30 per cent P concepts. This applies to a record of 30 to 60 associations. (As an absolute number, in records below 25 responses there should be at least 4 P's. In excess of 60 responses the percentage does not hold.) More than 30 per cent P engrams points to a prosaic outlook from which may be inferred an inability or lack of desire to stray from the beaten path. The higher the P percentage the more "clicheish," banal, and socially stereotyped the person's thinking. The individual is too steeped in sterile reality at the expense of flexibility and creativity of thought and perhaps action.

An underproduction of popular concepts may point either to originality with or without minimal social conformity, or to a pathologic disregard for society's demands. The latter may be characteristic of the protocol produced by the mentally retarded, the markedly anxious individual, or the psychotic who is tenuously tied to reality. The oligophrenic is unable to handle the inkblots acceptably due to limited experiences, while the anxious person is so ego-involved that he either rejects his need to conform or deliberately chooses to minimize involvement with his social world.

If the popular concepts are forthcoming in the Inquiry or limits-testing phases, it would seem as though the testee is either above banality and has to be prodded into typical perception, or familiarity with situations results in the expected responses to stimuli. The greater the pressure necessary to elicit the popular concepts (see next two sections) the less stereotyped is the individual. This does not necessarily imply that the subject is not in touch with reality; it may disclose the nonconformity of the extremely intelligent person who approaches "average" behavior expectancy only when it is called to his attention as in testing the limits. On the other hand, it may reveal the extent to which the subject has to be prodded in order to bring him into contact with the real world, as in the extremely anxious and psychotic person.

THE POPULAR RESPONSES

Some responses have a fourth symbol in the scoring scheme. These percepts have an unusually high frequency of occurrence and are labeled popular or P responses. Because frequency and good form-level accuracy are the criteria for these percepts, the list is bound to change with the accumulation of protocols. Beck (1950, pp. 196-199), Klopfer and Kelley (1942, pp. 179-181), and Hertz (1970) differ in their lists of popular responses. There are many concepts common to different lists and some concepts which appear in only particular lists as populars. Experience has led to the acceptance of the following as popular responses (Figure 15):

Card I: W — as bat, butterfly, moth, batman.
C — (Beck's D4) — center detail as human figure, usually female.

Card II: W — as two humans, usually clowns or female figures.
S + S — entire black portion of the design as two dogs or two bears up to the shoulders or entire animals.
D3 — as butterfly.

Card III: S + S — both side black details seen as two humans.
D3 — center red as bowtie or ribbon bow.

Card IV: W — as an animal skin, bear skin, hearthrug.
D6 — lower side detail(s) seen as boot(s) or shoe(s).

Card V: W — as bat, moth, or butterfly ∧∨ .
D1 — as human or animal leg(s).

Card VI: W or D1 — perceived as an animal skin, hide, animal rug, or hearthrug.

Card VII: W, or D1, or D2 — seen as humans, usually girls or women.

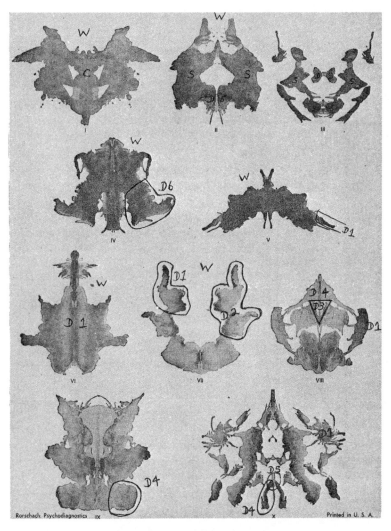

FIGURE 15

Location of Popular Responses
By courtesy of Hans Huber, Publishers, Berne, from Rorschach,
Psychodiagnostics.
The letters and numbers, D1, D3, etc., refer to Beck's numbering system.
See text for details (Beck, 1950, pp. 30-35.)

Card VIII: D1 — side detail as four-legged animal.
D3 — with or without space, seen as ribs or rib case of a body.
D4 — top gray detail seen as a tree or bush.
Card IX: D4 — lower side pink detail described as a man's head, usually that of Mark Twain, sometimes Santa Claus.
Card X: D1 — side blue detail seen as a crab, octopus, spider.
D5 — center bottom light gray as a rabbit's head.
D4 — center bottom green detail as caterpillar, worm, or snake.

The basis for popular frequency is the appearance of the concept in one out of every five records. Those appearing less frequently, but not rarely, are known as usual details and are not assigned any particular symbol.

Original Response — O

Concept-contents which appear once in approximately one hundred records are called original, O, responses. Hertz (1970) indicates original responses in her frequency tables. Basically, however, it remains for the beginner to accumulate a minimum of one hundred protocols before having an appreciation of the meaning of an O response. The O should be followed by a + or − in accordance with the form-level accuracy of the blot and the percept. Some of the fantastic productions of the psychotic and the inadequate perceptions of the deficient person are O −.

These concepts are the product of high intellectual ability, or the bizarre interpretations of the psychotic, or the distorted productions of the retarded and encephalopathic patient. In the record of the well-adjusted individual the original responses are characterized by accurate form (F +). In the disturbed, retarded, and brain-damaged patient the original concepts are poorly formed (F—) and are usually located in the Dr and Dd areas of the blots. In all instances O responses reveal an ability to deviate from the usual pattern of experiencing and behaving. O's produced only in the inquiry or limits-testing stages may be related to the subject's lack of confidence in his own ability; such responses are indicative of his need for the assurance of familiarity and permissiveness that characterized the later phases of the Rorschach testing situation, in order that he may produce creatively.

CRITIQUE

This chapter must certainly pose the issues of the validity and reliability of content usage in the interpretation of the record. Wittenborn's (1949) factorial approach appears to be as arbitrary as that of the extremely orthodox psychoanalytically inclined symbolist. Whereas Wittenborn seeks to achieve homogeneity and label it consistency, the symbolist utterly disregards the phenomenon of homogeneity and focuses on the individual, seemingly *in vacuo*. A point of view discussed by Hsu (1947, pp. 129-130) may help the beginner: "On the other hand [in contrast to factor analysis], there is a school of thought which represents the extreme psychologists and analytical therapists who refuse to take seriously the face value of a person's responses to a Rorschach plate, but insist on discovering its symbolic significance. According to this type of thinking, not only is one individual different from another but the same individual on one occasion is also different in himself from another occasion. The symbolic meaning of each response of an individual can be evaluated only according to that individual's past personal experiences and emotional background, and his experiences alone." Hsu prefers to equate the end product of numeration processes with (sterile) consistency while overlooking a basic tenet in personality theory, viz., that an individual's behavior will be consistent in terms of his own needs, tensions, and aspirations. Certainly the *verbal* symbols may differ from time to time.

The issues of validity and reliability in personality evaluation will have to seek for new modes of expression and solution in terms of behavior dynamics and concepts rather than the sameness of verbal reports and the face value of responses. When the sole aim in personality testing is to establish quantitative norms it becomes necessary to minimize the interrelationships among the discrete elements. There is no quarrel with quantification per se, but it must be recognized that the datum of the Rorschach investigation does not readily lend itself to measurement as does the length of a table or a pound of meat.

How shall the examiner know. By asking the subject rather than relying on unproved generalizations. Beck (1952, pp. 64-65) agrees with this rationale and relies on the clinical acumen of the experienced observer. He concludes: ". . . . in all instances I look on the theme as lead, not finding. It is an arrow directing the investigator or therapist to a personality area which he is to explore directly in the patient."

Chapter 22

THE CARDS AND THEIR MEANINGS

There seems to be agreement among Rorschach workers that the structure, achromatic, and chromatic hues and tones of the inkblots usually elicit common associations from subjects. This is demonstrated in the unique significance given to the popular responses. In addition to these commonly reported engrams, it is recognized that each blot engenders some characteristic ideas and feelings as the testee reacts to it. These associations (of the subject's reactions to the blots as a whole) are over and above such definite responses as "bat" to plates I and V, "animal skin" to plates IV and VI; more specifically, these are expressed as "a kind of feeling" or "train of ideas" aroused by the total blot upon exposure to it, viz., plate IV may represent an "authoritative figure" because of the looming quality of the blot.

Several studies report findings in regard to this aspect of the Rorschach Inkblots. Sanderson (1952) asked his subjects "to give each card a title" after the standard administration, inquiry, and testing the limits. He utilized this technique as an extension of the limits-testing phase with this rationale: "The shift in content is particularly interesting in those cases where the subject shows visible discomfort and anxiety during association, but still comes out with relatively innocuous responses, only to reveal the true meaning of the blot when requested to give it a label" (p. 28). This new task imposes on the testee an integrative assignment which calls for a review of the plate in terms of its total effect upon him rather than as a series of impressions or engrams. Rejection of the instructions to label a particular card, despite concepts given in the free association stage, may indicate that the subject can deal with parts of problems so long as he can avoid the self-concept-threatening aspects of the total situation. The advantage of the "label technique" is illustrated by Sanderson (p. 28): " A case in point is a young man who after struggling with card IV for some time produced such associations as 'insect crawling out' and 'line in the middle,' only to reveal his feeling toward the paternal image by labeling the entire card as 'Monster.' "

In a footnote Sanderson supports his reference to the "paternal image" with this statement: "According to some Rorschachers card IV brings forth associations that are psychologically connected with one's relationships and attitudes toward the father image (p. 28, n1). Halpern (1953) and Bochner and Halpern (1945, p. 81) agree that, "The heavy male figure may suggest the father or authority in general. . . ." The evidence for this general interpretation is clinical rather than experimental. However, Meer and Singer (1950) and Rosen (1951) have tested statements such as this with some interesting results. Meer and Singer investigated Bochner and Halpern's contention that plate IV represents the "father or authority figure" and that plate VII is identified by subjects as having "a feminine quality frequently with maternal applications" or the "mother" card. Fifty male college students were administered the standard Rorschach with additional instructions to designate a "Mother card and a Father card." Plate IV was identified as the "Father card" at the .01 level of confidence. Plates VII and X shared election as the "Mother card" both at the .05 level of confidence. Cards IV and VII were also regarded as the "best liked" cards by those students who chose these two as the "father" and "mother" cards. Rosen studied the symbolic meanings in the Rorschach plates "by a questionnaire which asked the subjects to choose, from among the ten Rorschach cards, that card which most nearly brought to mind the feeling or association of a male sex organ, masculine aggression, authority, father symbol, mother symbol, and family symbol, respectively" (1951, p. 239). Card IV was overwhelmingly associated with "masculine aggression" and "feeling of authority," while plate VII showed up clearly as the "mother symbol."

These few attempts to obtain controlled experimental evidence of the reactions of subjects to the Rorschach plates seem to support the findings in extensive clinical observations reported by those who have worked with this technique and have compiled responses and related feelings in psychological reports and at staff conferences. It is true that this compilation has been somewhat unorganized, that the reports have been passed on as information admittedly without experimental validity, yet this *clinical* evidence is being increasingly accepted by clinical psychologists and utilized in personality evaluation.

There are reports of several studies which have assessed the feelings, attitudes, and reactions of persons to the ten cards. Bochner and Halpern (1945), W. Klopfer (1954), Charen (1957), and Hirschenstein and Rabin (1955) obtained plate-significances from adults, while Halpern (1953) and Levy (1958) recorded the reactions of children to the plates. In essence, these investigations were concerned with the significances the cards held for their respective subjects. Most of the results yielded intercard meaning differences with the exceptions of Charen's. His findings indicated that the patient population used all ten cards as "father" or "mother" cards at one time or another. An indirect approach to ascertaining the meaning of the plates to testees is the semantic differential method. Little (1959) and Rabin (1959) employed this technique with results discussed below.

The following compilation is representative of the observations of the author and other Rorschach workers.[1] Beck's area numbers are used throughout.

CARD I

To the naive subject this represents an entirely new situation and therefore serves as an excellent indication of the effect of novel problems on the subject — especially when there are no familiar clues to serve as guides. Thus, the testee is literally thrown on his own resources for seeking out untried methods of problem solving in order to comply with the instructions (also see Alcock, 1963). The degree of organization and the alacrity with which this takes place in this circumstance will be reflected in the first concept and the reaction time. The possibilities are many, but these four loom largest: (1) an immediate good response; (2) an immediate poor response; (3) a delayed good response; and (4) a delayed poor response. The inferences respectively are: (1) A healthy constructive approach to new problems and confidences in one's own ability to cope with novel complexities. (2) This characterizes the impulsive doer; there is a need to comply as quickly as possible regardless of the quality of compliance. The motive may be quality ambition. The same performance may be given by the intellectually inferior person who believes his production to be good. (3) The

[1] At this point the mixture of logic and psychologic must certainly be at odds with the precise thinking of the experimentalist. Unfortunately, quantitative techniques and scientific constructs have not kept pace with developments in the understanding of behavior dynamics. This is no plea for discarding the scientific method. But it does seem necessary at this time to call to the attention of the rigid experimentalist that the whole issue of scientific methodology should be opened for rediscussion. In the context of dealing with the problems of people the traditional approaches are not quite satisfactory. It is time to examine new and more flexible attitudes toward gathering behavioral data and drawing inferences therefrom. In sum, the seemingly uncontrolled method of clinical observation appears to be in conflict with the rigorous demands of the scientific method. Is this actually the case?

ability to demur may reflect either the thinker, the person who prefers to examine a situation before plunging into it, or one who is habitually slow in responding (look for over-all slow average reaction time), or the person whose receptive and/or expressive processes are being interfered with by emotional and/or intellectual factors. (4) This would be the mode of responding usually seen in the markedly disturbed and deficient testee. Bell (1948, p. 119) ascribes rejection of plate I to "difficulty in adjustment to the test situation; possible shading shock." This refers to the subject's reactivity to the dark-light properties of the inkblot which, in the case of the neurotically disturbed, results in one or a combination of shading shock responses.[2]

The following ideas occurred to Rosen's (1951) subjects upon exposure to card I: "Night time. . . . Masculine aggression. . . . Feeling of Authority . . . . and Family symbol . . . ." (pp. 241-242).[3] In other words, these ideas categorize feeling

---

[2] The literature reports many indices of inefficiency accompanying the experience of the disturbing components of the inkblot — color and shading. These reactions are somewhat identical for both color and shading stimuli. The following are abstracted from a study by Allen, Manne, and Stiff (1952, p. 237): "1. Exclamations and emotional comments. 2. Refusals. . . .3. Decline in number of responses. . . . 6. Decline in F + ... 7. Decline in W . . . . 9. Decreased popular responses. . . . 10. Long reaction-time. . . . 11. Very short reaction time. . . . 12. Impoverished content. . . ." The student should reread the opening paragraph to Chapter 8 and the journal articles referred to therein.

[3] Klopfer and Davidson (1962, pp. 150-153) offer many aids for a sequential analysis of the Rorschach protocol based on: "a. The reaction time to each card. b. The variation and succession of form levels within a card. c. The content succession within a card. d. The color dynamics. e. The shading dynamics. f. The use of areas symbolic of sex. g. The intercard sequence in terms of formal and content categories. h. The handling of popular responses." The beginner is urged to read Klopfer's analysis of the plates. This technique should be used only after extensive experience with the more formal method of protocol interpretation based on the evaluation of the Location, Determinant, Content, and computational data. There is the danger of depending too much on easier so-called common sense and symbolism than on the more difficult grasp of the test elements and their interrelationships.

tones transcendental to the individual percepts reported by the subject. Whether or not the interpreter is justified in making use of these too-inclusive higher-order abstractions depends on the set of concepts which he brings with him into the clinical situation.[4] At least these are suggestive of attitudes that may require further probing by therapist or social worker.

In the middle third of this blot (D4) there is the popular H concept which has some interesting speculative possibilities. The subject's self-percept, or a facet of his attitudes regarding himself in a world of people, may be revealed in the nature of the human identification he makes. If the human figure is accompanied by kinesthetic tension or movement, the likelihood of his response bearing a direct self-reference is increased (Halpern, 1953). Self-devaluation may be reflected in a disparaging description of the figure. Feelings for dependency are experienced in the human as a supplicant. The role in life, as conceived by the subject, will usually be manifested in the response to this area of the inkblot.

The author agrees with Alcock (1963) who suggests that the testee's reactions (in terms of the formal *and* nonformal aspects of the verbal report) to the middle third as a female figure may contain clues to the ability to handle sex-related connotations. How does the person deal with the nudity that may be engendered by the transparency of the lower portion of the female figure in the plate? How are the "breast-like areas" perceived, if at all? Disturbance may be manifested by any one of a combination of complex indicators — poor form, denial in the Inquiry stage, use of shading determinants (with form secondary, etc.). Card I does invite disturbance.

Sequential analysis should be used *to supplement* rather than supplant the more formal evaluation of the personality as revealed in the scoring and their respective ratios.

[4] The author wishes to make it patently clear that this material, if used unwisely, will strengthen the attitude held by many regarding the cultish flavor of the Rorschach specifically and the projective method generally.

Card II

Rosen (1951, p. 241) finds that this card engenders associations of "human beings" (a popular response), "animals" (also P), and "emotional security." The closest to a rationale proposed by Rosen is this: "Emotional security, on the other hand, was associated with cards II and VII. *It is not clear what stimulus aspects of these cards motivated the choices"* (italics added). In regard to card II this reaction may be explained by the initial impact of the red area, its arousal of sexual ideation due to its position and form, and the attendant conflict that affects emotional security.[5] Bell (1948, p. 119) attributes rejection of this plate to "initial color shock." Experimental evidence suggests an alternate consideration, viz., that the color *plus* the structure (form) of the blot leading to these initially unacceptable ideas may be responsible for any deviation in responsiveness (Allen, Stiff, and Rosenzweig, 1953).

Card II, then, gives some insight into the subject's reaction to particularly disturbing stimuli based on the unique combination of the red color and form so distributed as to engender, in the sexually conflicted individual, overt manifestations of concern. The plate is highly charged for both male and female sexuality (D4, Ds5, and Dd24) so that the person who is sensitive to this type of conflict would give some sign or signs of this feeling.

---

[5] This is the core of the explanation given by several writers. Bochner and Halpern (1945, pp. 79-80) state: "The bright, splashy red incorporates an emotionally charged situation, pleasant or unpleasant, as the case may be. To most persons it represents danger, excitement, sex. . . . For some people, this card has particularly strong sexual implications. The white space surrounded by the black suggests the female genitalia. To some, e.g., homosexuals, this constitutes a sexual problem. To others, this female symbol relates to the mother, and the situation thus pivots about this relationship." In her book, Halpern (1953) strongly supported her earlier position, now fortified by years of clinical observations. Klopfer avers: "There are areas in this card often associated with sexual material. . . ."

The presence of the popular engrams — human and animals — discloses the extent of reality contact, conformity, and divulges the measure of recoverability available to an emotionally disturbed subject. The omission of the H concept in the free-association stage implies an interference with the testee's ability to make proper interpersonal ties. This impairment is also a function of how healthy or derogated the H concept may be. If the P responses are forthcoming in the Inquiry the inference may be made that the testee can recover from an initial upset and function acceptably in a more permissive and familiar atmosphere.

CARD III

Human identification is easily made in this plate, since it is an extremely popular reaction. All of Rosen's (1951) subjects associated "human being" in this card at the .0001 level of confidence. The absence of a human association is more pathological in this plate than in card II. Such exclusion emphasizes the subject's reluctance and/or inability to accept the implications of interpersonal identifications and relationships. The nature of the response to the usual H area, D1, will reveal the testee's attitude toward himself and/or others in his world. The use of, and the nature of, movement in connection with the human figure is also significant of self-perception.

This plate, according to Rorschach authorities, will reveal the extent to which an individual does recover from the disturbance engendered in plate II (if such did occur), or the degree to which the increasing conflict (inherent in the subject's continued experience of and reaction to the human figure and/or the red color) will eventuate in unwholesome responsiveness which is characteristic of his mode of adjustment under such circumstances. Another important consideration is the fact that the subject should be urged to identify the sex of the two figures.[6] In card II the significance of the sex identity is not as important as in card III. In the former, sexual confusion is readily covered up by emphasizing the lack of decisive body-structure cues. The subject may point to the clothing worn by the figures and easily justify male "clowns wearing baggy and colored costumes," or female figures such as "witches" because of the same ill-fitting colored costumes. In card III this rationalization cannot be advanced, and the subject should be required to establish the sex of the human figures on the basis of definite clues to such identification as are seen in the structure of the inkblot. Thus, the process by which the sex of the figure is established may disclose the presence, and perhaps the nature, of a sexual conflict. Lindner (1946) joins Klopfer (1949) in attributing to this plate a means of ascertaining sexual attitudes: "Card III — Homosexuals of either sex show confusion in assigning sex to the forms, being troubled by protuberances in the 'chest' region" (Lindner, 1946, p. 123). Klopfer (p. 7) writes: "Attribution of both male and female characteristics to the figures is, of course, an indicator of confusion regarding sex within the subject himself."[7] This is a widely accepted interpretation.

Card IV

Meer and Singer (1950, p. 482), and Rosen (1951, pp. 241-242) support the clinical observation that this plate elicits associations of "Father symbol," "Male sex organ," "Masculine aggression," and "Feeling of authority." Bochner and Halpern (1945, p. 81) believe that, "The heavy male figures may suggest the father or authority in general; this may be pleasant or unpleasant." Beck (1950, p. 198) stresses that the perception of

---

[6] The technique for this may be found in Chapter 20.

[7] The author urges using extreme caution and supportive evidence before attaching labels to subjects.

this blot as a "gorilla is popular. . . . A human form in itself . . . . giant, is not P." It would appear from these reports that there is wide recognition of the threatening aspect of this blot, particularly if the concept employs the shading tones, usual anxiety indicators. The tester should look for shading shock signs as tokens of the extent to which the subject is reacting emotionally to the "father" or "authoritative" associations elicited by this plate. Poor performance as manifested by F —, change in sequence, resorting to Dd or Dr in place of a healthy W, etc., do suggest to the interpreter that the testee's attitude in regard to what the father figure symbolizes (both toward the subject himself and/or toward significant persons in his environment) is in need of further scrutiny. In sum, the chief contribution of this plate for sequential analysis is to make accessible the individual's attitude, reaction, and adjustment to authority, the father figure.

The "father," "authority figure," and related significances have been widely researched. Hirschenstein and Rabin (1955) confirm the symbolization of the male parental figure by this plate. Levy (1958), using children as subjects, reported that plate IV was viewed as the male and father card. However, this was followed closely by the designation of plate VI as having male attributes. The semantic differential method employed by Rabin (1959), yielded "opposite meanings" for plates IV and VII. The former (plate IV) was seen as unpleasant, sinister, and generally in a negative vein. If this plate, according to Rabin, is not the father card, it does reflect a reaction toward the authoritarian figure. Rabin goes further in his interpretive caution to indicate that he has not validated the "father" symbolism, but he has confirmed the "masculinity" and "danger" signification of this plate (*in contrast to* the "feminine" and "security" representation of plate VII). Alcock (1963) suggests that the "father" engram elicited by this plate is not a tender one. This is attributable to the inherent massive and darkly achromatic structure of the blot design. Zelen and Sechrest

(1963) report a favorable association between this plate and the "father" idea, *along with* the same association for plate VII! While the literature does not show complete agreement, the evidence cited does warrant the interpretation of maleness and responsivity to the authoritarian engram in the phenomenal field of the testee.

CARD V

This is a buffer experience. The inkblot is simplest to organize as a W (Ranzoni, Grant and Ives, 1950, pp. 119, 132) and usually relieves tensions that have been accruing in the previous cards. This experimentally and clinically validated finding imposes serious implications on the rejection of this plate or the inability to report the extremely popular A response. The compact achromatic hue may play a role in its rejection or inferiority of productivity. Bell, and Bochner and Halpern agree on the potential effects of dark or "black shock" for the disturbed patient. Klopfer (1949, p. 8) calls attention to another possible reaction to area D 10: " An opportunity for the expression of aggression is also given by various animal responses, as the crocodile heads at the sides of the cards." Clinical observation by the author poses the feasibility of considering castration ideas in the subject's use of area D9 as pliers, scissors, or any other instrument that can mutilate by squeezing the "handles" together.

CARD VI

This plate is highly charged for male and female sexuality. Neither of these are popular responses. Probably it is well to recall Beck's admonition to the effect that sex concepts are not ordinarily voiced in our culture. Rosen's men and women students (1951, pp. 241-242) associated this card with "Male sex organ," and "Female sex organ," while only the men characterized this plate as "Feeling of authority" and "Father symbol." The latter two associated ideas were not as prevalent as the sexual connotations. Meer and Singer (1950) did not find significant "Mother" and "Father" associations with this card. Bell (1948, p. 119) attributes rejection of this plate to "sexual shock or texture shock." Little (1959) reports that his subjects identified this plate with those words on the semantic differential scale which were associated directly and indirectly with the "father" symbolization. Levy, as previously indicated, found this card to be almost as indicative as plate IV of the "male" and "father" memory picture. The author believes that these latter results are overt and socially acceptable expressions of male sexuality.

Card VII

Two ideas seem to predominate when subjects are questioned in regard to their immediate reaction to this plate: (1) "Mother" card, "Mother symbol" and (2) "Clouds," "Emotional security," and "Emotional insecurity" (Rosen, 1951, p. 241). This is an interesting combination of associations. While there may be an escape from the accumulation of "dark" or "black" shock, the disturbed anxious person finds other sources for arousing his concern. These are found in the shades of gray in D6 or in D 10, suggesting sex-related ideas. The light achromatic color and vague form engender a feeling of not being able to take hold—intangibility—which is characteristic of free-floating anxiety. The popular female percept elicited by the upper third or two-thirds of the blot at D1 or D2 is another potential source for the arousal of anxiety. This may be related to the "mother" or "mother surrogate" engram such as wife, girl friend, sister, or the feminine component of the testee's self-concept. A feeling of anxiety may be engendered by any one or a combination of these three loaded components of the blot.

The "Emotional security" and "Emotional insecurity" reported by Rosen's subjects may be related to female sexuality, the "mother" association, and the attendant or subsequent anxiety. The "Cloud" response is not unusual for this plate, so that an inference of anxiety is somewhat mollified. However, if these responses are accompanied by signs of discomfort and/or decrease in the quality of responsiveness the disturbing interaction of the suggested ideas (mother, sexuality, anxiety thoughts and feelings) assumes a more seriously adverse meaning.

Recent investigations affirm the emotional "security" (Rabin, 1959) and "mother" (Little, 1959; and Hirschenstein and Rabin, 1955) symbolizations in this plate. Two dissenting findings are reported by Levy (1958) and Zelen and Sechrest (1963). Alcock writes that the denotation of "mother card" to this plate "has considerable justification" since it often elicits mother-child associations.

Card VIII

Definite ideational association does not seem to be a factor in this plate for adults. Halpern (1953) assigns it a more significant role for young children because of the popular animal response and the nature of movement involved. Its most prominent feature lies in the possible impact of the colors on the perceiver. It is not a difficult card, and even the disturbed person should be able to use the well-articulated details to organize a response. The animals of D1 are the second most popular concept in the ten plates. Therefore, failure to elicit this in the main stage or to accept it in testing the limits points to a seriously disturbed and impaired efficiency in the face of an emotion-provoking train of ideas. Most Rorschach workers ascribe this to the engrams engendered by the multicolored areas which the subject is unable to handle adequately. Rejection of this card, coming as it does after four achromatic plates, is attributed to color disturbance. The nature of the determinants of the responses will disclose the extent to which the subject is able to cope with his emotional experiences in an interpersonal relationship. Flights into reality produce poorly assimilated and organized color-determined concepts. Rejection of this plate or the use of form alone unfolds the degree of personal involvement with others that the testee is desirous and/or capable of making. The sequential purpose of this plate is to ascertain how the testee adjusts to an abrupt change in visual stimulation, from achromatic to chromatic with its implications for the affective reactivity of the person.

Card IX

This is a difficult card to handle since the color-form combination does not lend itself to ready organization. Rejection of this plate is not uncommon among normal persons. The author has devised a method of differentiating, to some degree, between the delaying affect of the color and the intellectual difficulty of organizing the whole or details into an acceptable percept (Allen, 1948). That this should occur in view of the ease with which this plate is articulated into three distinct areas (orange, green, and pink) is quite interesting. The orange area, D3, the small pink detail between the D10 areas, and the accumulation of color impact on the subject contribute to the difficulty in dealing with this plate. The orange D3 presents an excellent opportunity for the arousal of derogated human associations in the subject who finds making interpersonal ties troublesome. The pink area between both D 10's is a sex popular which may stir up topical implications regarding the acceptability of such ideas. These two ideas occurring either separately or together account for the distress subjects experience in responding to this plate.

Card X

Lindner reports that, "This card is surprisingly sterile for content analysis" (1946, p. 128). Meer and Singer's (1950) study group labeled this plate as one of the two "mother" cards, while Rosen's subjects associated ideas of "Emotional security" and "Family symbol" with it. This feeling and conception revolve around the large pink areas, D9, which afford the perceiver an opportunity to identify himself as a child with its concomitant feelings of emotional dependence and reactions thereto. The ease with which details are organized decreases the subject's anxiety in complying with the tester's instructions, hence the feeling of emotional security. The rejection of this plate is serious because its structure invites responsiveness. The accumulation of color discomfort may manifest itself in decreased efficiency of production or, if the subject does have the capacity for demurring, he may recover sufficiently to perform more effectively. The latter, of course, is a favorable sign. Finally, this plate is so scattered it requires a high level of intellectual ability to produce a good W. Therefore, a W elicited by this inkblot discloses the effectiveness with which the testee can organize his experiences constructively and wholesomely. A poor W concept may mirror a quality drive or ambition to produce on a high level despite limited ability to do so. This is suggestive of a compulsive and rigid adherence to the self-percept.

Summary

This completes the analysis of the test plates. The suggestions given for each card should serve only as clues to be used *after* evaluating Location-Determinants-Content data. Sequential analysis should *not* replace formal analysis but should serve only as a final over-all review of the subject's conceptualizations and recourse to mechanisms for adjusting. Personality evaluation, based on clinical observation, has outstripped the rigid constructs of the more formal requirements of the experimental method. Is the one less scientific than the other in view of the subject matter.?

Chapter 23

TESTING THE LIMITS

INTRODUCTION

In the Main or free-association stage, the spontaneous reactions give insight into the more readily available facets of the personality structure. It would be interesting, indeed, to probe into those responses that are symptomatic of deeper-lying dynamics and of anxiety producing material not near the surface and consequently not easily accessible. Klopfer and Kelley (1942, p. 51) write: "In the testing-the-limits phase . . . the examiner exerts pressure in a systematic and controlled way in order to provoke reactions in directions avoided or not clarified by the subject in his spontaneous reactions." This phase of the testing is flexible and permits complete freedom of questioning since the answers are not scored. The ttl (testing the limits) data are treated qualitatively as expressions ordinarily hidden from observation. The essential point to this testing phase is the opportunity offered to clear up doubtful and nebulous angles of the test. It is as if the subject has been given one "last chance" to declare all.

The ttl is utilized for supplementing the richness or improverishment of the Main and Inquiry Stages. The more prolific these two stages are, the less will be required in the ttl. Fundamentally, the ttl is designed to elicit responses, details in location, determinants, and content, that have been omitted, distorted, and "avoided or not clarified."[1] An example of a directed ttl is the situation in which the examiner notes a dearth of popular responses. Because of the relationship between P responses and social conformity in thinking, the examiner should probe, not only the subject's ability to educe such concepts, but also the amount of psychological pressure necessary to overcome the resistance to such thinking. Again, a particular protocol may have emphasized D and be lacking in W.[2] Or there may be an absence of H content and too much A and Ad. The attempt to probe the subject's ability to produce these omitted, distorted, "avoided or not clarified" concept-components adds materially to the interpretive data. In short, ttl is a device for ascertaining the degree of pressure required to approach normal expectancy in Rorschach productivity.

THE TECHNIQUE—GENERAL

A separate sheet of paper should be used to make all ttl notes. Basic to all ttl inquires is this: all ten plates are spread out on the Test Table in this order:

I	V	VIII
II	VI	IX
III	VII	X
IV		

[1] Again the preponderance of evidence is in favor of a sound training for all Rorschach workers. The Inquiry and Testing the Limits assume an intimate knowledge of the test itself, otherwise the kind of information sought will represent trial-and-check fumbling rather than directed and purposeful questioning.

[2] Due to the necessity of having the ttl as part of the entire testing situation, the examiner must decide during the Main and Inquiry Stages what must be teased out in this final phase. There is no need to compute the percentages of W, D, etc. The lack of populars may be noted directly on the record sheet, while over- and underemphasis of location, determinant, and content elements may be "sensed" as the test progresses.

The Technique — Specific

A. LOCATION ttl: In this illustrative situation there is an overemphasis of D and Dd with only one W response. The examiner wishes to elicit W responses. He says, *Can you see all ten cards? I am going to ask you to do something for me. Many people are able to see something using the whole blot. Take this card, for example* (E points to plate I if S has not given a W concept to it, or another plate if card I has a W), *they can see a bat or butterfly or some other two-winged animal. Can you see it?* (If the answer is in the affirmative continue with—) *Now look at all of these other cards. Can you pick out any one or more cards in which you can see something using the entire card?* (If the reply to the illustrative question is in the negative the E should proceed as follows, still on plate I—) *Well, here are the wings, the body, and the feelers, seen all together people make out a bat or butterfly or moth. Can you see it now?* (An affirmative answer should be followed by an invitation to select other W concepts. A negative reply necessitates a further illustration with plate V, the easiest and most readily organized W—) *Let us try this plate. Some see this card as a butterfly, moth, or bat. Can you see it?* (If the response is still negative, the W ttl should be discontinued with its interpretive implications. A "yes" reply is succeeded by a request to indicate other W's.)

Essentially the same course is adopted for evoking D and Dd responses. For D: (E selects a well-delineated large detail blot area, circles it with his finger or pointer, and says—) *Many people can pick out a part of the blot and see something. For example, this part is usually seen as a—. Can you see it?* (If the reply is positive—) *Please look over these cards and pick out a portion of the card where you see something and tell me what and where it is.* (A negative reply to E's example implies further demonstration with other obvious details until S is able to comply with instructions or obviously unable to conform.)

All responses produced as a result of this process necessitate Inquiry, but the findings are not included in the final computations. An estimate of the pressure applied to elicit the lacking response is approximate: as the examiner finds it necessary to pursue one question with another, to that extent can it be indicated that none, little, moderate, or severe psychological pressue is required. The expression of the degree of pressure is obviously subjective, but the tester should apply the same criteria for the assignment of pressure levels.

B. DETERMINANT ttl: In this, an effort is made to ascertain whether a subject can organize a percept with a particular determinant that has been underemphasized or omitted during the earlier phases of the test. In the event that a protocol shows 100% F responses, it would be helpful to know if the testee can produce other-determined concepts, viz., M or FC. The procedure to follow: *There are people who use other factors besides shape to organize a response. For example, in this card* (plate III) *where you see a bowtie* (S has given this response in the Main Stage) *many people see it as a red bowtie, using the color as well as the shape. Please look over these plates and tell me where you can see more such form and color combinations that give you impressions of some kind.* (If the S does not seem to understand or cannot comply with this request, further illustration(s) should be given.)

To tease out the neglected M determinant, point to the human figures in plate II and say: *Most people who see two clowns or other human figures get the impression that they are alive and doing something. Can you see it that way?* (With an affirmative reply, invite the S to organize another human action concept in the other plates. Should the S prove unable to see the movement component, illustrate with the human in card III and again solict another such concept.) In each instance the elicited response should be probed for location, determinant(s), and content. This will assure the examiner that the solicited concept is actually seen rather than verbalized either to please the tester or evade the psychological pressure.

C. POPULAR ttl: The most frequent reason for testing the limits is to extract popular responses from the testee. During the Main and Inquiry Stages the tester should note the plates in which a popular response is missing.[3] A systematic method of keeping track of the popular responses is to list all the plate numbers with a note next to each for which a P response has been given:

I—ok	III—ok	V—	VII—	IX—
II—	IV—	VI—ok	VIII—	X—ok

The number of populars is below normal expectancy in the above protocol. Therefore an effort should be made to ascertain the testee's ability to evoke more P engrams and the psychological pressure necessary to bring these to the surface. The tester starts with plate II popular, since the P for plate I has been given: *Most people see two human figures or two animals like dogs or bears. Can you show me the card or cards that might give you that impression?*[4] (If S is successful, E should make the usual Inquiry and mark next to the plate number: card II: W M + H P (1) or D FM + A P (1) whichever of the two populars to plate II is given at the first pressure level. Inability to organize a P requires further questioning —) *Look at*

[3] Testing the limits for populars is called for when less than four such responses as an absolute number appear in a protocol or when less than 20 per cent of the total responses are P and O. The normal P expectancy is between 20 and 25 per cent of the total responses. These numbers apply only when the response-total is between 30 and 60. The maximum P concepts possible is 20 so that a prolific record of 100 responses could not easily have the required 20 to 25 per cent P's. It is not the goal of popular ttl to have the subject give all 18 P concepts. If the normal expectancy of 7 to 10 such percepts can be elicited the purpose has been served.

[4] This is the first level of psychological pressure—the content alone is suggested for the subject to seek out.

*the first column of cards, the two humans and dogs or bears
are usually seen in one of the plates in this column. Can you
see either or both of these concepts?*[5] (Success is followed by
Inquiry and proper notation on the record sheet: Card
II: W M + H P (2).[6] If the subject still fails to see the popular
percept the examiner points to plate II, circles the entire design and says—) *Many people see two humans here, two clowns
or two women. Can you make them out now?*[7] (An affirmative
answer leads to proper record sheet notation after Inquiry with
(3) for the level of pressure. A negative answer requires the
following additional demonstration—) *The two clowns or two
women are seen with this as the head, body here, hands and
feet. Do you get that impression now?*[8] (The testee's "yes" gives
(4) to the notation in the record sheet. A continued inability to
organize this precept leads to the final question—) *What is
lacking to make these look like two human figures?*[9] The response is recorded verbatim.

This procedure is followed for all popular responses omitted
or distorted by the subject. The order of pressure-questions
and demonstrations for popular ttl is:

1. Note the cards in which P's have been omitted or distorted in the Main and Inquiry Stages.

2. Point to the ten plates and state: *Most people see—.*

[5] This is the second level of psychological pressure—in addition to suggested concepts the choice of plate-possibilities is narrowed down.

[6] For the "two humans" popular concept the subject may very well point to
plates III and/or VII since the human figure is P for these cards too. This is
accepted and credited as an elicited popular if not given previously.
The tester should continue in the effort to secure the P for plate II with:
*Yes, that is good. Now can you see two humans in another card in this
column?*

[7] This is the third psychological pressure level, since it further restricts the
subject's choice to one card.

[8] This is the fourth level of psychological pressure—actually organizing
the percept for the testee.

[9] This is the fifth level of psychological pressure—the burden of proof for
the nonexistence of the concept is placed upon the subject.

Can you show me the plate(s) which give(s) you that impression?[10]

3. Each response elicited in ttl is followed by an Inquiry, and proper notation made in the record sheet, so that the ttl section for P may look like this:

$$I - ok$$
$$II - W \ M + \ H \ P \ (2)$$
$$III - ok$$
$$IV - D \ F + \ Clo \ P \ (1)$$
$$V - W \ FM + \ A \ P \ (1); \text{ etc.}$$

4. The levels of psychological pressure are characterized by:

(1) naming the popular concept only;

(2) giving the column in which the plate having the particular concept is placed;

(3) showing the subject the specific plate in which the percept may be seen;

(4) naming the concept and pointing it out on the plate in every detail, thus organizing it for the subject;

(5) asking the subject why the demonstrated blot area is not a—, i.e., what is lacking in the design to fulfill the requirements of a—. Thus the burden of proof for the nonexistence (from the testee's point of view) of the concept is placed on the subject.

5. An over-all estimate of psychological pressure—none, little, moderate, or severe:

a. none—the normal expectancy for P is given during the Main and Inquiry Stages;

b. little—the evocation of P responses in three or four plates at level (1);

[10] The words "plate" or "plates" and "give" or "gives" will be used in accordance with the P concept being sought. The popular H appears in cards I, II, III, VII, and possibly IX (human head detail); AObj (skin) may be given for IV and VI; A (butterfly, moth, bat) is P for plates I, V, and may be pointed out in II.

   c. moderate—admixture of (1), (2), and (3) pressure levels with (1) dominant;

   d. severe—a preponderance of (2), (3), (4), and (5) pressure levels.

D. SEX ttl: Pascal and his co-workers (1950) give as a rationale for sex ttl: "We do not feel that testing the limits for sex adds anything to the diagnostic value of the Rorschach with respect to seriousness of disturbance but we do feel that deviations from these more frequent responses in area and content have a particular significance for the sexual adjustment of the individual case" (p. 295). It may be true that the seriousness of the patient's problem is not affected, but most certainly the dynamics of the problem behavior stand a bit more exposed to exploration as a result of a thorough sex ttl. This phase is recommended, but *not in all cases*. If, in the judgement of the examiner, the pressure of exposure to utterly ego-alien material will be felt as a serious threat by the subject, this phase of the test must be abandoned. Probing for sex identification on a genital level may be dangerous for some subjects and nothing more than slightly embarrassing for others. If, during the process, the testee shows signs of becoming upset, it is best to draw the test to a close quickly (but unobtrusively so, and as gracefully as possible). The following is a list of sex responses in the ten plates, Figure 16:

Card I:	breasts;
Card II:	1. penis, 2. vagina;
Card III:	1. penis, 2. breast;
Card IV:	1. penis, 2. vagina;
Card V:	penis;
Card VI:	1. penis, 2. vagina;
Card VII:	vagina;
Card VIII:	vagina;
Card IX:	vagina;
Card X:	penis or penis and testicles.

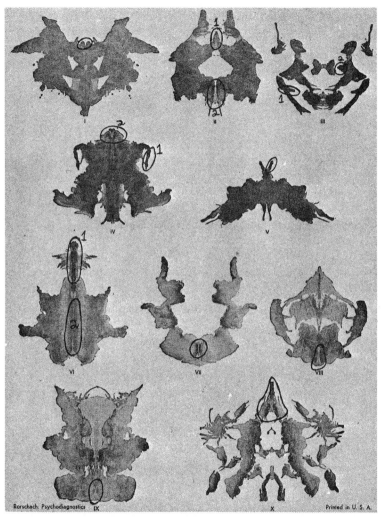

FIGURE 16

Location of Usual Sex Concepts

By courtesy of Hans Huber, Publishers, Berne, from Rorschach's
Psychodiagnostics.
The numbers refer to the concepts indicated in the text.

In the Main and Inquiry Stages male and female references may be made directly and/or indirectly or symbolically.Some samples of each are:

   Direct phallic—penis, male sex organ, "the real thing," scrotum, penis and testes;

   Symbolic phallic—snake, weird totem pole, stick, sword, arrow or spearhead;

   Direct vulvar—vagina, "snatch," "hot box," vulva, menstruation;

   Symbolic vulvar—walnut kernel (card VII), muff, open door, valley;

   Other sexual—breasts, two mounds, two hills with valley between, anus, backside, colon.

The verbalization of these items is some indication of the subject's ability to handle sexual concepts on a level-continuum from socially acceptable to crude social unacceptability. If a particular protocol shows an evasion or distortion of sexual concepts, the sex ttl offers an opportunity to plumb the subject's ability to deal with sex concept under pressure.[11] To carry out this ttl the examiner states: *Can you see all ten cards?*[12] *I would like you to look these cards over carefully and point out those parts of the cards which give you the impression of the male sex organ.*[13] (If the subject is unable to get started, point to the male sex popular[14] detail in card II and say—) *Some people identify this as the male sex organ. Can*

---

[11] Deviant sex responses, overemphasis on male or female concepts, complete absence of any sex concept (direct or symbolic), evasion of sex location-areas (in most plates the middle lower area) in organizing a percept point to a need for further query, *keeping in mind the caution stated previously.*

[12] If this question has been asked of the S before, it should not be repeated.

[13] This is equivalent to the first level of psychological pressure. The ensuing questions are analogous to the second, third, etc., pressure levels.

[14] This use of the term "popular" does not refer to the normal P concepts of this test. Certain of the sex-involved blot areas have been labeled "sex popular" by Shaw (1949, p. 274).

you see others like this in any of the cards? The same procedure is followed in the effort to elicit female sex concepts using any one of the female sex concepts in Figure 16. Substitute the word "female" for "male" in the questions.

SUMMARY

Testing the limits should be learned as *part* of the Rorschach Test and not as an appendage to be applied if the luxury permits. Important as the evocation of percepts may be, equally significant is the level of psychological pressure necessary to produce them. Another advantage of ttl is the freedom of the examiner without spoiling the protocol. The interpretive material is valuable. The testing the limits technique may also be utilized for sequential analysis purposes. However, the data obtained during this stage of the entire testing situation are open to the danger of flights of fancy by the tester. The interpretation of the added material should be used with extreme caution and then only to answer the specific question for which ttl was employed. Care must be taken not to introduce questions so threatening to the testee as to disturb him beyond the value of the information that might be gained. The tester should remember that during this phase there is no standardization of the questions to be asked or the method of calling the testee's attention to the various parts of the blot stimulus. This stage could be used to round out rather obvious gaps; it should not be abused to harm the patient. The material which has been successfully given, from the point of view of the testee, during the free association and Inquiry phases are the surface traits through which the personality expresses itself. There are facets of the individual's life which cannot be revealed either deliberately or with total unawareness on the subject's part. What is more likely, however, is that the defense mechanism employed, usually repression, has done quite an adequate job of protecting the self-concept from incompatible

thoughts and ideas without necessarily keeping out the emotional concomitants which are seeking expression in disguised
form. When this unacceptable material comes to the surface as
the subject verbalizes, it would be well to note behavior and record the overt signs of emotional discomfort and instability.
From these clues the tester will be able to make interpretive
inferences regarding the extremely sensitive areas in the life of
the testee.

Part VII

THE INTEGRATION OF THE PROTOCOL

Chapter 24

THE COMPUTATIONAL ASPECTS

Introduction

The early Rorschach literature in this country is replete with discussion, pro and con, on the question of standardizing the test. This is not at issue here.[1] It is fortunate that Rorschach's followers are sufficiently astute to educe (from empirical evidence) the inferential value of the distribution and relationships existing between the many factors in Location, Determinant, and Content. This is building on a solid foundation since the divergent is described in terms of the normally expected or convergent data.[2] In short, a description is couched in terms of the usual and serves as a base for the aberrant.

Tabulating Protocol Elements

There are many arithmetic manipulations that need to be accomplished with the accumulated information. Of prime importance is to have the scoring organized for use. It is suggested that the beginner use one of the printed record forms that are commercially available[3] or make up a convenient re-

[1] Actually this is not part of the testing situation but a formal preparation for interpreting the protocol. As such it is important even though the experienced Rorschacher leans heavily on sequential analysis.

[2] It further mitigates the oft-levelled charge of undue subjectivity with little or no norms for objective interpretation.

[3] Klopfer and Davidson's *Individual Record Blank*, published by Harcourt, Brace Jovanovich, is recommended.

cord form. A suitable record form should show Location, Determinant, and Content distribution for each of the ten cards individually for the main and additional factors in these scoring categories. The specific form is a matter of personal convenience but it should contain the following components:

1. Location: W and DW are tabulated in the W column; D has its own column; Dd, Dr, De, Di, and Do are summed up in the Dd column; S is tabulated in a separate column. The main and additional scores for each blot area are recorded in separate columns. When distributing a location-score such as WS for card I the W is checked in the main column and S in the additional column for the card. A final total column is included.

2. Determinants: The determinants should have main and additional tabulating columns for the ten cards separately and final totals. The determinant components are to be listed under these headings:

Imposed — M, FM, m (m, Fm, mF), k (k, Fk, kF), K (K, KF), and FK

Form — F (F +, F, F —)

Inherent — Fc, c (c, cF), C' (C', FC', C'F), FC, CF, C (C_n, C_{des}, C_{sym}).

In distributing a determinant combination for one response such as "FM, FC', cF," the main determinant is FM as a unit and not F, M, while the rest of the score, FC' and cF, are assigned as additionals in their respective determinant rows. All additions have equal weight if the beginner decides to give numerical values to additional factors in computing the final totals.[4]

3. Contents: The same plan is followed, i.e., for each of the

---

[4] The author treats only main elements in this quantitative portion of the protocol-preparation. The additional factors contribute to qualitative consideration.

cards the record form should show the main and additional content items with final totals for quick inspection. Include in this section, and in the same manner, the distribution of P and O responses. The alignment of content items for tabulation is semi-ordered. Because of their interpretive importance the human and animal responses appear at the top of the list:

1. H — H, (H)   3. A — A,(A)
2. Hd — Hd, Hdx   4. Ad — Ad, Adx

After the above items have been listed the remaining content categories may follow as:

AObj, At, Sex, X ray, Blood, Obj, Arch, Des, Geo
Cl, N, Pl, Fd, Clo. Vista, Fire, Sym, Others, P, O.

COMPUTATIONS

When individual Location, Determinant, and Content tabulations are completed, the final main totals for *each* of these should equal the total number of main responses for the *entire* protocol. For example, if a protocol has 24 main responses the total for main $W + D + Dd + S$ should be 24; the same should obtain for all the main determinants and contents in the record. The additionals usually do not add up to an equal sum since some responses may have none, one, or two additional components. The P and O concepts will not usually equal the response-total. With the scoring items distributed, tabulated, and checked the examiner is ready to continue with the remaining computations:

1. Total number of responses: +

Total number of responses is the final sum of all the main responses given to the ten plates. If there are additional concepts produced during the Inquiry they are totaled and recorded after the + : a protocol with 23 main and 3 additional responses is recorded as 23 + 3.

2. Total response time: seconds

The Total response time is obtained by adding up the response times for each of the ten plates, less than ten if there are card rejections. It will be recalled that the tester records two "time" observations for each plate. The first is the reaction time while the second is the response time: the fully elapsed time interval between presentation of the card to the subject and the subject's turning the card face down on the Test Table to indicate that he is through with the plate. A protocol has the following reaction and response times:

Plate	Reaction Time	Response	No. of R's*
I	1	27	2
II	2	48	3
III	4	67	3
IV	3	29	2
V	3	19	3
VI	9	43	2
VII	8	24	2
VIII	6	53	3
IX	10	36	2
X	10	44	2
Tot.	—	390	24

* The number of responses for each plate.

The total response time for this protocol is 390 seconds.

3. Average response time: seconds

The Average response time is found by dividing the total response time by the total number of responses. Referring to the data in #2, the Average response time is 390/24 or 16 + seconds. It is usually not necessary to go beyond the nearest whole number, e.g., in this illustration the time in seconds carried to two decimal places is 16.25 seconds, it may safely be considered 16 + seconds.

4a. Average reaction time for:

Achromatic		Chromatic	
I		II	
IV		III	
V		VIII	
VI		IX	
VII		X	
Tot.		✕	
Av.		✕	

This section is designed to show the Average reaction time for the achromatic and chromatic plates. The reaction time refers to the time interval between the presentation of the card to the subject and the subject's first intelligible response. Referring to the reaction time data in #2:

Achromatic		Chromatic	
I	1	II	6
IV	3	III	4
V	3	VIII	6
VI	9	IX	10
VII	8	X	10
Tot.	24		36
Av.	4 +		7 +

The reaction times for the noncolor and color cards are added separately then divided by the number of plates to which responses have been made. Ordinarily the total reaction times for the chromatic and achromatic cards will be divided by five since there are five plates in each series and a response is made to each. However, if a card is rejected the total reaction time for that particular series will be divided by four instead of five. For example, if in the chromatic series a testee rejects plate IX:

II   6
III   4
VIII 6
IX   0 (rejected)
X   10
Tot. 26
Av. $26/4 = 6 +$ seconds

When computing the reaction times the tester should list the ten plate numbers and the reaction time next to each, as in 4a. This will be especially helpful when making a sequential analysis since it will give a total picture of the changes in reaction times between the plates of the same series (achromatic and chromatic) and between the consecutive plates of the two series, e.g., I and II, III and IV, VII, and VIII, achromatic to chromatic, chromatic back to achromatic, and again achromatic to chromatic series.

4b. Average response time for:

Achromatic			Chromatic		
Card	Time	R's	Card	Time	R's
I			II		
IV			III		
V			VIII		
VI			IX		
VII			X		
Tot.			✕		
T/R		✕	✕		✕

This is an added feature devised by the author (1948) to determine the validity of possible time-determined color shock if revealed in 4a above. If the average reaction time for the chromatic series is one and one-half times longer than the average reaction time for the achromatic series one conclusion is that color shock may be present (Klopfer and Kelley, 1942, pp. 248-249, 385-386). This implies that exposure to the color cards resulted in a psychological disturbance of which one overt and observable manifestation is delayed reaction time in the color cards. If this is true supporting evidence may be found in an increase in the average response time to the color cards over the average response time for the noncolor cards; 4b will determine this. The procedure is as follows: (using #2 data)

	Achromatic Card Response R's Time			Chromatic Card Response R's Time	
I	27	2	II	48	3
IV	29	2	III	67	3
V	19	3	VIII	53	3
VI	43	2	IX	36	2
VII	24	2	X	44	2
Tot.	142	11		248	13
Av.	12 +			19 +	

Evidently color shock as manifested by the *longer average reaction time to the color cards* (4a) is supported by the *longer average response time for the color cards* (4b).

5a. Total F (including F +, F, F−):   +

Total F is the sum of all pure form-determined concepts with no regard for form-level accuracy. Additional F's appear after the + sign.

5b. $\dfrac{\text{Total F}}{\text{Total R}} = \text{F\%:}$ %

The total percentage of all form-determined responses is found by dividing the total F by the total number of responses. In a protocol of 21 responses the F tabulation is:

$$
\begin{array}{ll}
\text{F}+ & 4 \\
\text{F} & 1 \\
\text{F}- & 2 \\
\text{Total F} & 7.\text{F}\% = 7/21 \text{ or } 33\%
\end{array}
$$

5c. $\dfrac{\text{Total F}+ \text{ and F}}{\text{Total F}} = \text{F}+\%: \qquad \%$

Because of its interpretive value for an evaluation of the reality-testing function of the subject, it is desirable to know the F + %. It is obtained by adding the F + and F concepts, then dividing this sum by the total number of F responses. From the data in 5b: F + + F = 5; F + % = 5/7 or 71%.

6. $\dfrac{\text{A}+\text{Ad}}{\text{Total R}} = \text{A}\%: \qquad \%$

7. $(\text{H}+\text{A}):(\text{Hd}+\text{Ad}) = \qquad :$

8a. Total P: $\qquad +$

8b. $\dfrac{\text{Total P}}{\text{Total R}} = \text{P}\%: \qquad \%$

8c. Total O: $\qquad +$

Sections 6, 7, and 8 are self-explanatory and are computed by substituting in the formulae using only the main stage data. Additionals are recorded after the + sign and are not computed.

9a. $\tfrac{1}{2}\text{FC} + 1\text{CF} + 1\tfrac{1}{2}\text{C} = \text{Sum C}:$

9b. M: $\Sigma\,\text{C} = \qquad :$

The Sum C or $\Sigma\,\text{C}$ is obtained by adding together one-half of the main FC-determined percepts, all of the main CF-determined percepts, and one and one-half times the main pure C-determined percepts. For example, a protocol has 2FC, 1CF, and 4C responses; $\Sigma\,\text{C} = 1 + 1 + 6 = 8$.

The M: $\Sigma\,\text{C}$ is the ratio of the total M responses to $\Sigma\,\text{C}$ as obtained immediately above. This is the *Erlebnistypus* or Experience Balance (E.B.) ratio.

10. $(\text{FM}+\text{m}):(\text{Fc}+\text{c}+\text{C}') = $

This discloses the ratio of all main FM and m determined responses to all Fc, c, and C' percepts. In the following:

$$
\begin{array}{ll}
\text{FM} - 2 & \text{Fc} - 2 \\
\text{m}\left\{\begin{array}{l}\text{mF} - 1 \\ \text{Fm} - 1 \\ \text{m} - 0\end{array}\right. & \text{c}\left\{\begin{array}{l}\text{cF} - 1 \\ \text{c} - 2\end{array}\right. \\
\qquad\quad\; \dfrac{}{4} & \text{C'}\left\{\begin{array}{l}\text{C'} - 0 \\ \text{FC'} - 2 \\ \text{C'F} - 2\end{array}\right. \\
& \qquad\quad\; \dfrac{}{9}
\end{array}
$$

the $(\text{Fm} + \text{m}):(\text{Fc} + \text{c} + \text{C'}) = 4{:}9$

11. $\dfrac{\text{R's for plates VIII} + \text{IX} + \text{X}}{\text{Total R}} = 8,9,10\%$:   %

To obtain this percentage add all the responses given during the Main stage for the last three cards and divide by the total number of responses. This is known as the Color Ratio. In the data for #2:

$$8,9,10\% = \frac{3 + 2 + 2}{24} = 29\%.$$

12a.

	Total	$\dfrac{\text{Total}}{\text{Total R}}$	Description*
W		%	
D		%	
Dd+S		%	

* Normal Expectancy: W—20 to 30%
                                      D—50 to 70%
                                      Dd+S—less than 10%

This is obtained by filling in the number of main loca-tion-scores in the Total column and dividing each by the total number of responses to secure the percentage of each. Under-, normal-, and overemphasis is estimated by the extent to which the obtained percentage deviates from the Normal Expectancy Table, or refer to Beck (1950) p. 214.

12b. W:M =   :

This is simply the ratio of whole to human movement determined responses.

13. Succession

Description *				*Fixed _____
I		VI		Regular _____
II		VII		
III		VIII		Irregular _____
IV		IX		
V		X		

Rigid	Logical	Confused
Fixed	Regular	Irregular

A testee may have a fixed or rigd method of dealing with situations (the cards), or he may be regular and orderly, while the third possibility is a confused or irregular method. It is examined in this section in terms of the location-scores. Each card is considered separately and classified F, R, or I. These are noted in the "Description" column for each individual card:

F or fixed is assigned when there is only one response to a plate, or if more than one response is given to a card the location-score for the concepts is the same, viz., the concepts in the one card are all W or D or Dd.

R or regular is assigned to a card which has more than one response and in which the location-scores are in a definite ascending or descending order, viz., the first response may be W and it is followed by D, Dd or S. the converse of Dd or S to D to W is also considered R. The basic consideration for R is an orderly progression from larger to smaller or smaller to larger blot areas in making responses.

I or irregular is a confused mixture of W, D, Dd and S location of responses within a plate. Sequences such as these are I:

W-Dd-D-S-W or Dd-S-W-Dr-D.

Once having considered the cards individually and assigned F, R, or I to each, the tester then totals the number of cards assigned to each category. The final step is to indicate on the Rigid-Logical-Confused continuum an estimate of the subject's succession. A few guiding signs:

1. ten F's—extremely Rigid
2. ten or nine R's—Rigid
3. ten, nine, or eight I's—Confused
4. between the extremes of (2) and (3) above, the order of succession is Logical. The estimate of Logical should be tempered by the combination of R and I which make up the Logical evaluation.
5. if F, R, and I appear in one protocol the F's should be credited to either R or I whichever of these two is greater by at least two points. If R and I are equal or there is only one point difference between them the F's are divided equally between them. Examples:

> 5R, 3I, 2F becomes 7R, 3I—Logical succession with a tendency toward Rigidity;
> 2R, 6I, 2F becomes 8I, 2R—Confused order of succession;
> 3R, 3I, 4F becomes 5R, 5I—Logical order.

This completes the preparation of the protocol for the task of formal interpretation. From this data will emerge the bases for qualitative descriptions and inferences of the intellectual, emotional, and motivational aspects of the personality structure. It may seem difficult for the beginner to believe but this entire procedure should not consume more than two to four hours; one to one and one-half hours with the subject and the remaining time at the desk poring over the responses.

Chapter 25

INTERPRETATION OF THE
COMPUTATIONAL DATA

A Statement of an Issue

The issue is clear: to objectify and standardize or not to objectify and standardize. The solution is complex, but must begin with definition of terms. Objectivity is that attribute of a good test which minimizes the personal error by decreasing the variations in grading (or scoring, in the Rorschach Inkblot Test) and reducing the effects of the examiner's bias. Furthermore, a desirable test is standardized to reduce the error of interpretation by providing generally applicable norms. In paper and pencil (psychometric) tests these two characteristics join with validity and reliability to earmark a useful instrument designed to measure some personality dimension(s). These four qualities of an acceptable test contribute constructively to that task. The problem is much more complex in projective testing. The degree of structure of the stimulus, the qualitative responses, the conceptual background of the tester, and the unmeasureableness of the social interaction between the testee and tester render more difficult the goal of maximizing validity, reliability, objectivity, and standardization of an instrument such as the inkblot test.

Mensh (1952, p. 766) cites Munroe's plea for the use of scores in combination rather than each one in isolation because of the dangers inherent in the "sign" approach (i.e., separate scores) to labeling subjects. This is deceptive standardization. Hamlin and Kogan (1948) attempt to cope with the problem of objectivity and standardization of the Rorschach interpretive process. They write: "Eventually it may be possible to say of a Rorschach record: 'This Rorschach shows one degree of Type A perseveration, presence of Type C color shock, three degrees of organizational ability. . . .' This kind of objectivity suggests interesting possibilities" (p. 181). Mensh (1952) applauds the efforts of clinical psychologists who are concerned with investigating objectively their diagnostic techniques and their treatment of the resulting data. He looks hopefully for a more complete marriage of the group-centered and individual-centered approach to the handling of Rorschach data. Schneider (1950, p. 493), writing about Rorschach validation, cautions: "However, it is also agreed that results are highly dependent upon the skill of the interpreter. This is due to the fact that the relationships between the data yielded by the test and personality variables *have not been clearly ascertained and stated* [author's italics]. Consequently, the user of the method must rely upon the body of guesses as to the relationships involved. . . ." He deplores validation which "rests on unquantified clinical observations" even though he recognizes the value of such experience. Beck (1953), in an analysis of the problem of Rorschach standardization and validation, offers this criticism of past attempts to validate this instrument (pp. 604-605): ". . . . the observations they [Rorschach users] manipulate fail to respect any operational criterion. The ultimate value of any statistical findings, and the conclusions reached from them, can be no better than the operational value of the observations noted therein." He believes that the "final score" on the value of the Rorschach Test is "not yet in." Here the reader may see the two opposed points of view extant in regard to the use to be made of inkblot test data. The way out of this dilemma seems to be Ross' emphasis on personality description rather than attaching diagnostic labels. "Accurate descriptions of human behavior," Beck writes, "report significant behavior. To the trained mind, significant overt behavior, whether manifest in the usual methods by which people express themselves or in the language of a test, speaks of psychodynamics within. Give a description of the personality in terms of behavior, it is not necessary to worrry about diagnostic labels" (p. 610).

Discussions of validity and reliability are *not* purely academic. For the clinical psychologist, however, the price of waiting for all the final answers to be in is much too high in view of the urgency of the needs extant today. The psychologist is a rigorous scientist, but he is also directly involved in the problems of people. There is justification for considering clinical observations useful data for the descriptive foundations of interpretation to be incorporated into the framework of experimentally validated information appearing in the professional literature. The proponent of the projective method appreciates these important issues and must assimilate tested hypotheses into his system of clinically conceived rationale regarding the Rorschach variables. Are the vital problems of validity and reliability being avoided by the clinician? Should the Rorschach worker be satisfied with an "it works" philosophy for continued use of this device? In answer to the first question—validity and reliability—the evidence is contradictory. The weight of probability favors the continued use of the Rorschach Test so long as the definitions of validity and reliability are acceptable from the point of view of the clinical observer and investigator. At no time have clinical psychologists sought to evade these important considerations. The differences of opinion revolve around the semantics of the scientific method rather than the usefulness of the Rorschach Test. The second question is actually an interrogative statement of a fact amply supported by clinical evidence.

SECTION A: TOTAL PRODUCTIVITY

Number of Responses — R

The alertness of the testee is seen in the total responsiveness of the subject to the ten plates. The number of responses in the free association stage is inversely related to receptive and expressive restraint. Since the interpreter must be sensitive to extremes that indicate an impairment of adequate responsiveness to stimulation, the normal R expectancy limits are given prime consideration. Beck's Spiegel Sample averaged 32 responses per record. Cass and McReynolds (1951) arrived at a much lower average for their group — 25.[1] Neff and Lidz (1951) report varying means for their soldier population: "superior, average, and inferior" intelligence groups showed central tendencies of 25.6, 14.2, and 13.7 R's respectively, with an approximate average of 18 responses for the entire group. These findings, incidentally, disclose the relationship that exists between R productivity and intelligence. The normal range is 20 to 65 responses given in the free association stage of the test. The lower the total R, below 20, the more constricted the ego structure. Few R's with a low Sum C mirror the inhibited, emotion-avoiding individual who prefers not to become involved with other persons in his environment. It is essential to differentiate between the subject who produces sparsely because of limited ability, and one who is emotionally inhibited, cautious, overly critical, and otherwise blocked from spontaneity of association and verbalization. The former will produce in terms of poor form accuracy, with little differ-

---

[1] This variance of seven responses may be attributed to important differences in the composition of the sampling populations in such factors as intelligence, socio-economic levels, age distribution, and size of the groups. This emphasizes the importance of the interrelationships among the separate Rorschach elements since each population variable is reflected in more than one Rorschach factor.

entiation in the use of color and shading values of the plates —
the retarded and brain-damaged. The latter, the inhibited
subject, usually perceives and reports with excellent accuracy
of form, perhaps with too rigid control (high F and F + percentages), and with too little freedom of creativity (low M) and
affectivity (low Sum C). This type of responsiveness will include the intelligent but overly critical person, the atypically
depressed, and the extremely cautious subject who cannot afford the luxury of reflective self-indulgence for fear of what
this untrammeled free train of ideas might elicit that would be
ego threatening.

A protocol with more than 65 responses is the product of a
fertile intellect that is rich in associative ideation. The hypomanic will produce until the plates are removed from his
sight.[2] In this situation the prolific productivity will be highly
spiced with poor form, rare minute details, and bizarre content. This communicates caution thrown to the wind, lack of
criticalness in responding to stimuli, impaired judgment, and
paucity of association despite the high productivity. The latter
is evident in the small number of discrete content categories into which the responses may be distributed, so that
the high number of individual responses cannot be equated with healthy spontaneity, and constructive freedom of
thinking.

A prolific record, on the other hand, may reasonably be the
labor of high intelligence operating within a compulsive (obsessive ruminative) context. This is seen in the good form quality, absence of bizarre responses even though the subject uses
minutiae (dr, dd, de), and the deliberate thoroughness with
which the testee examines the plates (studied turning of the
cards, and long response time). The wealth of association results in an elevated distribution among content categories.
Moreover, test behavior itself differentiates the intellectually

---

[2] Overproductivity may be controlled tactfully; see Chapter 2.

superior and meticulous person from the elated, carefree, un-restrained producer of responses.

Rejections—Rej

Ordinarily rejections are not found in the protocols of normal subjects. Occasionally an adjusted person with low average intelligence may find difficulty in handling plate IX. This is usually attributed to "intellectual shock" rather than to neurotic interference.[3] However, the tester should regard every rejection with suspicion. The mentally retarded subject will usually encounter extreme difficulty with plate IX, but he will also find other cards a chore beyond his intellectual ken. (The general performance of the maldeficient is the result of an inability to organize and conceptualize because of restricted experiences manifested by limited responsiveness, few W, stereotypy, impoverished content, and the undifferentiated use of determinants.) The rejections of the depressed person will be found in the colored cards, especially II, IX, and X. Three factors are at play in this instance—the sudden burst of red in II, the greater energy required in IX to organize a pure form concept, and the scatteredness in plate X which might be suggestive of imminent calamity to the depressed patient. The rejections of the schizophrenic are unpredictable in view of the unevenness and fragmentation of ideation and hence association of ideas. Of the various behavioral categories the schizophrenic has the highest number of card failures. In the neurotic experience rejection may be confined to the shaded plates, IV, VI, and VII; and/or the colored plates, II and IX. The rejections of IV and VI may be ascribed to shading or dark shock *and* the particular topical memory picture educed by the form of the plate, viz., reaction to the authority figure or father symbol in IV, the double sexuality in VI. In regard to

---

[3] A method for determining this distinction has been suggested by Allen (1948).

card VII it is not the shading alone but its intangible diffuseness coupled with female sexuality or the mother figure that
troubles the emotionally ambivalent subject. Plates II and IX
are difficult for the neurotic perceiver because of the clash of
bright red with black (sex shock?) in II; and the vivid colors
combining with esoteric form in IX. Plate V is least often
rejected because of its almost self-organizing shape. In the
nonpsychotic rejection of card V may be an adverse reaction to
its blackness as in the depressed subject.

Rejection may be present in the protocol of the meticulous,
compulsive testee. The inflexibility inherent in high F per cent
and extreme F + adherence demonstrates the perfectionist nature of the adjustive mechanism at work — "meet my high standards of reality, or go by the board."

Section B: Time Determinants

Average response time — T/R

By definition *response time* is the fully elapsed time interval
between the presentation of a plate to the testee and his
placing the card face down on the table to signify he is through
with it. The *total response time* is the sum of the individual response time for all ten plates (excluding cards which have been
rejected, if any). The *average response time* (T/R) is this total
response time divided by the total number of responses for
the free association stage (i.e., do not count any responses
obtained in the Inquiry and Testing the Limits). Cass and Mc-
Reynolds (1951, p. 182) report a mean response time of 46.9
seconds for their standardization group. The middle 50 per
cent of this group ranged from approximately 24 to 52 seconds
(estimated by the author).[4] Rorschach workers generally

---

[4] The reported total of 15 to 357 seconds is misleading in view of the fact
that the spread between the tenth and nineteenth percentiles is from 18 to 78
seconds!

accept an average response time of between 25 and 45 seconds as normal. Too brief exposure to the stimulus may reflect impulsive decisions based on inadequate, partial views and judgments. The results are discernible in poorly assimilated stimuli and shabbily organized percepts. The euphoric patient is an example of this type of experiencing and responding—easy distractibility, jumping from one engram to the next as the eyes are attracted first by this then by that blot stimulus; and the pressure of speech sometimes entirely unrelated to the blot area as a stimulus.

An average response time of more than one minute must be regarded with suspicion. Any T/R over two minutes is definitely pathological. Organic brain-damaged patients and depressed persons will ordinarily give long T/R's. The former is unable to shift easily from plate to plate, and within the plate from one area to another. Due to the encephalopathy there is difficulty in organizing discrete parts into a gestalt. The patient's anxiety over his inability to handle the blots satisfactorily further contributes to delayed responsiveness. To these may be added the patient's perplexity and frustration attendant upon continued failure in order to understand an average response time of one minute or more. In the depressed subject there is a general psychomotor retardation due to blocked spontaneity of ideation and communication. The depressed is "tied up" with himself, his feelings of guilt and self-culpability, so that he first has to break through the wall of self-isolation in order to verbalize to the examiner. While both groups of patients have delayed response times, the difference between the two will be in terms of the adequacy of the concepts which are structurally more acceptable in the case of the depressed. Where repression and suppression play roles (in the neurotic and preserved psychotic) response time will be affected. It should be remembered, however, that averages mask individual deviations. The interpreter should examine the individual card response times to see if any one plate is unduly influencing the total (or average) time picture. For example, one plate may elicit only two responses in five minutes. This will distort the over-all picture especially if the other plates show responses and response times within usual expectancy. This one plate, then, should be considered as a significant lead for aberrant thinking rather than be lost in the anonymity of T/R.

Average Reaction Time—ART

By common agreement *reaction time* (as differentiated from response time) is the time interval between the presentation of the plate and the subject's first intelligible response. There is a reaction time for each plate to which the testee gives at least one response. The reaction times for the colored and non-colored plates are considered separately by obtaining the average reaction time for the chromatic plates and the same for the achromatic cards.

Before considering this dichotomy, it is first necessary to give some attention to the problems of reaction time in general. Beck et al. (1950, p. 273) give this advice: "Parenthetically it should be mentioned—this is more germane to the reports on the clinical groups—that anxiety shock and neurotic shock, in so far as they are indicated by time for the first response, *take as their base the patient's own average of first response time for the 10 figures in the group as a whole*" (italics). The core of this counsel is to use the subject as his own control rather than setting up an arbitrary or absolute figure as the referent for reaction-time interpretations. Sanderson (1952) investigated the reaction time for all ten plates and included in his report a "relative reaction time" index for the plates, using plate I as the base.

According to Table 2, card I has the shortest initial reaction time and is assigned the role of basic referent with a relative reaction-time value of 1.00. Plate II has an initial reaction time one half longer than the first plate giving it a relative re-

TABLE 2

Sanderson's Reaction Time Data for the Ten Plates*

Cards	Mean reaction time**	Range***	Relative reaction time	Rank
I	7.76	4-11	1.00	1
II	11.66	5-18	1.50	5
III	9.22	5-14	1.19	2
IV	13.02	8-18	1.68	6
V	9.66	4-15	1.24	3
VI	14.76	4-25	1.89	9
VII	14.26	7-22	1.84	8
VIII	11.46	4-19	1.48	4
IX	15.56	5-27	2.01	10
X	13.54	5-22	1.74	7

* Modified from Sanderson (1951, p. 128, Table I).
** Time in seconds.
***The range includes time limits between $\pm$ 2 standard deviations.

action-time value of 1.5. Beck (1949, p. 50) also breaks down his data for the individual plates. The reaction times are much higher for his study group with consequent variations in the rank orders of the plates. However, both studies accord card IX tenth place, i.e., as having the longest reaction time, and assign to cards I and IV low relative reaction times.[5] In the protocol of the adjusted person, plates I, V, III, VIII, and II should offer little difficulty from the standpoint of initial reaction. The remaining plates, VII, IV, X, VI, and IX, usu-

[5] The rank orders of plates from rapid to slow ART's:

Rank order	1	2	3	4	5	6	7	8	9	10
Sanderson	I	III	V	VIII	II	IV	X	VII	VI	IX
Beck et al.	V	I	III	VIII	II	VII	IV	X	VI	IX
Differences	1	1	2	0	0	1	1	2	0	0

The differences in rank orders and time values may be ascribed to the two sampling populations which have marked variations in size, educational background, and socioeconomic levels. These are important factors in Rorschach performance and emphasize the foolhardiness of attempting to utilize averages and other statistical data *in vacuo*.

ally elicit initial responses in delayed reaction times ranging from 67 to 100 per cent longer than the basic relative reaction time, i.e., the reaction time for plate I (1.00). This observation should give meaning to the individual reaction times of the testee. Long-delayed responsiveness to plate I (see Table 2), because of its primacy in the sequence of presentation, reflects the lack of alertness by the subject in the face of a novel situation in which familiar clues are absent and in which he must rely solely on his own resources. In regard to card V the reaction time should be almost similar to plate I because of the extremely popular, almost instantly self-organizing "bat, butterfly, or moth" percept. Response failures or inefficiency in these cards are expressions of a serious, interfering process at work. Slowness of first response to cards III, VIII, and II (the last especially) may stem from the presence of the color-form combination which limits the freedom of association, since two variables must be considered whether or not both enter into the final percept — form without color, form with color, or color without form; this is a selective process which requires time for completion. Tardy initial responses to plates VII and IV may be ascribed to the first impression or meaning of the plate — mother symbol, father figure, or parental authority — which plays a role for the adjusted as well as the maladjusted.[6] Plate X, on the other hand, is scattered. The average person will look over the major portion of the plate before responding overtly. This card has many opportunities, but they are dispersed and necessitate choosing from among the possibilities — a time-consuming process. This, however, is not the chief reason for delayed performance in card X; it lies,

---

[6] Assigning meaning to a plate does not necessarily imply an adverse affect, but meaning does infer an ideational process which requires a time dimension for the selection to take place. The perceiver will require more or less time for this depending on the nature of the meaning, the train of associations set off, and the consequent free translation of the idea into a verbal response or a blocking of this expression.

rather, in the highly variegated coloration which compounds with form to increase associational difficulty. Noticeable delay will occur in the case of the person with "quality ambition" to produce a W response.

Plates VI and IX are highest in mean initial reaction times. The combination of shading and obvious sexuality in VI comes as a surprise to the testee. Even the adjusted person requires time to recover and to verbalize a concept which is socially acceptable.[7] With regard to plate IX, it is accepted among Rorschach workers that intellectual or color disturbance will be manifested in long-delayed reaction time.[8]

In the effort to derive interpretive inferences from the reaction time data in a protocol it is best to apply the criterion of the subject's own performance rather than seek for absolute numbers as the measuring rod. Delayed reaction, i.e., those exceeding the relative values suggested by Sanderson,[9] need particular attention. In this way each testee sets up his own norms for the interpreter's use. It has been the author's experience to note the delayed reaction times on the summary recording form in this manner:

Achromatic plates	9	(15)	7	(18)	(19)
	I	(IV)	V	(VI)	(VII)
Chromatic plates	(II)	III	VIII	(IX)	X
	(14)	11	10	(21)	11

The overly delayed reaction times are circled. This method of recording calls the tester's attention to the deviated reaction times that are possible sources of difficulty for the testee.

[7] Beck's dictum with reference to sex content should be recalled: "The mean for sex content turned out very low: .03. The actual total number of overt sex content associations among the 157 individuals [of the Spiegel Sample] was 4. This need occasion no surprise. The censor is operating. This is no doubt an established habit in a normal population sample on the topic of sex" (Beck et al., 1950, pp. 270, 272).

[8] See footnote 3.

[9] See Table 2, column 3, this chapter.

The average reaction time for the achromatic plates (*ART-a*) I, IV, V, VI, and VII, should be similar to the average reaction time for the chromatic cards (ART-*c*) II, III, VIII, IX, and X.[10] Beck's (1950) chromatic-achromatic mean reaction times are 28.6 and 27.3 seconds respectively; Sanderson's ART-c and ART-a comparison is 12.3 and 11.9 seconds; while Cass and McReynolds (1951) contribute reaction time medians of 14 and 13 seconds for the five colored and the five noncolored plates respectively.[11] Clinical experience supports this validated trend of no significant difference between color and noncolor reaction times. In this particular test datum, "significance" is indicated when either one of these reaction times is one and a half times longer than the other, e.g., with ART-a of 12 seconds the ART-c would have to be greater than 18 seconds for significance. (When both average reaction times are 10 seconds or less, this rule of thumb cannot be applied.) The nature of the significance differs with the dominant ART. Color disturbance is reflected in ART-c delay.[12] One inference is the presence of color shock, of which delay in initial responsiveness to colored plates is a manifestation. The subjective predicament implied in the affective component of response to color, viz., degree of ego-controlled emotionality, receptivity to external stimulation and willingness to become part of the surrounding social world, is involved in the alacrity

[10] Note that there are two noncolored and three colored cards in the first five ranks; and three noncolored and two colored plates in the second five higher ranks as indicated in footnote 5, this chapter.

[11] Cass and McReynolds (1951, p. 182) also report the means for these two reaction times: 18 and 17.2 seconds for the chromatic and achromatic cards. Needless to say, the larger means (over the medians) are due to the extremely long reaction times above the 95th percentile. See footnote 4.

[12] ART-*c* delay should not be the result of only one extremely long initial reaction time to one of the colored plates. Should this occur, it is best to obtain the ART-*c* by excluding the reaction time for the unduly delayed plate. The author suggests that the tester seek supporting evidence for ART-c or ART-a delay in the average response time for the colored or the average response time for the noncolored plates.

with which the testee conceptualizes when faced with such stimuli. The neurotic is very sensitive to this type of experience and therefore is more likely to have long-delayed ART-c. The depressed may show some undue sensitivity to the colored plates but the over-all performance is so inhibited as to result in little difference between these two types of reaction times, i.e., both ART-c and ART-a will be high.

Shading shock is obvious in slow ART-a, especially for plates IV and VI in which card meaning and shading tones join to upset the neurotic subject. Shading-determined concepts are anxiety indicators: ". . . . of uncertainty, of a feeling of being exposed to danger, of considering the environment hostile, and doubt concerning the most suitable method of restoring security" (Brussel, Hitch, and Piotrowski, 1950, p. 72). The extent to which the shading tones of the achromatic plates incur these feelings in the subject, to that degree will attempts be made to evade responsiveness — a time-consuming process manifested by delayed ART-c.

The average response times for the achromatic and chromatic cards are found by totaling the number of responses and response times for the colored and noncolored plates separately, then dividing these reponse time totals (one for the colored and one for the noncolored plates) by their respective number of responses. These two sets of data are used to support the ART-c or ART-a.

Section C: Experience Balance (E.B) and Correlates[13]

M : Sum C

This is discussed in Chapter 12.

---

[13] The student will no doubt inquire why the Color Ratio (C, R, or 8-9-10%) is omitted from the main body of this text. Recent research has indicated that the conceptual basis for the interpretation of this formula (VIII + IX + XR/Total R) is much too speculative. Actual experimental in-

$FM + m : Fc + c + C'$

This is discussed in Chapter 12.

$W : M$

This is a ratio between the concepts built around the total blot, with its reflection of the testee's associative activity, and ability to deal with over-all situations, on the one hand, and

---

vestigation does not favor regarding this ratio as significant of an interpretation that could add to personality evaluation.

Sappenfield and Buker (1949) investigated Klopfer's assumption "that productivity on the last three cards is a function of responsiveness to color." By comparing subjects' 8-9-10 percentages for the Harrower-Erickson series (control) and achromatic slide reproductions of the standard Rorschach cards (experimental) they found for their group of 238 subjects evidence "contrary to the [Klopfer] hypothesis." Mean 8-9-10% for the H-E series was 31.84 as compared with 31.40 for the achromatic Rorschach slides.

Dubrovner, von Lackum, and Jost (1950), in a counterbalanced experimental design with standard and photographically reproduced Rorschach plates, tested the same assumption. They found (p. 336): "(1) there is no evidence in the present study to support the hypothesis that color affects productivity; (2) there is no support for the interpretation of the percentage of responses to color cards VIII, IX and X as an index of emotional resources. . . ." Allen, Manne, and Stiff (1951) employed a counterbalanced technique with standard and achromatically printed Rorschach plates (by Verlag Hans Huber, Berne, Switzerland) with the individual method of administration and inquiry. They found (p. 239): "With respect to the number of responses to cards 8, 9, and 10. . . . the test of significance between groups A (achromatic) and C (chromatic) mean per cent productivity on the last three cards, results in a t of .56 and a p of .50. . . . It may be concluded, then, that those who are fruitful in one ink blot situation are fertile in the other. The converse is also true—the barren producers remain sterile." The same hypothesis was tested with neurotic and psychotic groups of patients by Allen, Stiff, and Rosenzweig (1953) using the AB-BA technique with standard and achromatic plates individually administered and inquired. The difference between the C.R.'s for colored and noncolored plates VIII, IX, and X with both psychiatrically classified groups "was not sufficient to warrant the rejection of the null hypothesis (p. .30). It therefore remains tenable to assume that color has no effect in determining the color ratio" (p. 82).

One other study offers sufficiently important evidence of the futility, at present, of considering the C.R. as having interpretive value. Maradie (1953) executed an experiment with the ". . . . specific purpose [of investigating] the

the subject's capacity for imaginative living beyond the confines of the stern realities of life, on the other. Bringing these two Rorschach factors together "represents the drive for mastering the total situation, and . . . . the degree to which personal resources are used in this effort." (W. Klopfer, 1949, p. 5). Involved in the interpretation of this ratio is the subject's level of aspiration, W, and available intellectual resources to achieve this goal, M.

The range of normal expectancies recorded by Rorschach experts is placed at approximately 2W to 1M. Beck and Cass and McReynolds give as optimal ratios 1.7:1 and 1.5:1 respectively. The differences between these ratios is not significant.

An overemphasis of whole responses characterizes the individual who is attempting to reach beyond his intellectual means to achieve. He may be ambitious and therefore is under the constant need to perform at a high level in order to give as good a picture of himself as possible. Compulsive subjects tend to overemphasize the W location at the expense of spontaneity and freedom of thinking that would be manifested by a relatively sufficient number of M determinants. Young children and mentally retarded testees usually produce a high number

---

possibility that irrespective of the sequential positions of the cards, later-appearing cards will produce more responses than earlier cards. At the same time, this [latin square] design permits an evaluation of the productivity attributable to the cards themselves, independent of their order of appearance" (p. 32). He found: "(1) Irrespective of the order of the cards, the *position* of the cards is of importance with later-appearing cards producing more responses than earlier-appearing cards" (p. 35). Card X, regardless of its position in the presentation sequence, elicited the highest number of responses. Plate I, regardless of the its sequential position, produced the fewest number of engrams. This means that card pull for productivity is a function of the structure of the plate itself and/or its position in the presentation sequence. Attributing significance to responsiveness to plates VIII, IX, and X as something special as compared with plates I to VII is not justified since it would be necessary to attribute the same significance to *any* three plates in the last three positions. For these reasons the author has omitted the interpretive significance of C:R.

of W concepts but with very little evidence of intellectual capacity to support this façade of good achievement. In many instances an apparent picture of good W productivity will be contradicted by the poor form level accuracy of the W responses. In regard to the interpretation of the W responses in relation to M it is necessary for the tester to consider not only the W:M ratio *per se*, but also the quality of the W and M percepts. If both W and M are in the positive direction, that is, the responses are wholesome with good form accuracy, the interpretation will be more favorable than one in which there is high productivity but with a great deal of inaccuracy in form.

Underproductivity of W, i.e., the number of movement determinants outweighing the W responses by more than the expected ratio of two to one, suggests an interpretive inference in the direction of inner living outweighing productive ability. Whatever creative abilities the subject might have are not being properly utilized. Instead of achieving more objectively, this individual has strong tendencies to attain goals that are ideational rather than actual. This would range from the autistic person who accomplishes totally within his own fantasy world to the extremely intelligent individual who is less likely to produce his wares for the world to observe.

Klopfer and Kelley (1942, p. 277) have summarized this relationship as follows: "It is clear that W:M is an intra-individual ratio which indicates how well the contact between a rich inner life and mental activity is established."

H + A:Hd + Ad

This is discussed in Chapter 21.

W:D:Dd + S

This is discussed in Chapter 8.

Succession

This is discussed in Chapter 24.

Addendum

In this chapter the student of Rorschach interpretations has been exposed to the formal computational aspects of test interpretation. The author feels that this is a necessary part of the process of learning how to handle Rorschach data adequately. This is no plea for attempting to keep the student from appreciating the value of the sequential analysis of the Rorschach protocol. The author agrees that a sequential analysis does not depend too much upon the procedures just described. However, content of sequential analysis alone may have a place in Rorschach Test protocol interpretation, but only after a great deal of experience with this technique. Yet, to overlook the formal computational data is tantamount to using only part of the information available to the tester.

Part VIII

CASE REPORTS AND REPORT WRITING

Chapter 26

MAINTAINING DYNAMIC HOMEOSTASIS: THE NORMAL PICTURE

The protocol of the adjusted person reflects the group in which he lives. The process of everyday living consists of a constant flux of compromising ideation manifested as verbal and motor behaviors. The dynamics of the normal individual differ quantitatively and hence qualitatively from the motivations of the maladjusted.[1] It would be an error for the understanding of human behavior to think of the normal person as being unmotivated, static, and not coping with problems calling for constant and satisfying solution.

The Rorschach protocol of the adjusted person is a study of process in problem solving. It is difficult to present a characteristic normal record. The factors of age, sex, marital status, intellectual level, educational and social backgrounds, and present situations are variables which cannot be pressed into a single mold to give a typical record. At best, the em-

[1] This is a controversial issue in the study of behavior dynamics and behavior descriptions. The normal person resorts to adjustive mechanisms in order to maintain and defend his private idiosyncratic world (Frank, 1948). These mechanisms are utilized to *more or less* a degree by all persons.

The extent to which the person indulges himself in these tools for homeostatic maintenance will determine the consequent and subsequent activities. These behavioral manifestations may be so different as to defy all attempts at finding similarities. The occasional daydreams of the doctoral student may result in a constructive contribution to specific knowledge, while the pervasive daydreams of the autistic person produce uniquely unrealistic and bizarre fantasies that are highly topical and socially useless.

pirical approach is used for selecting an example of such a protocol. The criteria are necessarily practical.[2] In reviewing the
case history of the selected sample, the author's practical criteria are positive answers to these questions: Is the subject
meeting his everyday obligations satisfactorily? Is there an absence of conflict with social, legal, and religious institutions? Is
the subject functioning without disabling inefficiency? Can he
smile? Does he meet problems and cope with them in a socially
acceptable manner?

The following is the record of Mary R., who was referred to
the author for personality evaluation in connection with a
marital problem. She is 38, a high school graduate, married,
and the mother of a small son.

RORSCHACH PROTOCOL

I. 7"

1) ∧ This l.l. a large butter-fly.

1) It's a first impression as I see the whole blot. It may be flying, or it may not, I'm not sure. I've never seen a black butterfly but its color is suggestive. W FC' A P

2) ∨ This reminds me of an emblem on an Army officer's cap, not exactly, but a general impression.

2) It has the symbols of war and peace in its claws. W F + Emb.

3) > ∧ I see a woman holding her hands up.

3) The neck, waistline, and a rather full skirt. She has large hips and feet close together. I don't see the head. (D4) D M + Hd P

47"

[2] This criterion of normalcy is in contrast to the ideal and statistical standards. From the point of view of the practicing clinician it is more essential
to deal with adjustive norms than to reach for highly esoteric standards.

II. 9"

1) ∧ L.l. two bears.

1) Their noses are together, ears back here and front paws. (D6) These dark and light stripes give me an impression of fur. (? parts) I see only up to the front paws. D F +, Fc Ad P

2) ∧∨∧ This is a colored butterfly, down here.

2) It's shaped like a butterfly. (D3) D FC + A

3) >∨ Now the bears l.l. two scottie dogs in this position. These look alive even though I see only the heads.

3) Here are the ears. They must be smelling each other. (D6) D FM + Ad

4) ∨ This small part reminds me of a rooster's head. 68"

4) (Dd22) The outline of the coxcomb and the beak. Dd F + Ad

III. 4"

1) ∧ This looks just like two men, perhaps dancing or bowing.

1) The faces are not clear but the general shape reminds me of two men. They are being polite to each other. (D1) D M + H P

2) ∧ Here is a gaily colored ribbon.

2) (D3) The shape and color are exact. D FC + Clo. P

3) ∨ Looks like the head of a negro with curly hair and facial features.

3) The skull is shaped like a negro's and it's darker back here where the short curly hair is located. (D4) D F +, Fc Hd

4) ∧ In this position this part here (Dd26) is something sexy . . . the man's organ, you know what I mean. 72"

4) The shape of it and it's in somewhat the right place too. (Dd 26) Dd F + Sex

IV. 10"

1) ∧ My first reaction is see-ing a giant walking toward me. He's quite hairy all over. This thing in the middle does not seem to fit into the pic-ture at all (D1).

1) Here's the head, and his arms are at an awkward angle. (?) Position. He has big feet and seems to be walking toward me. (? hairy) The light and dark shadings all over. D M + , Fc (H)

2) ∧ Oh, I know, it's a head of a bull now.

2) Up here are his horns, and the eyes seem to be bulg-ing out. (D1) D F + , Fc Ad

3) < This is a statue of a dog barking at the moon with his tail up in the air.
    46"

3) (D2) His snout is up, mouth open. It's a cute piece for the house. D F + (A)

V. 4"

1) ∧ This seems to be easy, the whole thing l.l. a bat.

1) Here is the head and feelers, the body and wings. (?) Well, it's stretched out but I can't imagine it flying. W F+ A P

2) ∧ This is part of a wo-man's foot.

2) (D1) This bulge is the exact shape of the woman's foot. D F + Hd

(1a. ∨ This l.l. the profile of a man with the eyes, nose, and mouth here and a promi-nent chin — Dd23 Dd F + Hd)

    21"

VI. 8"

1) ∧ The bottom part re-minds me of a rug like I've al-ways wanted to own.

1) Might have been skinned but the head is missing. (?rug) A fur rug. (?fur) These light and dark differences in the picture. D Fc + AObj. P

2)∧ Looks l. cats whiskers up here.

3) ∧ The whole thing l.l. sort of an Eskimo tribal symbol on a large hill. My little son has one like this he got for box tops.

4)∨ Like this I see two faces.

57"

2) (Dd26) These long thin lines. Dd F + Ad

3) This (D8) is the pole dug into the bottom (D1) so that it l.l. it's being seen from the foot of this large hill. W FK + Obj.

4) (D4) Here's one face and the other is on the other side. The long nose, chin, and eyes here; a profile view. DS F + Hd

VII. 6"

1)∧ This is two women talking to each other, reminds me of women who are always supposed to be gossiping over the backyard fences.

2)∧ This is a mask like you see in a theater program.

3) >This is certainly a dog, it l.l. my son's dog.

4) ∨ The head of a man, an old-fashioned idea.

52"

1) (W) Here are their faces with fancy combs. They are turned toward each other. W M + H P

2) (D3) It might be "comedy and tragedy" symbols. (?) The shape. D F + Mask

3) (D2) The large head, short body, and sort of bent legs. D F + A

4) (S) You can't see the facial features, just the outline of a statue of a head. S F + Obj.

(1a. ∨ Down here I see what l.l. two people, they are not too distinct but here they are. (Dd27 Dd F + H)

VIII. 8"

1) ∧ Here are two wolves looking for prey, something to eat.

1) They're shaped like those I've seen in the zoo; yes, that's it. (D1) D FM + A P

2) ∧ A colorful design.

2) (W) (?design) Well, like you see on the Holy Torah at services only more colored. The lions on the side and the rest of it. W FC + Emb.

3) ∧ This l.l. a tooth.

3) (Dd26) It's the shape of a front tooth. Dd F − At.

4) V ∧ This l.l. two pillows.

4) (D5) (?) It's square and colored. (?pillows) I'd say the color reminded me of fancy pillows, silk ones. (?silk) Well, the color. D CF + Obj.

(1a. This l.l. a wishbone. [Dd29] Dd F + At)

70"

IX. 10"

1) ∧ This is a hard one, let's see. . . . this l.l. a witch or Mother Goose character.

1) (D3) The peaked cap and long flowing robe reminds me of Mother Goose and her rhymes. I read them to my son when he was younger. (? robe) She is dressed in a colored costume. D FC + (H)

2) ∧ V The cherry tree is in full blossom right here.

32"

2) (D9 and center D) I've seen 'em in Washington. The shape and color. D FC + Pl.

X. 10"

1) ∧ This l.l. a bunch of small bugs on a slide. They're

1) (W) They are all different shaped and can l.l. any-

stained to show each one separately.

2) ∧ This l.l. a spider, but a blue one.

3) ∧ > < ∧ The branch of a tree here, sort of tube-like in shape and gray.

4) ∧ This colored part is of a flower, like part of a yellow orchid.

5) > ∨ ∧ For some reason this l.l. pink cherubs to me; like you see in your imagination or Disney cartoon.

64"

thing a doctor sees in his microscope. I imagine they're colored. W FC A

2) (?blue spider) I've never seen a blue spider but there it is, the outline and it's blue. (D1) D FC + A P

3) (D14) D FC' + Pl.

4) (D15) The whole flower doesn't l.l. this. It's just a part of it. D CF Pl.

5) (D9) They look pink and cuddly. D FC + (H)

Summary

W	7	M	4	F%	43
D	34	FM	2	F+%	93
Dd	4 + 2	FK	1	A%	37
S	1 + 1	F	15 (1 −) + 2	P%	26

R 35 + 3

Fc	1 + 3	H + A: Hd + Ad	13:9
FC'	2	M:Sum C	4:6
FC	8	FM + m:Fc + c + C'	2:3
CF	2	W:M	7:4

Succession: between logical and rigid

Analysis of the Normal Protocol

The analysis presented below is *not* the usual type of report that would be relayed to the referring agency; it is *as if* the interpreter were talking out loud to himself in order to illustrate how the inferences and conclusions were reached. Suggestions for writing the report for other professional colleagues are discussed in Chapter 29.

Intellectual Aspects of the Personality

The first clue to this subject's ability is the vocabulary she employs to communicate her percepts. The general impression is word usage beyond the high school level and verbalizations appropriate to the context of her ideation. Other test data that reveal the adequacy of her behavior in this problem-solving situation (intelligence) are:

R — The total number of responses is adequate and discloses a fairly wide range of interests. However, the variety of contents is not exceptional since 22 of the 35 responses are assignable to the H, A. Hd, and Ad categories. The remaining 13 percepts show content variety but with no startling orginality. Her productions are popular or easily organized and require average intellectual ability.

W — The six whole responses are not unusual, rather they are mostly of the popular variety, almost self-organizing; yet their number and proportion disclose an ability to attain an over-all view of problems. While Mary prefers to deal with the obvious aspects of a problem she can fill in the small details so essential for a more complete grasp of a problem. Mary tends to emphasize the minutiae at the expense of a broader, all-inclusive approach. This gives the first inkling of one mechanism being used to maintain dynamic psychological balance — meticulous intellectualizing (check F and F + percentages and Succession).[3]

[3] In this and in the succeeding chapters the text in the parentheses indi-

M — The four movement responses are ordinary. Three are popular and to be expected from the subject. The fourth (in plate IV) reveals her attitude toward authority and her weak, controlled dependency feelings. Originality and unusual creativity are prominently absent.

W:M — This ratio discloses that Mary can achieve her goals since they are not set at too high a level. She can do better than her test performance seems to indicate; therefore, her present level of intellectual functioning is not entirely in keeping with her intellectual potential. This implies a slight degree of decreased intellectual efficiency, which, however, is not disabling. At the level she desires to operate there is good congruence between her "drive for mastering the total situation, and . . . . the degree to which personal resources are used in this effort" (W. Klopfer, 1949, p. 5).

F% and F + % — Both are adequate; 43 and 93 per cent respectively. Contact with reality and use of the objective features of the field are optimal. Fortunately Mary's interpretation of her perceptions are not as rigid as other aspects of the test findings would lead one to assume.

P and O — The presence of the former (26%P) and complete absence of O concepts support the growing impression that the present intellectual level is average or slightly higher. Her ability to deal with the objects, events, and phenomena of her environment meets the needs of her style of life. There is some reserve for achievement at a higher level *if the challenge were forthcoming* (as seen in testing the limits). Mitigation of the need for intellectualizing should result in decreased meticulousness and should open the way for a broader approach to problems with consequent lessened dependence on impersonality as a means to a solution. This would narrow the gap between current functioning and her potential. Mary is not so

---

cates sources or evidence for the inferences and conclusions reached by the author. The references will be to the protocol itself.

rigid as to render this goal improbable. There is an absence of stereotypy despite the seeming unimaginativeness of her percepts. (Animal percentage is low and no other category has replaced A% as an indication of intellectual impoverishment.)

The summary of Mary's intellectual picture is favorable in that disabling trends are not present. She is "on guard" and therefore functions somewhat less efficiently than she could with complete freedom from personal problems (but then, who would not?). Mary is in the upper limits of the average-intelligence category. Her "true" ability is probably within the high average classification. She can deal with problems acceptably [can obtain an overview in addition to the gross and essential details that make up any situation (D!! Dd + S! W)]. She is inclined at times to give undue attention to small details that could very well be overlooked with little harm to the process of problem solving. (Evidence of one mechanism at work.) Her mode of communicating (word usage) is on a higher level than the substance of her verbal reports (the content of the message), thus creating an exaggerated impression of her intellectual ability. The breadth of ideation is acceptable but not markedly rich or variegated.

Emotional Aspects of the Personality

Mary is a practical person, not given to fantasy living and preferring to seek solutions and act them out in the real world, the world of people which she accepts. Her self-percept is passive. If any emotional upheavals are involved they center about her reaction to others (plates IV and VII). Mary may occasionally lose control in a socially stimulating situation (CF and F—) but recovery is excellent (FC much greater than CF, F— followed by a partial recovery, while the CF percept in Card X does not appear to be vigorous).

The extraversive trend (M:Sum C 4:6) is not a new or superficial mode of behavior. Under stress, with its consequent reorganization of behavior to a chronologically earlier age level,

Mary will also act out her solutions and seek actively in her environment (M:Sum C 4:6 compared with FM + m:Fc + c + C' 2:3) but her self-concept [under this condition of lowered cortical control] would be more aggressive (the FM in plate VIII is more vigorous and potentially hostile than any of the M's). Any aggression, either under undue influences or in the normal state, would be directed toward the environment, toward other persons, rather than toward herself. (The protocol is lacking in conscious self-critical remarks, and the descriptions of the human figures are mostly passive, dependent, and noncommittal. An inkling of outwardly directed aggression, or at least hostility, may be seen in the first response to plate IV; in card VII there is a trace of resentment in her characterization of the social stereotype of gossiping women. Furthermore, the sequence of responses to plate IV as an indication of an area of conflict will be discussed below.) It seems that the provocation necessary to cause Mary to lose control over emotionality is not attained in the ordinary course of events (absence of pure C and other signs of loss of control or serious interference with reality contact, no marked and prolonged changes in her mode of perceiving and reacting to stimuli).

As previously noted, Mary is extraversive; along with this experience balance (*Erlebnistypus*) there is an evident interest in and an ability to accept other persons in her world. However, these interpersonal relationships are inclined, for the most part, to be somewhat impersonal, formal, and rationally considered. (FC much greater than CF with no indication of more than a momentary weakening of intellectual control when faced with emotion-provoking stimuli.) However, Mary can loosen up to show some warmth in her emotional response to others. (The presence of CF which, upon analysis, proves to be less passionate, less violent, and certainly less assertive than CF concepts could be. All of this emphasizes a lack of desire and/or ability to become emotionally involved with others in her external world despite her excellent responsiveness to their stimulating values.)

Mary is emotionally dilated (M:Sum C 4:6). She is capable of responding to prompting from within (M) as well as stimulation by her surroundings (Sum C). Does she have any safeguards against the possibility of too much buffeting from her fantasy (M) and "internal drive" world (FM)? Can she inhibit overreactivity to external stimuli? The answers seem to be in the affirmative (1FK + 15F + 1 (+3)Fc). Consider first the promptings from within, the drives to action, the ability to tolerate change and to reconcile self-perceptions with the role to be played in a situation. Mary is not an assertive, aggressive person. Her fantasy life is not a threat to her adjustment in the world of reality. Moreover, her basic physical and physiological drives are mild, passive, and lacking in urgency. While they are a source of energy for carrying on activities, they do not represent a threat to making an adequate adjustment. For these reasons it is not too essential that she have strong buffers (FK) between reality-testing function (F) and the urge to achieve in fantasy. She has grown in emotional maturity in that she exercises, socially and personally, acceptable control, over her inner drives (M's are popular, FM's are not aggressive or hostile, while m is absent).

The other side of the coin, her tendency to act out quite easily, needs elaboration. While the protocol reveals this disposition to seek satisfactions for her needs both within and outside herself, it is more likely that she will go in the latter direction if given the opportunity. (The M responses are popular at best, and are not creatively satisfying for Mary, so she is pushed into achieving in reality.) Her sensitivity to social amenities (Fc) is supported by an ability to demur and inhibit (FC') impulsive overreaction to the forces in her external world. It should be noted, further, that there is present an undercurrent of sensuality (four additional Fc) which is well-controlled and not likely to erupt into embarrassing proportions under ordinary circumstances. This inference is additionally borne out by her impersonal and objective manner of testing reality and responding to it in an orderly to rigid approach. This bolsters her adjustive mechanism of intellectualization by controlling the emotional component of a personal difficulty — her relationship to the symbol of the father figure (plate IV) and its topical meaning for her.

A reconsideration of Mary's performance in response to card IV may be helpful at this point (sequential analysis). Plate III reveals no signs of difficulty — the reaction and response times are within normal limits, all concepts are sharply and well perceived, popular responses are readily elicited, verbalizations are appropriate, and there is a direct and frank recognition of sexual ideation with no overt behavioral discomfort. (The ability to handle sexuality by this married woman is not unusual and certainly should not be construed as unwholesome in one who is married and the mother of a child.) The sequential-analytic picture shifts only slighlty with the presentation of card IV — the reaction time is raised, but not unduly. (This time dimension is not supported by a significantly long response time; as a matter of fact, the average response time for the percepts in this plate is approximately equal to the average response time for the entire protocol.) Moreover, referring again to plate IV, the percepts are at a high level of form accuracy. The noticeable deviation is in the ideational content of the first response: "A giant walking toward me, he's quite hairy all over. This thing in the middle (D1) does not seem to fit into the picture at all." An area of interpersonal difficulty comes to the fore. The "giant" represents an attitude of insecurity in her relations with a significant male figure. It should not be inferred from this response alone that the "giant" symbolizes father, brother, husband, even mother or another facet of her own self-percept. The answer lies with Mary and her own interpretation *as well as* her case history. The second and third concepts in this plate are objectively per-

ceived (both F +), but the content may be symbolically re-
warding, especially for the analytically oriented interpreter —
the use of the previously rejected D1 which now turns out to be
the "head of a bull" with "bulging eyes" (note that D1 was a
source of irritation to Mary in that she was unable to fit it into
the over-all engram of the first concept). The position and
form of D1 is suggestively phallic and differs from the previous
mode of handling such associations, as in plate III, response 4.
This possible phallic rejection is related to the male figure and
its meaning for her. The avoidance of the use of this detail in
connection with the threatening significant male figure
strongly implies an inability to unwillingness to accept sexuality in the particular setting of the personal significance of the
male figure.[4] Where this ego involvement is not dominant and
in situations in which she can accept the male figure (as in
plate III), sexual ideation is nonthreatening and can be handled more objectively and detachedly. In Card IV, however,
topical symbolism engenders imminent anxiety. Mary must
protect herself, and she does this by means of the mechanisms
of evasion — "This thing in the middle does not seem to fit into
the picture at all" — which alleviates the *immediate* threat, but
is not sufficient for complete release from the fear of consequences. An inference may also be made that her ambivalent
attitude toward the male figure symbol has imbedded in it an
unhealthy sexual component.

---

[4] This appears to be contradictory to the previous characterization of
Mary's ability to deal directly and frankly with sex ideas. While this is true,
there is no reason to assume that contradictory trends cannot exist side by
side within the same individual. Not only may these contradictions arise out
of the varying aspects of the self-percept of the individual in different situations (without implying a lack of consistency, since this attribute of consistency is a function of the individual *in a situation*), but these inconsistencies
of attitudes need not be incapacitating. For example, a person who is pre-
judiced against a minority can function very well in his social milieu even if it
becomes necessary for him to deal occasionally with a member of the minority group.

A favorable note must be introduced into this conjecture of a "soft" spot in Mary's personality structure; her recoverability from stress. This process of recovery is the mechanism of intellectualization at work. It is *as if* Mary must react to the forces in her phenomenological field, but sticks closely to the facts as a means of avoiding subjective productivity and what this unguided train of ideas might elicit. Complete recovery and the protective armor of reality contact follows in her responses to card V.

Interestingly enough, her performance in plates VI and VII is adequate. She displays a sensitivity to social demands, insight, and a grudging acceptance of the social stereotype of the female figure. There may be some contempt in her response to card VII: "This is two women talking to each other, reminds me of women who are always supposed to be gossiping over the backyard fences." The possibility also arises that she resents this too-inclusive generalization about women. In either event, she is not disturbed.

In sum, Mary is a fairly well-adjusted person with no disabling incompatible trends to interfere with her getting along acceptably in her social milieu. She is emotionally dilated, can relate well to other persons in her environment, and is not given to emotional outbursts or impulsive behavior. She is quite sensitive to social demands and is capable of exerting sufficient restraint to keep from overreacting to external forces. Her basic drives are not intense, and she has a passive and submissive conception of her own role in life. Under stress, she functions a bit less efficiently and maturely than usual but recovers readily. Resort to mechanisms of intellectualization and evasion (or denial) appear in the event of ideation involving a particular male figure perception (father? husband? son? brother? or some other masculine facet of her own self-percept?). On this note ends the evaluation of Mary's protocol.

It may thus be seen that normalcy is not a passive state of the organism, it is a process state empirically identified in terms of the absence of crippling inefficiencies and the presence of a constant flux that eventuates in the maintenance of homeostasis — a dynamic procedure that abhors the vacuum of *status quo*.

Chapter 27

THE COST OF DYNAMIC HOMEOSTASIS: THE NEUROTIC PERSONALITY

S. R. was referred to the author by his family physician for help with "an adjustment problem." This case is interesting because it illustrates the struggle of the neurotic to maintain a psychological balance among the forces that are constantly impinging upon him and driving him on in a search for security, happiness, and surcease from unremitting tension.

The 43-year-old male is married, has a college education, and is a high school teacher of chemistry in a large east-coast school system. His chief complaint: "I'm up and down too quickly for no sensible reason most of the time. I'll go along feeling on top of the world, and then someone says something, usually trifling, it may have no importance, and I'll go down into the dumps. Many times I slip down for no apparent reason, at least for no reason on which I can put my finger. It isn't normal, either I'm happy or sad, but I can't seem to be in between for any length of time." Other complaints include lack of friends and an inability to get along with people. The case history is replete with social failure in his youth and in his present relations with his wife and child. He worked hard to obtain his professional education and always paid a high price to maintain some degree of stability in an ever threatening world. He served in World War II as an officer and was separated because of emotional instability. The following is S.R.'s Rorschach protocol:

RORSCHACH PROTOCOL

I. 3"
1) ∧ This l.l. a bat.

1) The whole thing. It's gliding to a stop, to alight on something. W FM + A P

2) ∧ This middle part l.l.a woman. She seems to be stand-with her hands up, as if in prayer — a headless woman.

2) You can see her body through the skirt. (?body) The darker part. (D4) D M +, Fc Hd P

3) > Can I turn the card? Well, this side l.l., or at least reminds me, of a donkey. Sort of a Walt Disney animal.

3) Its ears are long and I get the impression it's turned its head, cocked is the term, as if listening to Pedro to urge it on. (D2) D FM + A

4) ∨ This l.l. an officer's insignia, a large eagle.

4) (W) The details are not clear but that's my total impression when I hold the card this way. W F + Emb.

5) ∨<∧ A cat's face — cross-eyed cat at that!

5) Here are the eyes and mouth, it's shaped remarkably like one. (WS) WS F + Ad

(1a. ∨ This l.l. the head of Abe Lincoln. (D6) D F + Hd)

187"

II. 5"
1) ∧ This resembles two circus clowns in colorful costume.

1) (W) They are playing a game like clapping hands. They have red and black costumes. W M +, FC, FC' H P

2) ∧ Now I see two . . . bears, up to the shoulder.

2) L. l. pictures of bears, I don't know what this thing between the nose parts is for. (D6) D F + Ad P

3) ∨ This l.l. a top.

3) It's shaped exactly like one. (S) S F + Obj.

4) ∨ Old Man of the mountain statue.

4) (Dd22) L.l. a carving seen in the mountains outside of Atlanta. Dd F + Obj.

5) ∨ The red l.l. flames of an explosion going off.

5) L. l. it's exploding, and that is the vivid coloring shooting up. (D3) D C, m Expl.

6) ∨ L. l. two wire-haired terriers. Looks as if they're sniffing each other.

6) (D6) These really look alive, ears perked up. (?wire-haired) Jagged edges and stripe-like effect here. D FM + , cF Ad

178"

III. 4"

1) ∧ Two actors doing an Alphonse and Gaston politeness act

1) They're bowing to each other — it must be a stage and these red are curtain decorations. (W) W M + , CF H O

2) ∧ A red bowtie in the center.

2) L. l. it. I'm a bowtie disliker myself. (D3) D FC + Clo. P

3) ∧ ∨ A negroid head.

3) (D4) The head is shaped exactly as a negro's. Even the close-cropped hair and the coloring. (?coloring) It's black. D FC' + Hd

4) > A fish.

4) (D5) Just like a fish swimming in the water. D FM + A

(1a. ∧ L.l. a red rooster. I never saw one so red all over but it does remind me of it. (D2) (D FC + A)

87"

IV. 10"

1) ∧∨∧ L. l. a huge ape with his barrel chest puffed up and arms akimbo. He seems to be approaching me.

1) (W) He's a hairy monster, it's enough to scare you. That threatening stance. I don't know what this might be (D1), can't be a tail, perhaps a tree behind him. W FM cF A

2) ∧ That l.l. a snake.

2) The shape of it. (D4) D F + A

3) >∨∧ That's an orchid.

3) (D3) You can see the fine pistils in it. It's delicately shaped and shaded. D Fc + Pl.

155"

V. 2"

1) ∧ That's a bat, too.

1) (W) It's shaped like one and it is the same dark color. W FC' A P

2) ∧>∧∨∧ L. l. a pair of pliers.

2) (D3) Either that or a nut cracker. D F + Obj.

3) >A woman's leg.

3) The calf effect here makes it l.l. a woman's leg. (D10) D F + Hd

66"

VI. 12"

1) ∧ That's a totem pole up on top.

1) (D3) I've seen these in some of my travels; the wings are especially characteristic. D F + Obj.

2) >A submarine surfacing, the conning tower looks quite realistic.

2) It's at sea; the camouflage is very good. All battleship gray, like the ocean. (D4) D FC' + Obj.

3) >V An animal skin, I'd say a bearskin rug.

3) (W) The whole thing. (?skin) A fur skin. (?fur) These mottled effects. (?mottled) Shadings here. W Fc + AObj P

4) ∧ L. l. a bed post in here.

4) (D2) Shaped exactly like one. D F + Obj.

5) ∧ This bottom l.l. a photo of some island or other. It's not too definite, in fact is quite vague.

5) (D1) It's vague, I guess it's the type of map taken from composite aerial photos. You can see the mountains and valleys. (?) These dark and light areas. D FK, kF Geo.

158"

VII. 16"

1) ∧ L. l. clouds.

1) All of these are different shaped clouds. (W) (?clouds) Fluffy, seem to be floating. W, KF, m Cl

2) ∧ This is a walnut kernel.

2) (D6) Shaped just like it, as if one half is opened up. Dd F + Fd

3) ∧V This is medical corps insignia.

3) (light Dr on top) I've seen 'em on army medics and nurses. Caduceus, I believe. Dr F + Emb.

4) V L. l. a bust of George Washington.

4) Just the outline of the head with its bobbed hair. (SW) SW F + (HD)

5) ∧ Now I see two figures, like women. They seem to be stereotypes of gossipers, like

5) (D2) Just like 'em, seems to be going in two directions at once. D M + H P

as if they are pointing in different directions, but looking at each other.
    190"

VIII. 3"
1) ∧Two animals on the
side

    1) I'd say they were bears,
like as if they're walking or
getting ready to spring on
some prey. (D1) D FM
A P

2) ∧ Two blue flags.

    2) I don't know what they
symbolize but they are crossed
flags. (?) Color and shape.
D FC + Emb.

3) ∧ L.l. strawberry ice
cream down here.

    3) (D6) Color of it. D C Fd

4) ∧ This l.l. a ghost.

    4) (Dd25) Vague outline as
if it were a ghostly, shrouded
figure. Dd F + (H)

    78"

IX. 9"
1) ∧V∧V A cello here.

    1) (S in middle) It's shaped
very much like one. S F +
Obj.

2) V> Mark Twain's head
nicely portrayed.

    2) (D4) Complete even to
the mustache and light hair.
D Fc + Hd P

3) >V∧ Antlers of a deer.

    3) (D7) Shape and color.
D FC + Ad

4) ∧ Spine.

    4) (D5) L.l. an X ray of the
spine. D Fk X ray
    (1a. ∧ This (D3) l.l. a preg-

| | | nant woman, here's her swol-len stomach. D F—H) |
| 62" | | |

X. 3"

1) ∧ A rabbit's head.	1) (D5) Here are the two ears, nose and mouth. (?nose) White half circle and darker eyes. D Fc, FC' Ad P
2) ∧ L. l. a spider here.	2) Looks all legs attached to a round body; it's crawling. D FM + A P
3) ∧ Two blue birds, looks as if they are flying in formation.	3) (D6) The color and shape. D FC, FM A
4) ∧ Pawnbroker's sign.	4) The gold color especially. (D3) D FC Obj
5) ∧ This l.l. a tooth.	5) (Dd34) Dd F + At
6) ∧ Just like a caterpillar down here.	6) It's colored. (D4) D FC + A
74"	

Summary

W	9 + 1	M	4	C'	3 + 2	F%	35
D	28 + 3	FM	7 + 1	FC	6 + 2	F + %	100
Dd	5	m	0 + 2	C	2	A%	33
S	3 + 1	k	1 + 1			P%	27
R	45 + 5	K	1			O	1 +
		FK	1	H + A:Hd + Ad			14:10
		F	16 + 2	M:Sum C			4:6
		Fc	4 + 1	FM + m:Fc + c + C'			7:6
		c	0 + 2	W:M			9:4

Succession: between logical and rigid.

ANALYSIS OF THE NEUROTIC PROTOCOL

The following is an analysis of this record. It is not intended as a final report, but illustrates how the interpreter would go about teasing out the various facets of S. R.'s personality structure in an effort to understand the dynamics involved.[1]

Intellectual Aspects of the Personality

S R.'s intellectual potentialities are very superior. His form level rating is maximal (100% F+) indicating a highly developed critical faculty. (This is also borne out by the nature of his professional work in chemistry, requiring exactness to a high degree.) S.R.'s superior potential calls for an abundance of inner resources (M), and it is precisely here that the first indication is found that all is not well in his personality make-up. (The four movement responses with human content are, for the most part, popular concepts. The actions expressed are prayer, bowing down, clapping hands, and gossiping. The first two are decidedly submissive, while the other two are a bit more outgoing but not vigorously so. He is thus an unaggressive exacting person.) His W responses show a quantity and quality at the average level and are not up to his possibilities. There is only one good original W response that uses a popular concept as its base. In those plates with difficult W's he apparently does not even make the attempt to do better than average, showing that he is not striving to achieve above his present level as represented by four M. Variety of content is

[1] The author administered and scored the above protocol and the one detailed in the previous chapter. The subjects are married to each other. They were given the Rorschach test as part of the larger problem of ascertaining possible causes of marital discord and preliminary to counseling and individual therapy. In some respects both records read alike, but there are significant differences to enable the student to note the neurotic make-up of S. R. as contrasted with the relatively stable picture of Mary R. The author wishes to thank Mrs. Margaret Stiff for her assistance with the case of S. R.

wide, but here again the impression is gained that he is dampening his natural spontaneity (35% F in an emotionally expansive context implied by the M:Sum C of 4:6).

Intellectual efficiency is apparently stressed above everything else by S. R. (F + is 100%, high and consistent). That he is too effective in controlling interpersonal relationships is evidenced by high FC. An indication that his efficiency is not maximal is the presence of only four M responses and the dominance of basic drives (7FM as compared with 4M) which interfere with a more fully mature and creative responsiveness on his part. While intellectual impairment is evident in this protocol, the current functioning level is not so low as to characterize his being incapacitated.

He can deal with the practical aspects of living, recognizing them for what they are and disposing of them in a logical manner. At times, however, he tends to lose himself in details and is unable to grasp an entire problem (approach: Dd!!D! W), he loses efficiency. (Card X, for this subject, should not have proved too difficult for some sort of W response; yet it was not forthcoming.) This suggests that he does not strive for achievement when challenged, being satisfied to go along at this lowered rate and to deal with separate problems individually. While he reasons effectively with abstract concepts, he prefers to do only the obviously necessary organizing and grouping; he does not choose to take a chance on anything of whose outcome he is not certain. The mechanisms S. R. must employ for maintaining homeostasis may be classified, thus far, as intellectualizing (100% F +, overemphasis of Dd, meticulous turning of the cards to make certain all aspects of the problems are covered, and the preciseness of his elaborateness to ensure that the examiner understands he is aware of the inaccuracies in the blots), the rationalization (a form of intellectualization with an element of self-protection from facing imminent unpleasantness).

His ability to think along conventional lines is highly developed (as shown by his popular responses). That he prefers to function in this manner is reflected in the fact that the popular responses are the first ones to be given in each card, with the exception of those plates in which he was blocked so that they did not appear until later. (Card IV so upset him that S. R. did not give the popular concept at all, although he was able to elicit them in all the other cards.) Plates VI and VII also held threatening and disturbing portent for S. R. so that he produced inefficiently at first; his mode of perceiving obviously mirrors his anxiety and lowered effectiveness. It appears that intellectual adequacy suffers when S. R. is faced with the necessity of dealing with parent or authoritative symbols, and with sex-related ideas.

While S. R. sometimes produces an original idea, this is not his strongest sphere of endeavor by any means. Range of interests is wide quantitatively, but there should be greater variety. (A and Obj. categories contain over 50% of the total R, adding H percepts raises the proportion to approximately 67%. A Ph. D. in chemistry should be able to do so much better.) Level of aspiration is not consistent with his abilities.

Intellectually he is tied to reality very strongly (26% P; form level extremely accurate; human concepts are vital and alive; good FC combinations; and all responses are easily within the range of possibility, i.e., they are not bizarre). The tie is so rigidly ingrained that conflictual material comes to the surface with difficulty, i.e., the weakening of control has to run its course before S. R. explodes into a deterioratedly violent and inefficient reaction (response 5 in plate II, "The red l.l. flames of an explosion going off," toward the end of the total productivity).

Affective Elements

The availability of inner resources for adjustment is a soft spot in S. R.'s psychological repertoire. His drives to self-actualization are weak and submissive rather than strong and aggressive; the same is true of his basic drives. The former (M) are less available for constructive, wholesome use because of interference with the more mature discharge of energy offered by the latter drives (FM greater than M). He perceives his world as hostile and unfriendly (3S in an extraversive setting) yet he leans upon it for satisfaction of his dependency needs. Ordinarily he controls the drive to satisfy his need for recognition (Fc), but under pressure he sheds this impersonal sensitivity and compliance with the demands of society to become crudely and grossly sensuous (c) in his drive for satisfaction of his need for affection from his external world. There is little satisfaction for him in his private, autistic world, therefore he must go outside of himself. His energy is directing him into his external world, and when this becomes excessive he acts out violently. He is aware, though, of social amenities and does try to inhibit himself. That he does have conflict caused by the frustration of his drives is evidenced by an explosive m concept. He would like very much to disrupt the present state of things and change them around to suit himself.

There is reason to believe that S. R.'s extraversive orientation is a recent development (FM + m:Fc + c + C' is 7:6 as compared with 4:6 for M:Sum C; note that the high Sum C is due to the two pure C responses so that the extraversiveness is due more to uncontrollable impulsiveness than to wholesome and warm interpersonal relationships). This contention is also enhanced by the fact that movement and form responses are always given first to a card, never the color. He is not visibly disturbed by the colored plates, as seen in the absence of qualitative remarks to that effect and the consistency of good form level. (However, it should not be overlooked that S. R. may have been tested during a period of cyclothymic transition between extraversive and intratensive responsiveness, especially since the Sum C is due mostly to the two pure C or emotionally deteriorated concepts.) The one exception is his interpretation of the red area in plate II (D3). This isolated emotional challenge is significant of frustration and conflict. (It should be noted that uncontrolled affectivity is present in plate VIII, but in a much milder form.) This suggests that S. R.'s personal difficulty comes to the surface when two stimulating conditions are present: (1) when responding to other persons, and (2) if there is sexuality involved in his interpretation of a situation. This will be discussed further. Apparently when given an opportunity to discharge energy, his emotional explosiveness is usually less aggressive than when the defensive lid of repression is violently removed because of the futility of the repressive process in some extreme instances. (Note the responsiveness in plate VIII as compared with his performance in Card II.) This leads to the inference that controlling forces in S. R.'s emotional reactivity are almost as strong as in the intellectual area. (All responses have form control except the two pure color-determined concepts.) Thus, there appears to be little capacity for entering into warm emotional and spontaneous relationships with other people. He reacts either objectively and impersonally, or he swings to the other extreme to become completely uncontrolled. The former appears to be the more usual mode of life, but there are those periods during which he responds in a "wild" sort of way. The latter uncontrolled behavior seems to emerge when the field proves too threatening for him. The picture now unfolds to include two more mechanisms at work: (3) repression dominates his ordinary way of life, thus depriving him of the opportunity to make warm interpersonal and emotionally satisfying ties. Related to this repressive process is S. R.'s compulsivity—a need to indulge in idea-absorbing activities in order to support the repressive process and keep ego-alien material from coming to the level of awareness. The fourth adjustive mechanism at work is a "flight into reality" which represents for S. R. a means of acting out against the environment his pent-up hostility (pure C and S). The impression is gained that if pushed hard enough he might be drastic in his actions, caring for nobody, including himself, and doing violence in the process.

S. R. appears to be extremely critical both of himself and of other persons. His motto might be: "There is no excuse." His conception of his own life role is another source of difficulty. Of his moving figures (the indices of his self-percept) two are women and two are men. The women are clearly defined, while the men are clowns and actors, thus disguised. The women are interpreted as being submissive, devoted to prayer and womanly gossip. The men are costumed and clapping their hands, an activity which is not aggressive. Perhaps S. R. is inclined to act a role rather than be himself (and so he interprets the blot-associated males as actors rather than playing their real selves).

While his human figures are clear as to what they are doing, their moods and affects are less certain. However, there is un-attached anxiety associated with his responsiveness to the female representation. This relationship needs further probing. Closer analysis of plate VII sheds some light on his attitudes and consequently his own conception of role-taking. The female figures in this plate are submissive and at the same time stereotyped as gossipers. That he is greatly disturbed by the female concept is also revealed by his long reaction time. The first response is "clouds," an anxiety indicator; then "walnut kernel," suggesting that the anxiety is engendered by the female sexual concept. Finally, after two more responses which do not appear to be particularly significant, comes the "gossipers" which, if seen at all, is frequently the first response to the plate. It is interesting to note that his only F— response is contained in a reference to a female percept, viz., "pregnant women," in plate IX given as an additional response. This mode of perceiving the female concept is seriously impairing his intellectual and emotional responsiveness (as indicated by the sudden appearance of F— as a determinant).

His attitude toward men is also unwholesome. Card IV

clearly evidences this. The father figure is fearful and threatening. He is seen as a "hairy ape." Other men in action are seen as clowns and actors. This suggests a lack of clarity of his own role as a male and perhaps an unwillingness fully to accept his own masculine role. The fact that maleness and femaleness (and the masculinity and femininity involved) threaten him so much may be related to his attitude regarding heterosexuality as an activity. He may find it a disturbing notion because of his interpretation of heterosexual activity as an act of aggression (or at least one in which the male must be ascendant) that is incompatible with his own self-percept as a passive individual. This is not society's definition of the male role in sex activity, i.e., to be passive and a male. He therefore feels uncomfortable when faced with the necessity of assuming the expected role because of the conflict between the need to be accepted by himself and by society. His passiveness might suggest the possibility of homosexual interests. Little wonder that dependent S. R. approaches his environment with a great deal of caution in the search for affection and recognition.

S. R. is a man of superior intelligence, with concomitant intellectual possibilities, who feels visibly disturbed by women and threatened by the father figure. He has been forced into reacting in an intellectualized and compulsive manner in order to alleviate and/or avoid anxiety. When faced with emotion-arousing situations as projected onto the blots he gives his best performance first and then gradually lapses into lack of control. He takes refuge in a burst of aggression to relieve unendurable tension. Furthermore, he employs another neurotic method of coping with anticipated and actual anxiety feelings, viz., empathy is not stressed, thus avoiding emotional relationships that might bring unpleasantness. His strong points are his ties to reality and the fact that he is intellectually efficient under most circumstances under which he will operate in his present socioeconomic situation. The overall mood is not definite, though the prevailing mood at the time of testing was somewhat depressed. (Blot concepts are not seen as being spontaneously happy and there are several dysphoric, C', responses. The latter, of course, act as a brake on less than severe provocation to impulsive behavior and therefore have their value for S. R.)

Addendum

At this point it does not become too difficult to understand S. R.'s life history, his complaints, his attitudes, and his way of life. He is aware of his inability to get along with people, that he is lonesome, that he has mood swings that are uncomfortable and a source of unhappiness. He does not understand these attitudes and reactions as dynamic processes that have an economy and a purpose, that they keep him functioning as he does, even with lowered efficiency, rather than resulting in a complete breakdown and in zero functioning efficiency. From the point of view of society, the cost is high; for S. R. the cost is negligible as compared with the alternative of breakdown and personal failure.

Chapter 28

MECHANISMS OF FUTILITY:
THE PSYCHOTIC PROCESS

Observation of the behavior of the seriously mentally ill person leaves little doubt about the failure of the "less than extreme" use of adjustive mechanisms. It is difficult to present a typical psychotic protocol, just as it is unusual to speak in terms of the typical psychotic person. The behavioral manifestations vary from the incipient psychotic, through the ambulatory disturbed patient, reaching the extreme in the chronic, deteriorated and obviously ill individual who requires no testing for classification.

The protocol of I. A., a 34 year old married male, father of two children, and educated through high school, is interesting because it exemplifies the lack of *exact* congruence between Rorschach performance and other clinical tests. His chief complaint is: "People say that I do not like them. I hate people. I even hate myself." Other complaints include an extreme "hate for the Jews" (I. A. is Jewish), dislike of a utility company for refusing to give him service, and "no use for my wife and children." He was given the Wechsler-Bellevue Intelligence Test for Adults, form 1; Sentence Completion Test; Draw-a-Person Test; and the T. A. T. All of the test findings will be presented in brief form prior to the Rorschach protocol:

Wechsler-Bellevue Intelligence Scale

Test	W. S.	Remarks
Inf.	15	Overideational, verbose
Comp.	7	Extreme pressure to speak. 1. Envelope: "Put it in your pocket, go home, and see if there's money in it. I used to do otherwise, mail it. Honesty does not pay any more. I do not believe in being good." Then repeated this in French. Uneven productivity on this entire subtest.
D. Sp.	10	
Arith.	7	
Sim.	13	"This is interesting, I'm in a good mood today." Responses were generally short and to the point.
V	12	
PA	11	Verbal I. Q. 109
PC	10	Perf. I. Q. 110
BD	10	Full I. Q. 110
OA	11	
D. Sy.	11	

The over-all performance is irregular. Failure is followed by a diatribe against Jews, the United States of America, the utility company, and other irrelevancies.

Draw-a-Person Test

Remarks: The male figure expresses I. A.'s attitude toward people. The drawings are essentially as barren as his own mentation. The facial features suggest a paranoid trend, with aggression directed toward the environment overtly, and toward himself covertly. The former is quite obvious. The latter may be inferred from the heavy band around the neckline suggesting self-decapitation and elimination. The patient is hostile, and the figures express it. The female figure is especially childish and presents psychotic features in its entirety. See Figures 17 and 18.

SENTENCE COMPLETION TEST

A summary of the expressed attitudes in various areas:

Family—rejection of his own and parental family members with a great deal of hostility.

Past—as a youngster he was always happy when alone, dreaded having to come home.

Drives—unable to accept a challenge, strong conflict between the need to consider others and to please only himself.

Inner states—(Contradictory and ambivalent attitudes are expressed here.) He is emotionally labile; despite his dislike for his home, he does want to be at home and is actually afraid to stay away from his family, decries being alive and is afraid of being alone.

Goals—I.A. is a nihilist, wants to devote himself to annoying people (how is this related to his fear of being alone?), a great deal of confused thinking is immediately evident from the test items in this area.

Values—in this area I. A. is contradictory and shows extreme confusion of what factors in life hold value and meaning for him.

Energy—not much at best, uneven in expenditure of effort, but usually gives in when faced with a difficult problem.

Outlook—sees the future as hard, bad, and full of grave discouragement.

Reaction to others—poor, confused, hostile.

Interpretation of reaction of other persons to him—thinks other people regard him as kind, there are occasional flashes of insight. Thus far it is not difficult to arrive at some inferences regarding the personality structure, and his modes of experiencing and behaving.

DRAW-A-PERSON TEST

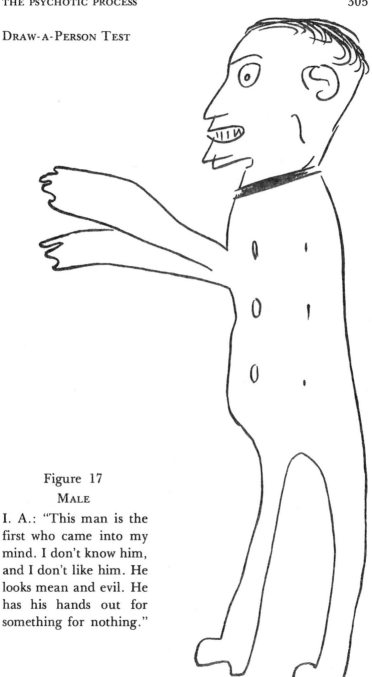

Figure 17
MALE

I. A.: "This man is the
first who came into my
mind. I don't know him,
and I don't like him. He
looks mean and evil. He
has his hands out for
something for nothing."

Figure 18
FEMALE
I.A.: " This is supposed to be a woman. It's the best I can do."

RORSCHACH PROTOCOL

I. 4"
1) ∧ This is a bat.

1) It's gloomy, the black color, it's not cheerful, looks dead to me. (W) W FC' A P

2) ∧ It also l.l. the inside of a walnut; and am I right?

2) The ragged edges. I'm looking at the center of one half of a nut. (W) W F— Fd

3) ∧ l.l. a bug.
   35"

3) (denies this response — W F A)

II. 7"
1) ∧ This l.l. inside the mouth of a lion or big animal.

1) (WS) I'm looking into the mouth here (S) and the rest is the head. WS FC, Fm Ad

2) ∧ This l.l. an X-ray picture of something . . . . the lungs, I believe.

2) It's a negative film like a doctor uses. (W) W Fk X ray

3) ∧ Also l.l. two dogs' heads.

3) They're standing in an up-right position, almost rubbing noses. (D6) D FM + Ad P

   40"

III. 3"
1) ∧ These (D6) l.l. ostriches.

1) Exactly as I've seen them in the Central Park Zoo, the heads of the ostriches. Do F + Adx

2) ∧ l.l. two men sitting, one on each side.

2) (D1) They look as if they are about to get up from a sitting down position — a rocking chair — they are raising themselves up. D M + H P

   30"

IV. 10"

1) ∧ This l.l. a bat.

    1) (W) The shape of it —
but it's an ugly black bat and
it's a dead one. W FC' A

2) ∨∧ Also l.l. the inside of a walnut.

    2) (W) The ragged shape reminds me of it. W F— Fd

3) ∧ L. l. lungs.

    3) It's like the other one I saw — an X ray of lungs. (Di in D7) Di Fk X ray

     37"

V. 7"

1) ∧ L. l. a butterfly.

    1) (W) It's flying or gliding through the air. W FM + A P

2) ∨ Now it l. l. a bat, a small baby bat.

    2) (W) It's sprawled out and I get the feeling it's flying, wobbly-like. W FM + A P

     25"

VI. 7"

1) ∧ The top l. l. . . . . a caterpillar.

    1) (D7) (points to portion of blot very carefully and identifies it again as a caterpillar) D F+ A

     28"

VII. 14"

1) ∧ What the hell is this! . . . L. l. two small bears, Teddy bears.

    1) (D1) It's just the head and face of a bear cub. D F+ Ad

2) ∧ L. l. clouds, rain clouds.

    2) (W) The picture is gloomy, not bright, black clouds. W KF, C'F Cl

     32"

VIII. 5"

1)∧ That's pretty . . . these l.l. squirrels on each side, they're sneaking up on something.

2)∧ Fir, f-i-r, tree.

26"

1) (D1) (points to the blot area but comments only, "The red ones.") D FM + A P

2) (D4) The shape and the color green make it l. l. a tree. D FC + Pl

IX. 15"

1) ∧ Gee! I don't know what this l. l. . . . . It l. l. the inside of a person, internal view, got all kinds of colors, lungs, ribs, neck, kidneys — all the right colors.

45"

1) (W) I remember this from my biology. One thing equal to some things are equal to each other. (Does not explain this irrelevancy.) W C/F — At

X. 13"

1)∧ A crab.

2)∧ This l. l. two moles biting into a tree.

3)∧ This l. l. a rabbit's head.

4)∧ This l. l. two birds in flight.

56"

1) It's very active, moving about. (D1) D FM + A P

2) (D8) Seems as if they are trying to sharpen their teeth on the bark of the tree. D FM + A

3) I couldn't draw one better than this myself. (D5) D F + Ad P

4) (D6) They seem to be flying together in formation. D FM + A

Summary

W	10 + 1	M	1		F%	20	
D	11	FM	7 + 2		F + %	67	
Ds + S	1 + 1	Fm	0 + 1		A%	63	
R	22 + 2	Fk	2		P%	32	
		KF	1		H + A:Hd + Ad	10:5	
		F	6 + 1		M:Sum C	1:2	
		FC'	2		FM + m:Fc + c + C'	6:2	
		C'F'	0 + 1		W:M	10:1	
		FC	2		Succession:	Rigid	
		C/F	1(−)				

The behavior of the patient is just as revealing as his verbalizations and test findings. The following is an analysis and report of all the test data as made to the referring pyschiatrist:

Examination of Intellectual Processes

Patient obtained a full-scale I.Q. of 110 which places him in the upper limits of the average adult level of intelligence. There is no difference between his verbal and performance results. This is not a true picture of his native capacity. He is capable of doing as well as the high average or bright normal individual. He did very poorly in the comprehension items. This was due to his hostile attitude rather than his lack of knowledge. For example, on the envelope item he replied as follows: "Put it in your pocket, go home and see if there's money in it. I used to do otherwise, mail it. Honesty does not pay any more. If you put it back you're a nice guy, but I don't believe in being a nice guy." This type of reasoning characterized most of his responses to the items. This reflects his antagonism more than his lack of judgment. Furthermore, it is more serious in view of the fact that he does apparently know the right thing to do from the ethical desideratum, but harbors thoughts of doing just the opposite. His bitterness is not covered up; on the contrary, it is very much on the surface and comes out at the slightest opportunity.

During the testing he displays tangential thinking and functions quite unevenly. He intersperses facetious remarks with sober responses to individual questions. For no ascertainable reason he breaks into his answers with irrelevant remarks, e.g., tirades against Jews, people in general, request for a telephone, and a request for a position in South America. This is a frequent occurrence. He constantly seeks approval and encouragement from the examiner. He attempts to "beat" the examiner to the completion of a problem so that he could snap out the responses in shorter time. He feels he is in a race against time.

The test pattern and intratest analysis suggest that we are dealing with a psychotic personality involvement and that the patient is functioning rather tenuously in the environment—probably an ambulatory schizophrenic, paranoid reaction type. Intellectual efficiency is being markedly impaired.

Examination of Personality Structure and Dynamics

The projective tests reveal an individual who has quality ambition beyond his ability to achieve. Constructive planfulness so necessary for positive productivity is absent, thus leaving the subject bereft of resources for emotional stability, inner creativeness, and intellectual control. When he "leaves off" going beyond his intellectual depth, he can perceive concrete details. The progression from the "bird's-eye-view" (W) to an interest in the "near at hand" (D) aspects of problems represents a step down for the patient rather than a critical and analytical approach to coping with these problems.

He has a great deal of drive which is pushing him to find some outlet. Some of it is being released in social reactivity, but the greater portion finds expression as vague and generalized free-floating anxiety. He is unable to absorb any of the energy in creative productivity or in fantasy. The outward signs of his ventilation of energy may be seen in his psychomotor restlessness and press of speech. He is constantly on the go and makes anyone in his immediate vicinity the recipient of verbal tirades. While he is emotionally puerile, he does try to control its social expression until it piles up and he becomes explosively labile.

At present the patient is attempting to intellectualize his anxiety so that he might be able to deal with it. He is not successful because of his lack of insight into the nature of his conflicts. The chiaroscuro elements in his concept formation (of the Rorschach) further reveal active repression and an associated atypical depression.

Despite overt restlessness and garrulousness, the patient maintains a cautious and guarded attitude toward his environment. He does take cognizance of outer reality and tries to limit the freedom and violence of his emotionality. Obviously he is not always successful. Ideationally, he is quite sterile, a fact which his verbosity fails to mask. He enters new situations with some enthusiasm, but uses only a superficial rather than critical approach. The only concern he may show regarding his percepts is in terms of a need for reassurance rather than an intelligent evaluation of his ideas. Disturbing stimuli bring about a cautious reactivity coupled with anxiety features. He does not readily identify with people, but his extraversive inclination literally forces him to empathize. He compromises this press by seeing his human figures in less than acceptable modes, viz., "half-man and half-ostrich." The anxiety trend becomes most pronounced, reflecting severe neurotic disturbance, when sex-associated engrams are elicited (as in the Rorschach plates). In a basically psychotic structure this is a favorable element indicating that the break is not complete and that I. A. is still sufficiently "in contact" to be concerned about his behavior, overt and ideational. His greatest difficulty is in the area of accepting the female concept. (The usual penile concept is disguised and therefore acceptable. In card VII this is seen more clearly—the first response is derogatory and in effect renders the association quite harmless, to be followed by a percept that mirrors the extent of his free-floating anxiety as engendered by the preceding idea. The second response also indicates the extent to which female ideation renders him unable to intellectualize and concretize his feelings.)

The male and female figures he drew express his attitude toward people. The male looks "mean and evil. He has his hands out for something for nothing." With the exceptions of the facial features, both are barren reproductions of his own body image. The facial features suggest a vivid suspiciousness directed toward the environment. The aggression is not at all disguised, rather it it so dramatically depicted as to be inferred quite readily. Both figures show a desire to cut off the body at the neck line as if rejecting the rest of the body and at the same time executing it. The female figure is much poorer than the male, indicating the discomfort of female-tinged ideation. His attitudes toward women become very clear in the T.A.T. stories. "The man is crying [13MF], his wife must have died on him [laughter]. What is he crying for? *A lot of them hope for that.* His wife died. Maybe she did not have insurance and he's crying . . . ," and so on in this vein. He expresses an intellectual interest in suicide and remarks that he used to think about it but "something holds me back." Another story also reveals the extent to which he cannot accept society: "This guy [card 15] looks like the chief devil and he looks like an undertaker [contamination?]. Oh, yeah! An undertaker, either praying or counting his customers on the cemetery."

I. A. seems to be incapable of taking advantage of adjustive mechanisms that might contribute to a more stable balance. He is sterile of personal resources and too tenuously in contact with reality to make beneficial use of interpersonal relationships in the process of adjusting adequately.

Summary

1. This patient has potential high average intellectual ability. He is functioning much below this level. His poor evaluation of social situations and bizarre thinking tend to impair the effectiveness of his intellectual productivity.

2. The data suggest a basic psychotic structure — ambulatory schizophrenic involvement with movement in the paranoid direction.

3. Superimposed on this basic structure may be seen a free-floating anxiety reaction.

4. It is not recommended that I. A. be considered for group therapy. He would probably be a disturbing influence in such sessions. He should be seen on an individual basis for the time being.

Chapter 29

THE TESTER'S REPORT

The value of the clinical psychologist's efforts also revolves around his ability to communicate findings to the referring agency or professional colleague. In regard to the rationale and the elements of the total report the reader is referred to Hammond and Allen (1953). It is not usual for the psychologist to write a separate report for each of the tests administered in a battery. Rather, the entire series of tests, each selected and administered for a definite purpose, should be organized to answer the questions raised directly and implied by the referring source. This may range from a simple request for an evaluation of intellectual level to the complex appraisal of the personality structure for differential diagnosis, basic structure, modes of experiencing and responding to reality, and therapeutic indications. While this chapter is devoted only to the writing of the Rorschach test report, it must be understood by the reader that all other test data will ordinarily be interwoven, compared, and cited in one organized report.

THE RORSCHACH REPORT

This report, like any other, should deal with two aspects of the individual's behavior and then resolve itself into a higher order of abstraction called the *summary*. The first of these should describe the intellectual functioning of the testee while the second phase would be devoted to the affective personality picture.

315

Intellectual Functioning

The interpreter should be able to indicate, from the proto-col, the subject's present functioning efficiency and whether or not it is at variance with his optimal level of performance. The former is found in the F + percentage, the W:M ratio, as well as the absolute number of whole and movement responses, freedom from stereotypy (A%), and original responses. Each of these may be considered separately with a view to combining them into a smoothly reading over-all description of the intel-lectual maturity with which the subject meets and deals with problems. A nonscorable but vitally important contribution to intellectual status is furnished by the testee's word usage.

F + % approaching the maximum discloses the potential of the individual as he relates to objective reality and utilizes this in problem solving. The structure of the language and the level of word usage, viz., functional or categorical, *plus* the organi-zation of the verbal symbols in a meaningful context reflect the ability to deal with verbal concepts, a valid index of intel-lectuality. If there is a discrepancy between past achieve-ment (schooling, socioeconomic and occupational status) and test functioning, the examiner is in a position to make some in-ferences regarding ability and present efficiency. The quality and number of W's and M's contribute to the estimate of in-tellectual functioning efficiency. The desideratum is *not* maxi-mum W and M but the optimal use of these factors for per-ceiving and organizing concepts. Best efficiency is the two W to one ratio with good form. Closely joined to this is the testee's relative freedom from impoverished and banal ideation which are mirrored in the A percentage and absolute number of dis-crete content categories.[1] The subject's capacity and/or ability may be higher than his current functional efficiency as seen in the uneven use of good form (F + with some F−), an occa-

[1] The interpreter is cautioned to analyze the entire protocol to make cer-tain that another category is not a stereotype substitute for low A percentage.

sional original but with an emphasis on popular responses, and minimal use of movement responses. This variance should be noted, and the tester must seek out the reasons for this discrepancy. This impairment should be ascribed to the interfering process, either simple maladjustment, neurotic disability, or psychotic reality loss. However, ascription is not enough, the interpreter must describe the particular functional processes which result in good, fair, or poor intellectual efficiency.

Since intelligence may be defined in terms of the adequacy with which problems are faced and handled, it is necessary to give some consideration to the manner in which the testee meets situations in an effort to cope with them. Thorndike's attributes of abstract, social, and concrete intelligence may be derived from the Rorschach record. Abstract intelligence and the quality of this approach is seen in the proportion of W responses given by the subject. It is necessary to describe the adequacy of this abstract approach, i.e., the ability to deal with total concepts; therefore, this should be evaluated in terms of the form level and also the consistency with which the W responses are related to the objective reality of the blot stimulus. The second aspect of the approach to problems is the perception of the large details (D). This reflects the testee's handling of the concrete everyday aspects of life. Again form level accuracy is important. In order to complete the picture of intelligence, it is also necessary to see if the subject is capable of handling the smaller facets of a situation which are so essential for both constructive abstract thinking and appropriate concretistic manipulation of the environment. The social aspect of the attributes of intelligence is manifested in the human figure percepts given by the testee. If they are healthy, constructive, and wholesome, they indicate the subject's ability to relate well to social stimuli. This becomes more evident if the human figures are seen in acceptable and nonderogatory action. The testee's intelligence, of course, cannot be separated from the total personality picture.

Emotional Aspects of the Personality

This section of the report is best approached by a discussion of the testee's intra- and interindividual relationships. The first of these, intraindividual processes, includes the self-concept and the adjustive mechanisms essential for the maintenance of this role. Intraindividual relationships may be derived from the movement responses, the nature of the use of space, safeguards (FK) between the subject's reality-testing function (F) and promptings from within (M, FM, m), consistency of the self-concept, and the amount of subjective discomfort in the social field. It is necessary that the tester report the nature of the subject's self-percept and how this is related to the regard for people in the social milieu. The changes in role are also important and may be obtained from the consistency or inconsistency between the M:Sum C and the FM + m: FC + c + C' ratios, i.e., do both go in the same direction or are they opposite to each other?

The testee's response to inner drives is inferred from the nature of the movement responses: The M is related to the accepted and recognized impulses: FM stems from the less acceptable, less mature motivating forces (physical and physiological): while m indicates those driving forces that are unacceptable but which are forcing their way to the level of awareness. The flexor or extensor direction of the movement is related to the passive or assertive tendencies of the individual. (These may or may not be consistently in one direction, as seen by the two ratios noted above.)

The use of denial, evasion, intellectualization, or other mechanisms, to meet actual or imminent anxiety may be implied from the manner in which the testee experiences and relates himself to his world. Hostility directed inwardly against the self or outwardly in an effort to satisfy some need is derived from the use of space in an experience balance context. This leads to a consideration of the interindividual relationships and how the subject handles them.

The use of color, control of this use (FC in relation to CF and C), the ability to demur (presence of C' responses), and the nature of the human figure and animal descriptions disclose the extent and nature of the subject's interpersonal ties. Changes in the rhythm or style of responsiveness should also be noted. Breaks or changes in the testee's manner of approach to the blot stimuli serve as referents for elaborating descriptions of the testee's perceptual and behavioral processes.

Finally, all this is summed up by abstracting from the above descriptions and inferences the strengths, weaknesses, and clinical impressions regarding the testee. The question of diagnosis is an important consideration. Unless it is required by clinical team procedures, the psychologist could contribute most efficiently by giving other members of the team a behavioral description with dynamic inferences, leaving diagnosis for the staff conference.

Sample Rorschach Report

The following report was submitted to a local agency which referred a fourteen-year-old girl, Rose H., for psychological evaluation. The Rorschach and summary findings included immediately below:

I. 4"
   1)∧ L. l. a bat.

                       1) (W) The whole thing, l. l. a bat, over-all picture l. l. a bat; grayish in color. L. l. a regular bat—one that flies. (?flies) Seems to be flying, wings would have to be folded more if not flying; could be like sailing. W FM +, FC' A P

2) ∧ (smiles) Can't find anything else. (Urged by E.) Part up here (upper half D4) l. l. the way a heart is shaped, or something.

3) ∧ This part l. l. a turkey turned upside down.

2) Particularly this up here l. l. pictures I've seen, reminds me of it, a heart in the science books. D F— At

3) (Dd24) L. l. it's running, no, hung up in a butcher shop; the bottom is the head. It's facing the opposite way, can't see it; shape I guess. Dd F Ad

(1a. ∨ lower half D2; The sides should l. l. something but I don't know. L. l. the wind blowing, the head, eye; wind man. Dd cF, mF N)

54"

II. 4"
   1) ∧ L. l. a heart.

∧ ∨ ∧ I don't know of anything else it l. l.

1) (WS) Veins and something connected with the heart. The opening (S) l. l. pictures of the heart; the color a little bit too, and the shape of the heart. WS F/C At O—

(1a. ∧ S; L. l. the beak of an A and the rest of the A; don't know what kind of A, sort of a fat one, shaped like a beak. DS F— A contamination

(2a. ∧ D6; L. l. an elephant but not too much. [? parts] Ears, trunk, built something like one but not too much,

one on the other side too.
D F + A

(3a. ∧ D2; L. l. there should be something in these two red up here. Looks a lot like someone's hand working a puppet, of a human; face, nose, mouth, and high hat. Nothing to do with the color.
D F + (H) O + C̄)

35"

III. 10"

1) ∧ Part of it l. l. a poodle dog.

1) (D11) Nose, sort of, does not really look too much like one, just the nose, the shading helps. Dd F −, Fc A

2) ∧ And a bow in the middle.

2) (D3) Shaped just like a bow, color makes it a prettier bow but I guess it would still l. l. a bow. D F/C Clo P

3) Some sort of a bird.

3) (D11) Head at the top, wings. The bird is stuffed and there for exhibition, shading. D Fc + A

(1a. ∧ (D10; Hand with a finger pointing [demonstrates]. D M + Hd

(2a. ∧ D7; I saw a heart but I did not say it. All pictures are different. The shading makes it l.l. a heart. D Fc − At

(3a. ∧ D2; Animal with a tail, looking back. The shape of it. D FM A

(4a. ∧ D5 minus Dd26; L.l.
an arm if it wasn't for this.
41"   D F— Hd)

IV. 6"
    1)∧ L. l. a heart again.   1) (W minus D2) The bot-
tom part from the heart to
wherever it's connected, the
top is the top of the heart.
D F— At

    2)∧ And a boot.   2) (D2) Toe, heel, kind of
small for one. D F + Clo

    3) ∧ Roots of a tree.   3) (Dd 26 and Dd 28) The
whole middle is now the trunk
if these are the roots. DdD
F + Pl

    4)∧ Icicles.   4) (D4) The way they are
shaped, the way they're hang-
ing in a downward direction.
D F N

    5) ∧ A leaf.   5) (Dd 30) These things go
in it, the way it's shaded, got
lines in it looking something
like a leaf. I changed my
mind, I see the whole thing as
a leaf, no, leave it as before.
Dd F + Pl

(1a. ∨ W; L. l. something
the body of a butterfly. These
42"   l.l. sort of wings. W F + A)

V. 3"
    1) ∧ Butterfly.   1) (W minus D10) Things
that come out of here, wings,
and the shape. (?) Could be

on exhibition, pinned to wall.
D F+ A P

2) ∧ Legs.

2) (D1) Thicker part, could
be a human leg, or an A leg
too. Dog or horse leg, not
shaped too distinctly. D F +
Ad P

3) ∧ A heart again (snicker).

3) (W minus D3 and D6)
The shape. When I say heart
I do not mean heart-shaped,
I mean the organ. DW F— At

28"

VI. 4"

1) ∧ It l. l. a caterpillar
turning into a butterfly.

1) (D3) Whiskers, head,
half way between caterpillar
and butterfly, it did not get
'em all. (?) It does not have
all the parts of each. D FC',
Fc A

2) ∧ ∨ Some sort of organ,
body organ, I don't know
what.

2) (D1) (?) Could be a heart
or maybe a liver. The shape
at the bottom. DdD F— At

40"

VII. 4"

1) ∧ Heart organ.

1) (W) I don't know what
made me think of it. It looks a
little bit like a heart, but not
too much. W F— At

2) > Lion, when I look at it
this way ∧ >< this is the
tail.

2) (D2) The head, mane,
tail. It should be more straight,
but it still l.l. a lion; shading
here. D Fc A

47"

VIII. 3"

1) ∧ A heart every time.

1) (D7) The bottom, this (yellow) l. l. the liver or heart, maybe the color. Dd F/C At

2) <> Some sort of creature, like a rat or cat, I don't know just what.

2) (D1) The pink here, the shape, head; looks more like a cat. (?) A real one. (?) It's alive. (?) It's walking on the side as if real. D FM + A P

3) ∧ Rocks.

3) (half D7) On each side, just the way they are sitting there, shape and color. Dd F/C N

4) ∧ Sort of a skeleton.
   41"

4) The white and the color. (DS3) DS FC + At P

IX. 14"

1) ∧∨ Hmmm . . . .
∧ heart again.

1) (Dr) (difficulty in selecting blot area) This is the heart. Dr F— At, $\overline{C}$

2) ∧ Icicles.

2) (Dd25) It comes to a point and is shaded. Dd Fc N

3) ∧ Roots.

3) (D5) The roots are in the ground and the bottom is the underground. D F Pl.

   50"

X. 11"

1) Rats.

1) (D8) Shape and shading, darker at the sides. D Fc + A

2) Antelope.

2) (Dd27 and Dd28) It l. l. it. Dr F— A

3) Reindeer.

3) I can't see it now, did I say that?

4) Stem.

4) (D14) The shape of the stem of a tree or plant. D F + Pl

5) Leaves.

5) (D13) The color and shading. D CF, cF Pl

6) Lion.

6) (D2) Shape. D F + A

7) Branches.

7) (D35) The shape. Dd F Pl

(1a. D4; L. 1. a heart, the shading and shape. D Fc − At)

(2a. D5; L. 1. a bunny's head, ears particularly. D F + Ad P)

72"

Summary

W	4 + 1	M	0 + 1	F%	59
D	17 + 9	FM	2 + 1	F + %	58
Dd	11 + 1	mM	0 + 1	A%	37
S	0 + 3	F	19 + 4	P%	16
R	32 + 14				

		Fc	4 + 4	H + A:Hd + Ad	10:2
		cF	0 + 2	M:Sum C	0:3.5
		FC'	1 + 1	FM + m:Fc + c + C'	2:5
		FC	5	W:M	4:0
		CF	1		

Succession: orderly to rigid with definite confusion when upset.

This fourteen-year old young lady was given the Rorschach Inkblot Test and Draw-A-Figure Test on March 17, 1953. Her test behavior was cooperative, and she manifested some interest in the proceedings. There was very little overt indication of anxiety, and only one protest was forthcoming when she told examiner that she could not draw and therefore could not complete the figure-drawing test. After some reassurance she complied with the instruction.

Intellectual Aspects of the Personality

Rose's functioning efficiency is poor, markedly impaired by a pathological process which is not, as yet, overtly manifest. The nature of her responses to the blot stimuli strongly suggests a psychotic-like development.

Her ties to reality are vacillating and tenuous. Her ability to solve problems fluctuates widely; on the one hand, she can produce creatively, yet this is followed almost immediately by a regressive quality in her responsiveness which becomes perseverative, poorly conceived, and almost bizarre. These three attributes characterize her thinking: conceptualization becomes impoverished (F —), perservation of a response (due to lack of congruity between percept and blot area) indicating a repeated break with reality in which her preconceived ideas prevail over the blot contours, and, finally, shallow affect.

Her range of interests is quite barren and reflects a dearth of richness in thinking. Her drive toward achievement does not have the requisite energy and the basic intellectual productivity characteristic of the efficient person. Examiner believes that Rose's striving to function on an acceptable level, in keeping with her innate ability, is all façade and will not bear up under scrutiny.

In her present state Rose cannot go beyond mere conventionality. She is sufficiently sensitive to social amenities so that her behavior is not antisocial. This is a favorable sign in that it serves as a cover for the underlying pathological proceses at work. It is this superficial conformity that gives the impression that she is a "nice quiet girl."

Affective Aspects of the Personality

Rose has very little in the way of adjustment resources, little drive, and only a slight indication of adjustment potential. While she is a dependent teen-ager, there is a remarkable lack of the restlessness and rebelliousness that is characteristic of her peers. What are the responsible factors?

Unfortunately, Rose is unable to find a source of satisfying her needs within herself. At the same time she is afraid to act out the satisfaction of her needs in her social milieu. She is striving to adhere to an impersonal and objective interpretation of her world in order to guard against psychological trauma. This is the defense of intellectualization in which she is attempting to evade emotional involvement with the people around her and at the same time "sit tight" on her basic drives, which are a source of threat and imminent anxiety to her should she indulge herself in them. This dependent, sensuous child is in a serious conflict situation—she cannot channelize her energy inwardly for fear of what might be engendered should she give free rein to her fantasy thinking. On the other hand, she cannot seek help from the significant figures in her external environment, again because of the threatening import these persons hold for her. The enigma for Rose is: Where shall I turn for help at this time?

For the moment the defense of intellectualization is covering up her basic distress. Should it become less effective, and the protocol would seem to indicate this possibility, she will have to resort to more intense utilization of mechanism(s) to maintain homeostasis. The indices favor a movement in the direction of an overt schizophrenic breakdown, i.e., a marked reorganization of her interpretations of her life space so as to alleviate the encroaching anxiety. Insight is lacking, and she is adhering to an unimaginative and sterile interpretation of her world as a means of maintaining integrity. There seems to be some hostility directed toward the mother figure, at least much more so than is evidenced against the father figure. Her human identifications are deeply personalized, unhealthy, and destructive. Examiner suggests further probing in the area of mother-daughter relationships. The perseveration of the "heart" concept would seem to suggest that this holds some direct or symbolic topical meaning for Rose. During the short time for free associating, examiner learned that she had a boy friend who suffered from a weak heart and from whom she was parted, having lost him to a prettier and far more active girl.

Another significantly poor aspect of the personality structure is the almost complete emotional coarctation, revealing her apathy and lack of interest in what might be going on about her. There are some indications of her inability to handle sex-associated concepts. Examiner did not probe into this because the general situation did not indicate the wisdom of this. She cannot handle sex concepts and deliberately avoided such areas and responses in the projective situation.

Clinical Impression and Recommendation

Beneath the thin veneer of a seemingly well-adjusted young lady there is a strong indication of incipient psychotic involvement. Rose does not relate will to herself and to her social environment. The facade may not serve too long. It depends on the stress that will continue to impinge upon her. Examiner is of the opinion that this young lady should be referred to the psychiatrist for individual therapy.

ADDENDUM

The value of the report is enhanced by adhering to descriptions of behavior rather than relying on the extensive use of technical or esoteric terminology. There is no doubt that technical terms read impressively, but their interpretations differ too widely among psychologists, psychiatrists, and caseworkers for comfortable use in communicating concepts. This is much less a disadvantage when the report cites behavioral descriptions, i.e., the testee's reactions to the blot stimuli, as the bases for making dynamic inferences. Beck's point of view holds a great deal of merit: "Accurate descriptions of human behavior report significant behavior. To the trained mind, significant overt behavior, whether manifest in the usual methods by which people express themselves or in the language of a test, speaks of psychodynamics within. Given a description of the personality in terms of behavior, it is not necessary to worry about diagnostic labels" (1953, p. 610). It is good advice for the beginner.

Chapter 30

THERE IS AN ALTERNATIVE
TO THE I. Q.

The usual psychological evaluation of the mentally retarded child includes a standard verbal, academically oriented intelligence test to establish an I. Q. and/or Mental Age (MA). The Revised Stanford-Binet or Wechsler scales meet the criterion of measured intelligence for a diagnosis of mental retardation (MR). However, the second criterion for MR, social or adaptive behavior, may be overlooked. While the I. Q. rating places the child at some point in relation to the general population, it tells very little about his way of coping with the problems of daily living.

It is possible to demonstrate how the second criterion, social intelligence, may be evaluated in a formal psychological testing situation through the child's verbal behavior, the overt expression of adaptation to social demands. A by-product may also be some notion of the child's measured intelligence, perhaps not as precise as the Stanford-Binet I. Q., but much more meaningful in terms of *the child's* stage of cognitive development. The test is the Rorschach Psychodiagnostic Inkblot Test. This verbal non academically oriented technique focuses, not on predetermined correct answers to test items, but on how the child perceives, organizes, and responds to the re-

This chapter was published in the *Journal of Personality Assessment*, 1975.

latively unfamiliar and unstructured inkblot card stimuli. Thus, the focus shifts to the child and how *he* interprets and responds to the world around *him* using *his* language to express *his* ideas rather than trying to guess what a test author had in mind when a particular item was included in an intelligence test.

The three young subjects of this demonstration are:

Jeff, nine years old, I. Q. of 106, and MA of nine years, six months; he is in the average range for measured intelligence.

Allen, ten years, ten months old, I. Q. of 43 with an MA of four years, four months. He is in the moderately retarded range, at the -3 level of measured intelligence.

Steven, fifteen years, ten months of age, I. Q. of 66 and MA of ten years. He is mildly retarded at the -2 level of measured intelligence.

It should be noted that:

1. Jeff and Allen are chronologically closer to each other than either is to the much older Steven.

2. Jeff and Steven are almost identical in mental ages.

3. Allen and Steven have in common only that Allen has a CA (Chronological Age) of ten years, ten months and Steven has an MA of ten years.

This affords an opportunity to see:

1. How two boys of similar CA but differing levels of measured intelligence — normal and moderately retarded — cope with problems.

2. How two boys of similar MA but differing CAs handle problems.

3. How two retarded boys who are matched only for mental and chronological ages respond to stimuli.

The inkblot test represents for most people an entirely unfamiliar situation. How do Jeff, Allen, and Steven behave verbally in the face of this unfamilar, relatively unstructured situation?

Within seven seconds after being handed Card I Jeff spontaneously said, "Butterfly," which has good form and included the whole blot. He was able to encompass the entire situation, so to speak, and deal with it relevantly.

Allen responded within one second to the same card and as nearly as could be made out he uttered the word "Sun," an irrelevant poor response which he denied during the Inquiry stage. Nineteen seconds later, after persistent questioning, Allen gave his first intelligible percept, "Hands." He constantly touched the card, tapping it with fingers, in a sort of ritualistic manner from which he probably derived some security and a sense of being in contact with the situation. His behavior was perseverative, speech barely intelligible, spontaneity entirely lacking, and at no time did he organize the total inkblot into a single percept.

Steven, the chronologically older mildly retarded testee whose MA is equivalent to that of younger nonretarded Jeff, said, after ten seconds, "I see a butterfly." This is very much like Jeff's well-organized percept, but later inquiry showed a marked difference in accounting for the response. Whereas Jeff named and pointed to the "butterfly" parts accurately, Steven simply stated that the colors—blue, gray, and black—reminded him of a butterfly.

Three questions may now be posed:

1. How does the child of average, just below average, and significantly below average intellectual maturation approach a new, unfamiliar situation?

2. How does each perceive the situation?

3. How does each organize and respond to it?

In essence, what may be the important contributing variables in dealing with life's stimuli?

From this brief observation of the three youngsters, it may be seen that Jeff almost immediately organized the new situation, in this instance, the entire blot, into a single, popular, and well-formed percept. An unfamiliar situation did not incapacitate him, rather, he rose to the challenge of the new and related acceptably to the stimuli. Time taken for thought culminated in a free-flowing verbal expression.

Allen also indulged in thought when faced with the unfamiliar, but the end result reflected impulsivity and an extremely concretistic view of the situation. Having been instructed to "see something," he plunged in, figuratively speaking, with both feet and gave a percept he could not account for during the subsequent Inquiry. He responded only because he felt he had to. The situation as represented by the inkblot was secondary to the psychologist's demand that he "see something." After a long pause and much prompting, during which he looked at and tapped the plate, he was able to select a small detail which was familiar to him — the "Hand" percept. The area selected does indeed resemble a hand. He gave four additional responses, but each one was emitted only after persistent urging. These were one-word unintegrated percepts marginally related to the inkblot.

The second question — how did each perceive the situation, organize it and respond to it — may be evaluated from the manner of verbally expressing the content. There is sufficient contrast to reveal how the normal ten-year-old and the retarded ten-year-old reacted to stimulation.

Note the language used by Jeff: On Card IV he talked for quite a while, slowly building up to a total concept. Using the whole card, Jeff stated, "Looks like somebody's arm and head, and there's the feet and a big tail. A person who has a long tail." His facial expression and later inquiry revealed that he was evidently not satisfied with this response. This is not unusual for a young person reacting to authority as represented by the basic figure. In the Inquiry he was manifestly ambivalent about the "person-with-a-tail" percept. This self-critical ability is not present in the responses of the other two youngsters.

Steven, the chronologically oldest of the three, with a level of intellectual development equal to Jeff's and far above

Allen's and whose MA is equal to Allen's CA, immediately organized the whole of Card IV into a contaminated or spoiled response, "I see a tree with two feet." His later explanation does not refer to the card or to any part of it. Rather, he verbally recalls seeing trees with feet. No effort is made to account for the incongruence between his percept and reality. This verbal expression in no wise approaches that of the chronologically younger but intellectually brighter self-critical explanation by Jeff. Steven still adheres to the world of fantasy.

Allen, as suspected, perceives, organizes, and responds in bits. His response to Card IV is "Shoulders, shoes, back, legs, hair, ankle." He was unable to bring these parts together to form a human or animal figure. The elemental language is neither descriptive nor explanatory. His verbalization reflects his poverty of ideation and configurational deficiency.

The third question asks what may be the important contributing variables to each youngster's response to life's stimuli as represented by the inkblots. The simplest and least explanatory answer would be their intellectual differences. This is a tautology. It is necessary to look elsewhere for possible answers. From a Piagetian point of view the level of development, or cognitive maturity, is stage- not age-related. Jeff built well on the reflexes of the sensory-motor stage and was able to assimilate from learning experiences. This in turn developed the symbolic functions so that an inkblot on a card yielded a mental symbol, or engram, which had real meaning for him. Thought content could be expressed linguistically, and it is language that is the best vehicle for transmitting information to oneself and to others. His present level of cognitive development is at the stage of concrete operations, characteristic of normal children between seven and eleven years of age.

Allen, the ten-year-old with an MA of four years, four months, and I. Q. of 43, is currently functioning at a lower stage of cognitive development — at a stage that is more closely related to his MA than to his CA. Certainly his is beyond the first Piagetian stage of sensory-motor intelligence. His simple and at times unintelligible language places him in Piaget's stage of intuitive thought — the stage in which the child begins to use words to reflect the extremely concretistic nature of his thinking. This is seen in Allen's series of one-word responses to Cards I and IV, with no attempt to integrate these into a gestalt. Note also that he is still the center of his ideation: in Card IV the "shoulder" response is reinforced by pointing to his own shoulders. Allen is chronologically ten and intellectually somewhat interested in what is going on around him. Gradually, he is moving from egocentricity to social participation — characteristic of the four to seven-year old child.

Finally, Steven should be in the stage of formal operation — the highest level of cognitive potential. Despite his chronological age, he has not reached this stage. From the quality and content of his responses, he is intellectually at a level with Jeff — the stage of concrete operations. But the mode of verbal expression and the quality of his responses do reflect a difference. For example, on Card VI, Jeff sees the skin of a tiger and he is looking down at it. He encompassed the whole card. Steven, on the other hand, used only the top third and called it a Tom and Jerry "cat," re-emphasizing his fantasy, childlike approach to life. Steven named, but did not describe. Jeff's operational thinking went beyond the mere concretism or realism of the blot and introduced a dimension of space between himself and the percept. This is a step beyond concretistic thinking, on the way to abstract thinking — the ability to deal with objects and events not actually present. Jeff is well on his way to Piaget's highest cognitive level — the stage of formal operations.

Now, what does all this mean behaviorally, socially, and intellectually? While measured intelligence, the I. Q. rating, has traditionally been a major criterion for mental retardation, it tells us very little about the child except for the rate of development and his place in relation to the normative population.

This may satisfy a legal requirement for institutionalization, or a regulation regarding admission to a special-education class, or exclusion from the public school system. For social, behavioral, and perhaps diagnostic-remedial concerns, the I. Q. has little to contribute. Therefore, turning to an alternative to the traditional view, to an assessment technique that taps linguistic manifestations of how the individual perceives, organizes, and responds to stimuli or the forces in his phenomenological field may afford better insights into the relevant strengths and weaknesses in coping with the activities of daily living. After all, isn't this what should be known about our young retardate?

REFERENCES

Alcock, T. (1963), *The Rorschach in Practice*. London: Tavistock Publications.

Allen, R. M. (1948), A simple method of validating color and shading shock. *J. Consult. Psychol.*, 12:360.

―――― (1951a), A longitudinal study of six Rorschach protocols of a three-year-old child. *Child Develpm.*, 22: 61-70.

―――― (1951b), The role of color in Rorschach's Test: The influence of color on reaction time in a normal population. *J. Proj. Tech.*, 15: 481-485.

―――― (1953a), *Introduction to the Rorschach Technique*. New York: International Universities Press.

―――― (1953b), The M determinant and color in Rorschach's Test. *J. Clin. Psychol.*, 9: 198-199.

―――― (1954a), Continued longitudinal Rorschach study of a child for years three to five. *J. Genet. Psychol.*, 85: 135-149.

―――― (1954b), *Elements of Rorschach Interpretation*. New York: International Universities Press.

―――― (1955), An analysis of twelve longitudinal Rorschach records of one child. *J. Proj. Tech.*, 19: 111-116.

―――― (1957a), A longitudinal Rorschach analysis. *Tohoku Psychol. Folia*, 3-4: 25-29.

―――― (1957b), A note on persistent responses in longitudinal Rorschach protocols. *J. Proj. Tech.*, 21: 362-365.

―――― (1958), *Personality assessment procedures*. New York: Harper.

―――― (1960), The place of projective technique in the university curriculum: They do belong there. *J. Genet. Psychol.*, 96: 321-325.

―――― (1965), *Variables in Personality Theory and Personality Testing*. Springfield, Ill.: Charles C Thomas.

―――― (1966), *Basic Issues in Psychological Tests and Measurements*. Coral Gables, Florida: University of Miami Bookstore Press.

―――― (1975), There is an alternative to the IQ. *J. Person. Assessment*, 30: 377-380.

―――― and Dorsey, R. N. (1954), The effect of suggestion on human movement productivity in Rorschach's Test. *Zeit. diagnost. Psychol. Personalichkeitfrsch.*, 2(2): 137-142.

_____ Manne, S. H. and Stiff, M. (1951), The role of color in Rorschach's Test: A preliminary normative on a college student population. *J. Proj. Tech.*, 15: 235-242.

_____ _____ and _____ (1952), The role of color in Rorschach's Test: The influence of color on the consistency of responses in the Rorschach Test. *J. Clin. Psychol.*, 8: 97-98.

_____ Richer, H. M. and Plotnik, R. J. (1964), A study of introversion-extroversion as a personality dimension. *Genet. Psychol. Monogr.*, 69: 297-322.

_____ Stiff, M. and Rosenzweig, M. I. (1953), The role of color in Rorschach's Test: A preliminary study of neurotic and psychotic groups. *J. Clin. Psychol.*, 9: 81-83.

Allison, J. and Blatt, S. J. (1964), The relationship of Rorschach whole responses to intelligence. *J. Proj. Tech.*, 28: 255-260.

Allport, G. W., Vernon, P. E. and Lindzey, G. (1951), *Study of Values— Manual of Directions*. Boston: Houghton, Mifflin.

Altus, W. D. and Altus, G. T. (1952), Rorschach movement variables and verbal intelligence. *J. Abnorm. Soc. Psychol.*, 47: 531-533.

APA Committee on Training in Clinical Psychology (1947), Recommended graduate training program in clinical psychology. *Amer. Psychol.*, 2: 539-558.

_____ (1950), Standards for practicum training in clinical psychology: Tentative recommendations. *Amer. Psychol.*, 5: 594-609.

Atkinson, J. W. and McClelland, D. C. (1948), The projective expression of needs, II. *J. Exp. Psychol.*, 38: 643-658.

Balloch, J. C. (1952), The effect of degree of shading contrast in ink blots on verbal response. *J. Expt. Psychol.*, 43: 120-124.

Bark, B. and Baron, S. (1943), Neurotic elements in the Rorschach records psychotics. *Rorschach Res. Exch.*, 7: 166-168.

Barnett, I. (1950), The influence of color and shading on the Rorschach Test. Ph. D. dissertation, University of Pittsburgh.

Baughman, E. E. (1958), The role of the stimulus in Rorschach responses. *Psychol. Bull.*, 55: 121-147.

Beck, S. J. (1943), The Rorschach Test in psychopathology. *J. Consult. Psychol.*, 7: 103-111.

_____ (1948), II, Rorschach F plus and the ego treatment. *Amer. J. Orthopsychiat.*, 18: 395-401.

_____ (1949), *Rorschach's Test: A variety of Personality Pictures*. New York: Grune & Stratton.

_____ (1950), *Rorschach's Test. I. Basic Processes*. New York: Grune & Stratton.

_____ (1952), *Rorschach's Test. III. Advances in Interpretation*. New York: Grune & Stratton.

_____ (1953), Rorschach Test. *In:* Weider, A. (ed.), *Contributions toward Medical Psychology*. New York: Roland, pp. 599-610.

_____ Rabin, A. I., Thiesen, W. G., Molish, H. and Thetford, W. N. (1950), The normal personality as projected in the Rorschach Test. *J. Psychol.,* 30: 241-298.

Bell, J. E. (1948) *Projective Techniques.* New York: Longmans, Green.

Benton, A. L. (1952), The experimental validation of the Rorschach Test. II. The significance of Rorschach color responses. *Amer. J. Orthopsychiat.,* 22:755-763.

Bergman, A. and Schubert, J. (1974), The Rorschachs of normal and emotionally disturbed children: A review of the literature. *Brit. J. Proj. Psy-Chol. Person. Study,* 19: 7-13.

Bernreuter, R. G. (1935), *Manual for the Personality Inventory.* Stanford, Calif.: Stanford University Press.

Binder, H. (1937), The "light-dark" interpretations in Rorschach's experiment. *Rorschach Res. Exch.,* 2: 37-42.

Binet, A. (1903), *Etude experimentale de l'intelligence.* Paris: Schleicher.

Blatt, S. J. and Allison, J (1963) Methodological considerations in Rorschach research: The *W* response as an expression of abstractive and integrative striving. *J. Proj. Tech.,* 27: 269-279.

Bleuler, E. (1912), The theory of schizophrenic negativism. *Nerv. Ment. Dis. Monogr.,* No. 11. Washington, D.C.: Nervous and Mental Disease Publishing Co.

Bochner, R. and Halpern, F. (1945) *The Clinical Application of the Rorschach Test.* New York: Grune & Stratton, 2nd edition.

Brady, G. G. (1953), A study of the effects of color on Rorschach responses. *Genet. Psychol. Monogr.,* 48: 261-311.

Braly, K. W. (1933), The influence of past experience in visual perception. *J. Exp. Psychol.,* 16: 613-643.

Bridgman, P. W. (1927), *The logic of modern physics.* New York: Macmillan.

Brittain, H. L. (1907) A study in imagination. *Pedagog. Semin.,* 14: 137-206.

Brown, F. (1953), An exploratory study of dynamic factors in the content of the Rorschach protocol. *J. Proj. Tech.,* 17:462-464.

Bruner, J. S. (1948), Perceptual theory and the Rorschach Test. *J. Pers.,* 17: 157-168.

_____ and Postman, L. (1949), Symbolic values as an organizing factor in perception. *J. Soc. Psychol.,* 27: 203-208.

_____ _____ and McGinnies, E. (1947), Personal values as determinants of perceptual selection. *Amer. Psychol.,* 2: 285-286.

Brussel, J. A., Hitch, K. S. and Piotrowski, Z. A. (1950) *A Rorschach Training Manual.* Utica, N. Y.: State Hospitals Press, 3rd edition.

Buehler, C., Buehler, K. and Lefever, D. W. (1948), *Rorschach Standarization Studies. I. Development of the Basic Rorschach Score with Manual of Directions.* Los Angeles: Rorschach Standardization Studies No. 1. mimeographed.

Cass, W. A. and McReynolds, P. A. (1951), A contribution to Rorschach norms. *J. Consult. Psychol.*, 15:178-184.

Charen, S. (1957), Pitfalls in interpretation of parental symbolism in Rorschach cards IV and VII. *J. Consult. Psychol.*, 21: 52-56.

Clark, R. W. (1971), *Einstein, the Life and Times.* New York: World.

Cox, F. N. and Saranson, S. B. (1954), Test anxiety and Rorschach performance. *J. Abnorm. Soc. Psychol.*, 49: 371-377.

Cronbach, L. (1948), A validation design for qualitative studies of personality. *J. Consult. Psychol.*, 12: 363: 374.

Cureton, E. E. (1949), The principal compulsion of factor analysts. *Test Service Notebook*, No. 4. Princeton, N. J.: Educational Testing Service.

Dubrovner, R., von Lackum, W., and Jost, H. (1950). A study of the effect of color on productivity and reaction time in the Rorschach test. *J. Clin. Psychol.*, 6: 331-336.

Duncker, K. (1939), The influence of past experiences upon perceptual properties. *Amer. J. Psychol.*, 52: 255-265.

Elizur, A. (1949), Content analysis of the Rorschach with regard to anxiety hostility. *J. Proj. Tech.*, 13: 247-284.

Erlemeier, N., Monikes, W. and Wirtz, R. (1974), Rorschach organization and form level indices of intelligence. *Diagnostica*, 20: 106-116.

Fiske, D. W. and Baughman, F. F., (1953) Relationships between Rorschach scoring categories and the total number of responses. *J. Abnorm. Soc. Psychol.*, 48: 25-32.

Fonda, C. P. (1951), The nature and meaning of the Rorschach white space responses. *J. Abnorm. Soc. Psychol.*, 46: 367-377.

⸻ (1960), The white-space response. *In:* Rickers-Ovsiankina, M. A. (ed.), *Rorschach Psychology.* New York: Wiley, pp. 80-105.

Frank, L. K. (1948), *Projective Methods.* Springfield, Ill.: Charles C. Thomas.

Gibby, R. G. (1952), Examiner influence on the Rorschach inquiry. *J. Consult. Psychol.*, 16: 449-455.

Goldfarb, W. (1945a), The animal symbol in the Rorschach Test. *Rorschach Res. Exch.*, 9: 8-21.

⸻ (1945b), Organizing activity in the Rorschach examination. *Amer. J. Orthopsychiat.*, 15: 525-528.

Goldstein, K. (1939), *The Organism.* New York: American Book. Co.

Graham, S. (1963), Interaction in the life space. *Acta Psychologica,* 21: 16-22.

Haan, N. (1964), An investigation of the relationships of Rorschach scores, patterns, and behavior, to coping and defense mechanisms. *J. Proj. Tech.*, 28: 429-441.

Halpern, F. (1953), *Clinical approach to Children's Rorschachs.* New York: Grune & Stratton.

Hamlin, R. M. and Kogan, W. S. (1948), Objectification in Rorschach interpretation. *J. Pers.*, 17: 177-181.

Hammer, E. F. and Jacks, I. (1955) A study of Rorscach flexor and extensor movement responses. *J. Clin. Psychol.,* 11: 63-67.

Hammond, K. R. and Allen, J. R. (1953), *Writing clinical reports.* Engelwood, N.J.: Prentice-Hall.

Hanfmann, E. (1952), William Stern on projective techniques. *J. Pers.,* 21: 1-21.

Harris, J. E. (1960), Validity: The search for a constant universe of variables. *In*: Rickers-Ovsiankina (ed.), *Rorschach Psychology.* New York: Wiley, pp. 380-439.

Harrower, M. R. (1952), *Appraising Personality.* New York: Norton.

Hathaway, S. R. and McKinley, J. C. (1951), *Manual for the M. M. P. I.* New York: Psychological Corp.

Hertz, M. R. (1940), The shading response in the Rorschach ink-blot test: a review of its scoring and interpretation. *J. Gen. Psychol.,* 23: 123-167.

_____ (1952), The Rorschach thirty years after. *In:* Brower, D. and Abt, L. F. (eds.), *Progress in Clinical Psychology, Vol. I.* New York: Grune & Stratton, pp. 108-148.

_____ (1970), *Frequency Tables for Scoring Rorschach Responses,* Fifth Edition. Cleveland: Case Western Reserve University Press.

Hertzman, M. and Pearce, J. (1947), The personal meaning of the human figure. *Psychiat.* 10: 413-422.

Hirschenstein, R. and Rabin, A. I. (1955), Reactions to Rorschach cards IV and VII as a function of parental availability in childhood. *J. Consult. Psychol.,* 19: 473-474.

Holzberg, J. D. (1960), Reliability re-examined. *In:* Rickers-Ovsiankina, M. A. (ed.), *Rorschach Psychology.* New York: Wiley, pp. 361-379.

Hsu, E. H. (1947), The Rorschach responses and factor analysis. *J. Gen. Psychol.,* 37: 129-138.

Huber, J. T. (1961), *Report Writing in Psychology and Psychiatry.* New York: Harper.

Hutt, M. L., Gibby, R., Milton, E. O. and Potthurst, K. (1950), The effects of varied experimental "sets" upon the Rorschach test performance. *J. Proj. Tech.,* 14: 181-187.

_____ and Shor, J. (1946), Rationale for routine Rorschach "Testing the Limits." *Rorsch. Res. Exch.,* 10: 70-76.

Jensen, A. R. (1959), The reliability of projective techniques: Review of the Literature. *Acta psychologica,* 16 (2): 3-67.

Kass, W. (1958), Commitee on training: Report. *J. Proj. Tech.,* 22: 120-121.

Kelley, E. L. (1950), *Training in Clinical Psychology.* New York: Prentice-Hall.

Kimball, A. J. (1950), History of form-level appraisal in the Rorschach. *J. Proj. Tech.,* 14: 134-152.

Klein, G. S. and Schlesinger, H. J. (1951), Perceptual attitudes toward instability. I. Prediction of apparent movement experiences from Rorschach responses. *J. Pers.,* 19: 289-302.

Klopfer, B., Ainsworth, M. D., Klopfer, W. G. and Holt, R. R. (1954), *Developments in the Rorschach Technique*. Vols. I and II. New York: Harcourt, Brace, Jovanovich.

_____ and Davidson, H. H. (1962), *The Rorschach Technique: An Introductory Manual*. New York: Harcourt, Brace, Jovanovich.

_____ and Kelley, D. M. (1942), *The Rorschach Technique*. New York: World Book.

_____ and Marguiles, H. (1941), Rorschach reactions in early childhood. *Rorschach Res. Exch.*, 5: 1-23.

Klopfer, W. G. (1949), *Suggestions for the Systematic Analysis of Rorschach Records*. Los Angeles: The Student Store, University of California, Los Angeles, mimeographed.

_____ (1954), Interpretive hypotheses derived from the analysis of content. *In:* Klopfer, B. *et al.*, pp. 376-402.

_____ (1960), *The Psychological Report*. New York: Grune & Stratton.

_____ (1974), The Rorschach and old age. *J. Person. Assessment.* 38: 420-422.

Korchin, S. J. (1960), Form perception and ego functioning. *In:* Rickers-Ovsiankina, M. A. (ed.), *Rorschach Psychology*. New York: Wiley, pp. 109-129.

Kouwer, B. J. (1949), *Colors and Their Character*, The Hague: Nyhoff.

Lazarus, R. S. (1948), An experimental analysis of the influence of color on the protocol of the Rorschach test. *J. Pers.*, 17: 182-185.

_____ (1949), The influence of color on the protocol of the Rorschach test. *J. Abnorm. Soc. Psychol.*, 44: 506-516.

_____ and McCleary, R. A. (1951), Autonomic discrimination without awareness: a study of subception. *Psychol. Rev.*, 58:113-122.

Lehmann, H. E. and Dorken, H. (1952), Stress dynamics in psychiatric perspective. *Psychiat.* 15: 387-393.

Leibniz, G. W. (1949), *New Essays Concerning Human Understanding*. LaSalle Ill.: Open Court Pub. Co.

Lewy, E. (1958), Stimulus values of Rorschach cards for children. *J. Proj. Tech.*, 2: 293-296.

Lewin, K. (1935), *A Dynamic Theory of Personality*. New York: McGraw-Hill.

Lindner, R. M. (1946), Content analysis in Rorschach work. *Rorschach. Res. Exch.*, 10: 121-129.

_____ (1947), Analysis of the Rorschach test by content. *J. Clin. Psychopath.*, 8: 707-719.

Little, K. B. (1959), Connotations of the Rorschach inkblots. *J. Pers.*, 27: 397-406.

Loosli-Usteri, M. (1950), 100 hommes "normaux" à travers le test de Rorschach. *In:* Hertz, M., The first international Rorschach conference. *J. Proj. Tech.*, 14: 42-43.

Lord, E. (1950), Experimentally induced variations in Rorschach performance. *Psychol. Monogr.,* 64: 1-34.

Lubar, G. H. (1948), Rorschach content analysis. *J. Clin. Psychopath.,* 9: 146-152.

Machover, K. (1947), A case of frontal lobe injury following attempted suicide. *Rorschach Res. Exch.,* 11: 9-20.

Maradie, L. J. (1953), Productivity on the Rorschach as a function of order of presentation. *J. Consult. Psychol.,* 17: 32-35.

McClelland, D. C., Atkinson, J. W. and Clark, R. A. (1949), The projective expression of needs: III. *J. Person.,* 27: 311-330.

McCue, K. W., Rothenberg, D., Allen, R. M. and Jennings, T. W. (1963), Rorschach variables in two "Study of Values" types. *J. Gen. Psychol.,* 69: 169-172.

McGinnies, E. (1949), Emotionality and perceptual defense. *Psychol. Rev.,* 56: 244-251.

Meer, B. and Singer, J. L. (1950), A note on the "Father" and "mother" cards in the Rorschach inkblots. *J. Consult. Psychol.,* 14: 482-484.

Mensh, I. N. (1952), The experimental validation of the Rorschach test. III. Treatment of data. *Amer. J. Orthopsychiat.,* 22: 764-770.

Meyer, B. T. (1951), An investigation of color shock in the Rorschach test. *J. Clin. Psychol.,* 7: 367-370.

Mons, W. E. R. (1950), *Principles and Practice of the Rorschach Personality Test.* Phila.: Lippincott, 2nd edition.

Munroe, R. (1941), The inspection technique. *Rorschach Res. Exch.,* 5: 166-190.

Murphy, G. (1947), *Personality.* New York: Harper.

Murray, H. A. (1943), *Explorations in Personality.* New York: Oxford University Press.

Mursell, J. L. (1947), *Psychological Testing.* New York: Longmans, Green.

Neff, W. S. and Lidz, T. (1951), Rorschach patterns of normal subjects of graded intelligence. *J. Proj. Tech.,* 15: 45-57.

Norman, R. and Scott, W. A. (1952), Color and affect: a review and semantic evaluation. *J. Gen. Psychol.,* 46: 185-223.

Pascal, G. R., Ruesch, H. A., Devine, c. A. and Suttell, B. J. (1950), A study of genital symbols on the Rorschach test: Presentation of a method and results. *J. Abnorm. Soc. Psychol.,* 45: 286-295.

Piotrowski, Z. A. (1937), Rorschach studies of cases with lesions of the frontal lobes. *Brit. J. Med. Psychol.,* 17: 105-118.

―――― (1940), Positive and negative Rorschach organic reactions. *Rorschach Res. Exch.* 4: 147-151.

―――― (1942a), A Rorschach compendium. *Psychiat. Quart.,* 16: 28-35.

―――― (1942b), On the Rorschach method of personality analysis. *Psychiat. Quart.,* 16: 480-490.

―――― (1957), *Perceptanalysis.* New York: Macmillan.

_____ (1960), The movement score. *In:* Ricker-Ovsiankina, M. A. (ed.), *Rorschach Psychology*. New York: Wiley, pp. 130-153.

Rabin, A. I. (1959), A contribution to the meaning of the Rorschach inkblots via the semantic differential. *J. Consult. Psychol.*, 23: 368-372.

_____ and Sanderson, M. H. (1947), An experimental study into some Rorschach procedures. *J. Clin. Psychol.*, 3: 216-225.

Ranzoni, J. H., Grant, M. Q. and Ives, V. (1950), Rorschach "card pull" in a normal adolescent population. *J. Proj. Tech.*, 14: 107-133.

Rapaport, D., Gill, M. and Schafer, R. (1968), *Diagnostic Psychological Testing, Revised Edition*, R. R. Holt (ed.). New York: International Universities Press.

Rav, J. (1951), Anatomy responses in the Rorschach test. *J. Proj. Tech.*, 15: 433-443.

Ray, J. B. (1963), The meaning of Rorschach white space responses. *J. Proj. Tech.*, 27: 315-323.

Rickers-Ovsiankina, M. A., ed. (1960), *Rorschach Psychology*. New York: Wiley.

Roe, A. (1950), Analysis of group Rorschachs of physical scientists. *J. Proj. Tech.*, 14: 385-398.

Rorschach, H. (1942), *Psychodiagnostics*. Bern: Huber, 3rd edition.

Rosen, E. M. (1951), Symbolic meanings in the Rorschach cards: a Statistical study. *J. Clin. Psychol.*, 7: 239-244.

Rosen, E. M. (1952), M. M. P. I. and Rorschach correlates of the Rorschach white space response. *J. Clin. Psychol.*, 8: 283-288.

Rosvold, H. E., Ross, W. D. and Dorken, H. (1954), The Rorschach method as an experimental instrument. *J. Proj. Tech.*, 18: 227-232.

Sanderson, H. (1952), Card titles in testing the limits in Rorschach. *J. Psychol.*, 33: 27-29.

Sappenfield, B. R. and Buker, S. L. (1949), Validity of the Rorschach 8-9-10 per cent as an indicator of responsiveness to color. *J. Consult. Psychol.*, 13: 268-271.

Schachtel, E. (1943), On color and affect: contributions to an understanding of Rorschach's Test: I. *Psychiat.* 6: 393-409.

_____ (1945), Subjective definitions of the Rorschach test situation and their effect on test performance: III *Psychiat.* 8: 419-448.

_____ (1950), Projection and its relation to character attitudes in the kinesthetic responses. Contributions to an understanding of Rorschach's test: IV, *Psychiat.* 13: 69-100.

Schneider, L. I. (1950), Rorschach validation; some methodological aspects. *Psychol. Bull.*, 47: 493-508.

Schofield, W. (1952), A laboratory exercies in projective interpretation. *J. Gen. Psychol.* 46: 19-28

Shakow, D. (1945a), Training in clinical psychology—A note on trends. *J. Consult Psychol.*, 9: 240-242.

_____ (1945b), Report on Graduate internship training in psychology. *J. Consult. Psychol.*, 9:243-266.

Shapiro, D. (1960), A perceptual understanding of color responses. *In:* Rickers-Ovsiankina, M. A. (ed.), *Rorschach Psychology*. New York: Wiley, pp. 154-201.

Sharp, E. A. (1899), Individual psychology. *Amer. J. Psychol.*, 10: 329-391.

Shaw, B. (1949), "Sex populars" in the Rorschach test. *J. Abnorm. Soc. Psychol.*, 23: 466-470.

Singer, J. L. (1960), The experience type: some behavior correlates and theoretical implications. *In:* Rickers-Ovsianka, M. A. (ed.), *Rorschach Psychology,* New York: Wiley, pp. 223-259.

_____ Meltzoff, J. and Goldman, G. D. (1952) Rorschach movement responses following motor inhibition and hyperactivity. *J. Consult. Psychol.*, 16: 359-364.

Small, L. (1956), *Rorschach Location and Scoring Manual.* New York: Grune & Stratton.

Stern, W. (1937), Cloud pictures: a new method for testing imagination. *Character & Pers.*, 6: 132-146.

Taulbee, E. S. (1961), The relationship betwen Rorschach flexor and extensor M response and the M. M. P. I. and psychotherapy. *J. Proj. Tech.*, 25: 477-479.

Toomey, L. C. and Rickers-Ovsiankina, M. A. (1960), Tabular comparison of Rorschach scoring systems. *In:* Rickers-Ovsiankina, M. A. (ed.), *Rorschach Psychology.* New York: Wiley, pp. 441-465.

Ulett, G. A. (1950), *Rorschach Introductory Manual.* St. Louis Mo.: Educational Publishers.

Vernon, P. E. (1964), *Personality Assessment.* New York: Wiley.

Wallen, R. (1948), The nature of color shock. *J. Abnorm. Soc. Psychol.*, 43: 346-356.

Wetherhorn, M. (1956), Flexor-extensor movement on the Rorschach. *J. Consult. Psychol.*, 20: 204.

White, R. W. (1946), Interpretation of imaginative productions. *In:* Hunt, J. McV. *Personality and the Behavior Disorders.* New York: Ronald, pp. 214-251.

Willemaers, R. (1973), The human movement in the Rorschach Test: a validation study: II. results. *Psychologica Belgica*, 13: 313-340.

Wilson, G. P. and Blake, R. R. (1950), A methodological problem in Beck's organizational concept. *J. Consult. Psychol.*, 14: 20-24.

Wittenborn, J. R. (1949), A factor analysis of discrete responses to the Rorschach ink blots. *J. Consult. Psychol.*, 13: 335-340.

York, R. H. (1951), The effect of color in the Rorschach test and in selected intellectual tasks. *Ph.D. dissertation,* Boston University.

Zelen, M. and Sechrest, L. (1963), The validity of the "Mother" and "Father" cards of the Rorschach. *J. Proj. Tech.*, 27: 114-121.

Zubin, J. (1954), Failures of the Rorschach Test. *J. Proj. Tech.*, 18: 303-315. Also in: Hirt, M. (ed.), *Rorschach Science*. New York: Free Press, 1962, pp. 331-346.

———— Eron, L. D. & Schumer, F. (1965), *An Experimental Approach to Projective Procedures*. New York: Wiley.

Zulliger, H. (1953), The Case of Franz and Lotti. *J. Proj. Tech.*, 17: 61-65.

———— (1956), *The Behn-Rorschach test*. Berne: Hans Huber.

GLOSSARY

Achromatic—Absence of color, use of the black, white, or gray elements.

Additional—Indicates that the Location, Determinant, or Content of the percept makes use of more than one element, e.g., the Main Location may be W and the S is additional in a WS location percept.

Additional responses—All percepts given during the Inquiry stage are considered additional responses and scored as such.

Apperceptive mass—Person's storehouse of knowledge gained from experiences, all that is known to the individual.

Approach—The relationship of the Whole to Detail to Small Detail and Space Location elements; W:D:Dd + S.

Average reaction time—The sum of the individual reaction times divided by the number of chromatic and achromatic plates separately; usually divided by five unless card rejection(s) occur(s).

Average response time—The result of dividing the total response time by the total number of percepts.

c—*See* Surface texture: c, cF, Fc.

C—*See* Color symbols.

$\bar{C}$—*See* Color denial.

C'—The percept includes black, gray, or white in the description of the response. C', C'F, FC'.

C_{des}—*See* Color description.

C_n—*See* Color naming.

C_{sym}—*See* Color symbolism.

CF or C/F—See Color symbols: form secondary to color or form utilized minimally and secondary to color.

Card—Used interchangeably with "plate" referring to the inkblots.

Chiaroscuro—Rorschach (1942, p. 185) term for the shading determinant.

Chromatic—Color or colored.

Color denial, $\bar{C}$—Mention of color but not using it in the percept: this red, I don't know what it is; or the red part is a _____.

Color description, C_{des}—Testee only describes the color: this is a washed-out red.

Color naming, C_n—Testee simply names the color or colors: these are red and orange splotches.

Color ratio, CR—Number of responses to plates VIII + IX + X divided by total responses.

Color symbolism, C_{sym}—The symbolic or abstract use of color: this red reminds me of Spring.

Color symbols or determinants C, CF or C/F, FC or F/C—The use of the color(s) of the inkblot in a percept.

Confabulated whole, DW—Location symbol is used indicating that a small portion of a blot is used to give meaning to a larger part or to the whole blot.

Confabulation DW or DdD or DdW or even DD—A poor percept in which a small portion of the plate is used to give meaning to a larger part.

Contaminated response—The merging of two percepts to the same area of the blot resulting in a poor percept, despite the fact that each percept *separately* may be a good one.

Content—The culmination of the "where" or Location and the "how" or Determinant of the testee's percept; the result may be human, animal, an object, plant, etc.

D or Detail—Refers to the use of less than the whole inkblot in a percept.

Dd—See Small detail.

DdD—See Small detail.

De — See Small detail.

Di—See Small detail.

Do—See Small detail and oligophrenic detail.

Dr—See Small detail.

DW—See Confabulated whole.

Determinant—the manner in which the testee perceives the responses, using form, color, movement, and shading either singly or in combination.

Experience Balance or Erlebnistypus *primary, E.B.* – the M to Sum C ratio: M: ΣC.

Experience balance or Erlebnistypus *secondary, E. B.* —the ratio of animal and inanimate movement to texture shading and black determinants: (FM + m):(Fc + c + C').

F—See Form.

F + —See Form.

F— —See Form.

FC or F/C—See color symbols; color secondary to form.

FK—The use of shading to report distance or perspective as an attribute of the percept.

FM—Animal movement; *See* Movement.

(FM + m):(Fc + c + C')—See Experience Balance, secondary.

Form, F—The shape or contour of the selected blot area gives it meaning.

  *F + —*Percept and contour are congruent and specific: a rose.

  F neutral, F/—Percept and form refer to an object that may have any shape, e.g., a stone, a mountain.

  *F— —*Percept and contour are not congruent.

F per cent—The number of form-determined percepts divided by the total number of responses: $\dfrac{\text{Total F}}{\text{Total R}}$.

F+ per cent—$\dfrac{\text{Number of F + and F determinants}}{\text{Total Number of F}}$.

Imposed determinant—A scorable Rorschach Test element which is evoked by the blot, but is not actually present in the blot, e.g., human movement.

Inherent determinant—The determinant is present in the physical make-up of the blot, e.g., a black bat; also describes color and surface texture percepts.

Inquiry—The phase of the Rorschach Test administration during which the testee accounts for the Location, Determinant(s), and Content of the percepts given in the Main Stage or free-association phase.

k—*See* Shading depth.

K—Shading as the basis for reporting a feeling of diffusion or expanse: K, KF.

Location—Delineating exactly how much of the card is included in the percept and where it is located.

m, mF, Fm—Inanimate movement, movement that is not human or animal in nature; *See* Movement.

M—Human movement; *See* Movement.

M:Sum C—*See* Experience Balance, primary.

Main stage—the free-association phase of the Rorschach Test administration.

Movement—A subjectively imposed determinant which is accompanied by a kinesthetic feeling (of motion or movement) by the testee: M or human movement; FM or animal movement; and m, mF or Fm, inanimate movement.

Multiply-determined percept—The hierarchial order for scoring determinants in a percept which has more than one determinant: A black bat flying is scored W FM + , FC' A P: the agreed order is primacy to M, followed by C, FM, Fc; remaining other determinants are treated as additional determinants in whatever order they occur.

O—*See* Original percept.

Oligophrenic detail—Testee reports part of an animal or human where most people see the entire animal or human; Klopfer's dx: scored Hdx or Adx in the Content column.

Original percept, O—Signifies a response occurring as infrequently as once in 100 protocols.

P—See Popular response.

Percept—The testee's response to the Rorschach Test card.

Plate—Used interchangeably with "card" to refer to the 10 inkblots.

Popular response—Percept which has an unusually high frequency rate as a response to the plates, e.g., bat in card I.

*Position, ∧∨ >< —*Of the top of the card. Indicates whether subject turns the card or holds it only in the position in which it is presented to him. ⊚ indicates rapid turning of the card; ⁄ ⧵ indicates the position of the testee's head when he turns his head instead of the card.

Positional response—A detail deriving its content primarily from its placement in the plate and which tends to disregard other aspects of the selected blot area, e.g., bottom middle portion of most plates seen as female genitalia and accounted for by its position on the card and nothing more.

Protocol—The test record which includes the marked location chart, the distribution of the Location, Determinant, and Content elements, the response, and the scoring.

R—See Total response.

Reaction time—Elapsed time in seconds between the presentation of the plate to the testee and the first scorable percept.

Rejection—Testee does not give a scorable percept and/or gives no response to a card or cards.

Remark—An unscorable comment given by testee to the inkblot(s).

Response time—The total elapsed time in seconds between the presentation of the plate to the testee and his/her indication of no further response(s) to that particular card.

Shading as depth, k, kF, Fk—Variations in shading tones of the blot yielding a two-plane impression, e.g., X ray or a topographical map.

Shading determinants, k, K, FK—Use of shading in the chromatic and achromatic cards as depth, as a feeling of diffuseness, and as portraying distance or perspective.

Small detail,

Dd—Smaller than D and less frequently used portions of blots.

De—Edge detail is the use of the outer edge or contour of the inkblot without going into the blot itself.

Di—Interior detail scored when the chosen area of the blot is entirely surrounded by the other portions of the plate.

Do—Oligophrenic detail in which the testee reports part of an animal or human for those portions of the blot usually seen as a whole animal or human; Klopfer's dx, and scored as Adx or Hdx.

Dr—Rare detail given to an infrequently or rarely selected part of a blot.

Space, S—Use of the white parts of the plate in a percept.

Spoiled response—*See* Contaminated response.

Succession—The sequence of the W, D, Dd, and S Location elements within each card.

Surface texture—Testee's use of shading variations (lighter and darker) to describe the surface or single-plane impression in a percept.

Sum C, $\Sigma C = \dfrac{FC + 2CF + 3C}{2}$ —The number of main form-color plus twice the color-form plus three times the pure color determinants divided by two; *see* Experience Balance, primary.

Symbols, $\wedge \vee > <$ —Signify the position of the top of the Rorschach plate when the testee gives a particular response.

Ttl—*See* testing the limits.

Testing the limits—A supplementary technique to elicit Location, Determinant and/or Content percepts not given in Main Stage or free-association phase and during the Inquiry stage; an optional procedure to ascertain whether the testee can handle previously omitted elements of the Rorschach Test.

Total responses, R—The number of percepts given to the plates by the testee.

W—The use of the *entire* inkblot in the percept; whole responses Location.

W^x —Cut-off-whole. Used in some scoring systems to indicate a percept utilizing less than the entire blot but more than could be considered a large detail or D.

W-additive—Using one-half of a plate then pointing to the other half to repeat the percept, sort of doubling the response: this is a forest and down here is its reflection in the water.

W-creative—A creative or original percept using the entire plate; usually given in cards VII, IX, and X, although a creative W may occur in any of the plates.

W popular—A readily perceived and practically self-organizing response to the entire plate.

Z—Beck's (1950) "organizational activity" concept, ". . . an index to the energy at one's disposal for the organization drive" (pp. 58-82).

AUTHOR INDEX

355

SUBJECT INDEX